Expat is an epic non-fiction story about one young man's remarkable life in big-city, big-time Latin America. The book is high entertainment well worth giving it its due as a number one reader's choice. The book is historic and describes corruption in the cities and countries and adds a good dose of violence. I have been to many of the countries described in the book and can vouch for the authenticity of some of the events and how they are described in the book. Through the fast-action, Whitt is able to add clever and humorous events. It is interesting how he makes comparisons with his career and those of his friends in the United States. It is not only profoundly interesting to read, it will give the reader food for thought.

RAMON DIEZ FERNANDEZ, PRESIDENT
RD Publicidad/Mexico

If you've ever wondered how James Bond might have existed in a corporate environment, *Expat* is a must. Latin America has never seemed as threatening or as covert. Robert Ampudia Whitt certain would have made Ian Fleming take notice.

TAMARA HANSON, AUTHOR
Mastering the Dance

Expat is a provocative geopolitical true account of Latin America's struggle for moral normalcy in the face of an overpowering system of corruption and violence that transcends all moral codes. *Expat* tells how governments in Latin America really work and the part the U.S. plays in shaping their destiny.

DAVID A. WITTS, AUTHOR
Survivor of 50 combat missions
Forgotten War–Forgiven Guilt

I an investigative reporter contracted to write an in-depth cover story on the Cali and Medellin drug cartels. I acquiesced to write the story based on my trust of the author who cared for me and my family after the story was published. He walked a tight rope for many years and eventually fell but survived. *Expat* describes his twenty years of living on the edge in Latin America.

JUAN SIN MIEDO (NOM DE PLUME)
Retired Investigative Reporter
Formerly of Cali, Colombia
Now residing in the USA

As a Sea Captain and an explorer in Latin America, I have had the opportunity to find myself in the company of the author during his many years crisscrossing the hemisphere. Whether in a run-down saloon in Maracaibo, Venezuela or the beach of Callao, Peru, his indefatigable spirit in telling the real story of the rise and fall of dictators, presidents, and other wannabes is a rare and chilling account. *Expat is* right in the middle of all that goes right and wrong told by a man who lived it and mastered it.

CAPTAIN TAY C. VAN MALTSBERGER
Master unlimited tonnage
Turks and Caicos Islands Home Port

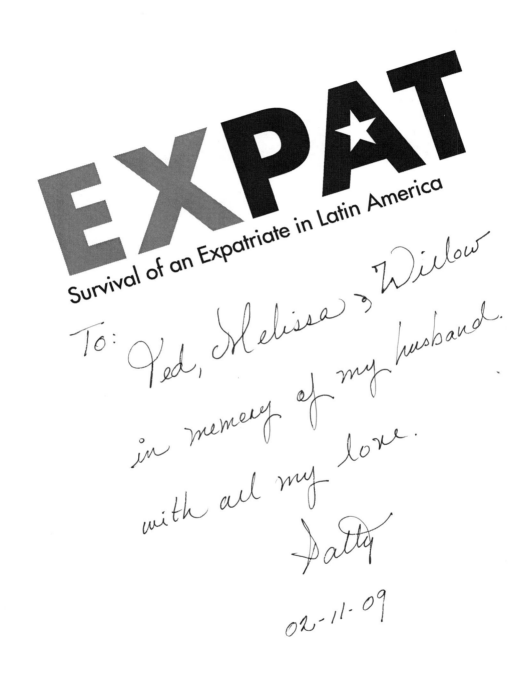

EXPAT

Survival of an Expatriate in Latin America

To: Ted, Melissa & Willow

in memory of my husband.

with all my love.

Patty

02-11-09

Survival of an Expatriate in Latin America

Robert Ampudia Whitt III

TATE PUBLISHING & *Enterprises*

Published by Tate Publishing & Enterprises, LLC
127 E. Trade Center Terrace | Mustang, Oklahoma 73064 USA
1.888.361.9473 | www.tatepublishing.com

Tate Publishing is committed to excellence in the publishing industry. The company reflects the philosophy established by the founders, based on Psalms 68:11,
"The Lord gave the word and great was the company of those who published it."

Book design copyright © 2007 by Tate Publishing, LLC. All rights reserved.
Front and back cover design and interior illustrations by RafiQ Salleh, www.rafiquesalleh.com
Interior design by Leah LeFlore
Cover illustrations:
Left: General Alfredo Stroessnor, declared himself President-for-Life of Paraguay
Center: General Hugo Banzer, President of Bolivia by a military coup
Right: Che Guevara, Castro's right hand man in the Cuban Revolution

Published in the United States of America

ISBN: 978-1-6024726-8-6
07.07.18

DEDICATION

To God Almighty, who allowed me to come this far, to my Mother who gave me all and asked for nothing in return and to my beloved wife, Patricia, who saved my life and cared for me ever since, like Florence Nightingale over a fallen soldier.

"No man can answer for his own valor or courage, till he has been in danger."

—LA ROCHEFOUCAULD

"He who never leaves his own country is full of prejudices."

—GOLDONI

ACKNOWLEDGEMENTS:

RUNNING THE LAST LAP

I was gently and lovingly coerced and cajoled into writing this book by my wife, Patricia, and inspired to finish it by my old friend Jerry Boyd, a.k.a. F.X. Toole, author of *Million Dollar Baby*, while sharing the *joie de vivre* and fierce competitiveness of my friend and mentor, Igor Gordevitch.

Table of Contents

FOREWORD

Expat is what life and working in Latin America used to be all about for an American executive. It is set before the homogenization of culture, which has made some of the excitement of a foreign assignment the stuff of history books. On the one hand, the effective offshore executive had to be self-contained, independent, working in an environment not many home office corporate types understood or even cared about. On the other, he or she was expected to operate without creating any surprises for the people back home. This tightrope of responsibility versus constantly changing and, at times, strange surroundings is what made the assumption of profit center responsibilities attractive to those of us who chose the challenge of earning a living in one or more of the countries south of the border. No mode of travel or destination was too bizarre to shy away from. If setting a course of action meant positively impacting the company's interests, then so be it, forward into action!

It is this spirit that Bob Whitt captures in *Expat*. I dare say some of Bob's solutions to the problem of the hour would never see the light of day in the US. But ingenuity and understanding the nuances of the local scene is what he was able to rely upon time and again to further his magazine's cause—and not at all coincidentally, that of the United States as well.

For the modern executive going to Latin America for the first time, there are lessons to take from this book. Lesson number one is learn all you can about the local culture. That is no easy task. It involves immersing oneself in the history and the various levels of society and having an appreciation of how it has affected the development of the marketplace being worked. Number two is learn the local language. Bob was blessed to be a native-born Spanish speaker, but the less fortunate will profit immeasurably from striving to speak and even live the Spanish language.

There are lessons for the seasoned expatriate as well. Don't take your surroundings for granted—savor them to the maximum. Not only will it make your unique experience more fulfilling, it will help make you a more effective manager or entrepreneur.

Expat is an exciting read, full of action, and laced with the wisdom that comes with the experience of more than twenty years working in one of the most interesting eras in Latin America's recent history, a great backdrop for sharing a life that many can only dream about. It will have you looking forward to the sequel that Bob alludes to in the finale.

RICHARD BACKUS

Mr. Backus' career encompassed more than thirty years in international banking. He lived and worked in Buenos Aires, Mexico City, La Paz, Bolivia, Hong Kong, and Singapore. He retired from banking in 1996 after serving six years as president and CEO of the New York subsidiary of a major Colombian banking concern.

PROLOGUE

Who in the world is Bob Ampudia Whitt?

My first encounter with Bob Ampudia Whitt was almost a half a century ago. I was director general of an advertising agency, and Bob was peddling space for his magazine. The magazine was a major publication in Latin America with political and editorial strength above other "foreign" and local publications.

It was my business to receive individuals such as this young man who were so well connected it was almost a duty to exchange commercial, political, and social information to be filed away and used at the right time. I discovered an interesting, albeit relentless yet entertaining individual. He was my kind of person, and we became close and fast friends.

He cut quite a figure when we were young, always careful with his gastronomic favorites that would not sidetrack his athletic physical appearance. Yes, he was vain but with good reason. He dressed like a dandy and was well known in Mexico City's nightlife.

We shared many pleasurable times over a good VSOP cognac when he was not off on some assignment in Latin America. Through the years I knew him better than most, even his own family. We had much in common, and I knew things about him that no one else in the world could possibly know.

So who is Bob? Many things: he is a traveler, an immigrant, explorer, adventurer, curious tourist, and, as he calls himself, an authentic expat.

Here today, gone tomorrow. Bob has been a spectator and witness to many events that have changed history. Bob's eyes had the ability to see, study, discover, contemplate, examine, and file away in his privileged memory and journals the events through the passage of time. Bob has been a witness of history and has asked himself many times what to do with so many accumulated memories.

Here is part of his life.

RAMÓN DIEZ FERNANDEZ
Professor of Semantics
President, RD Publicidad/Mexico

INTRODUCTION

When I was home on vacation, I found it difficult to explain my work in Latin America. Unless those listening to me were close friends, there was always doubt as to the veracity of what I was describing. Some who did not know me well would later say I was exaggerating or embellishing the stories.

On one occasion I was invited to the home of a close friend for a small party to talk about my adventures in Latin America. It ended in disaster. One guest in particular tried to shoot down everything I said. He couldn't believe that a person who accepted a business position in Latin America would have to face all the bumps in the road I encountered. He was right; my assignment was decidedly different. It was his manner, his attitude, and his verbal attack on practically everything I said that angered me. Foolishly, I retaliated in a very unbecoming way. Our encounter became a war of words. The other guests were stunned by what was taking place. In the end, I prevailed over my adversary, but I could tell by the look on my host's face and other guests that they were not pleased. Embarrassed, I left the party and later learned the commentary of the incident did not favor me. I didn't really care what people were saying, although I did feel they were being grossly unfair in taking my tormentor's side. I decided in the future to never discuss my work except with trusted friends and only the highlights.

The man was right. Not all American executives based in Latin America are faced with the kind of the extreme situations that I was a part of as described in this book. Many of the events had to do with my career in the newsmagazine publishing industry. In most Latin American countries newsmagazines are quietly undermined or attacked wherever and whenever possible by groups sponsored and financed by governments or groups with their own agenda hoping to intimidate or hurt the press. Still, some magazines persist and try to do their jobs by well-researched investigative reports, articles, and opinion editorials. Magazines, more often than newspapers, are the first priority for governmental retribution. This was due to the high socioeconomic level of magazine readership. The magazine reader was more intelligent, better educated, and wealthier than the common man reading newspapers. They represented a bigger danger to the government who was not able to manipulate them as easily. In the government's eyes, as well as those of special interest groups, it was the magazines that were the real threat with their editorial content. Magazines, therefore, became the ongoing target of those trying to either silence or buy the voices of honest magazine reporting.

At the end of the day, there is, has been, and always will be an adversarial relationship between the government and the press with those publications not secretly aligned with the government. This is no different than in the United States where we have political media bias. The difference in the United States is that the political media bias, by major newspapers and periodical publications, use every scheme and trick to influence the American people with deliberate partisanship but without overt sponsorship from the government, political party, or individual. The U.S. politicians happily go along with the printed bias that has been purposely leaked and abetted by lobbyists and others with vested interests.

This book is also about acculturation and how it plays an important role in the success or failure of an American executive in Latin America. It is essential for any senior executive considering taking a position in Latin America to study the country and city where he and his family will live and understand their respective social and business code of ethics and morals. Without the use of the Internet, research had to be done at a major library. The spouse should be brought in on the process at the outset. Contact with the consulate or embassy of the target country and city is also a prerequisite. If possible, locating citizens of the country in question and interviewing them at length would be a big help in getting the pulse of who they would be dealing with. Children, depending on their age, should also be given indoctrination about where they were going and why. Finally, the person who takes the managerial position has to make a stab at learning the Spanish language. There is nothing that impresses the local citizens and the management staff of the company he is taking over or has targeted as a client for the new man to speak some Spanish, even if he stumbles his way through it. If the assignment is to be taken seriously and if success is important to whoever is undertaking the challenge, these steps must be taken.

The common bond between Latin American countries is the Spanish language. However, each of the eighteen Spanish-speaking countries has their own slang words and vernacular speech. Each country has its own culture and standards, values, and basic moral code. The mindset of the Latin American business professional is very different from its counterpart in the United States. It isn't enough to rely solely on how good you are at your business area of expertise; if you can't handle the acculturation process, you and your career are in trouble.

My only early experience working in the United States was in my family's place of business, and I found it was not a career I wanted to pursue. Instead, I chose the international business arena because I felt especially suited for this line of business. I was certain that working abroad would provide the excitement and glamour I was searching for and a more interesting career. Over the years international business would give me a tremendous amount of satisfaction and all the action and adventure I had been seeking. Nevertheless, now and again I wondered what direction my life and career would have taken had I chosen to remain the United States. I kept up with my childhood friends, looking into their lives, families, and fortunes through the years. There was a marked difference in our respective careers. I doubt I could have taken their place or they could have taken mine. This book will also give the reader the opportunity to tinker with the thought of working abroad and whether or not it is worth the dramatic change in lifestyles.

My first step in venturing away from home was to enlist in our armed forces. I served as a paratrooper with the 11th Airborne Division during the Korean War. Shortly before my discharge, I was recruited by The University of the Americas in Mexico City and awarded a football scholarship. In addition, I also had the G. I. Bill. With the scholarship and the G.I. Bill, I was living very well for a college student. Studying in Mexico gave me an ample taste of living outside of my country. What I learned, the local people I met, the environment, the way everyone enjoyed life grew on me and led to my choice of a career based more on adventure than logic.

Shortly after I graduated, I was hired by a division of a Fortune-500 company and immediately sent to the New York headquarters office for "basic training." Several months of indoctrination would result in a permanent assignment to one of the branches in Latin America. The company was in the business of manufacturing graphic arts supplies for the printing and publishing industry. Eventually, this led to my career in the newsmagazine and book-publishing business. At the time I was hired, the industry of the company was immaterial to me since I didn't know one field of business from another. The most important thing to me was to have a job.

There are several levels of international assignments. Certainly Paris, London, Rome, and Madrid are more glamorous and comfortable but not nearly as exciting as Mexico City, Bogota, Colombia, Santiago, Chile, or Buenos Aires, Argentina. I didn't know that comfort, convenience, leisure activities, and quality of life were used to grade international assignments, and the country and city where I would be assigned were irrelevant as far as I was concerned.

Not everyone is well suited for work in the international business arena. Even the change in lifestyle in the glamour city assignments makes it difficult for everyone to adjust. Living and working in what had come to be known as "third world" countries is even harder to handle not only for the executive, but the family as well. Some have "culture shock" within months or weeks of arrival and are flown back to the States (one case that I know of had to be restrained by a straightjacket for the trip). It is a matter of not being able to adjust to the dramatic changes in lifestyles. I was in my late twenties and young enough to be able to adjust to any environment. Somehow the excitement of living and working outside the United States allowed me to close my eyes and mind to the frequent transgressions made by the public and private sectors against most laws of the land regardless of the consequences.

In addition, I had the advantage of having native fluency in

Spanish. Being able to communicate with the business community on all levels and deal with government officials to "fix" problems made my life easier and my career blossom. I later learned that my complete command of the Spanish language gave me a high priority by the hiring list of companies.

Businessmen and women and their families live privileged life-styles in their Latin American assignments. Most have company cars, drivers, school, and rent allowances, a country club membership, paid vacations including transportation expenses, servants, and a more exciting business environment than back home. With those kinds of benefits offered only to a few very senior management executives in the United States, why do so many Americans fail in foreign assignments? Unable to acculturate to the country of assignment is one of the factors.

Americans who make it through the acculturation phase learn to deal with individuals in power that lay down the rules of whatever game is being played. Depending on whose rules they are and what power to castigate he or she has, you decide whether or not to follow their program. If you understand this ruse, you have a better chance of succeeding in your international assignment.

THE WORLD OF EXPATS

Many of you are wondering what the word "expat" means and why it is important. Expat is a short version of the word expatriate. A dictionary will tell you that an expatriate is someone who has been banished from his country or is living in exile. The dictionary will also point out that an expat is someone who lives away from his home country but has not been banished. As far as I can remember, those of us who live and work steadily in a foreign country use the term expat. There is a kind of bond between Expats that probably comes from the marked difference in the American way of life and that of the foreign country in which we live and work. The acculturation process also includes the family, and to include them in the process is not an easy task. Expats are not given short-term assignments of one or two years. They have proven their worth to the company they work for or to their own entrepreneurial operation by staying the course, not blinking, and learning that the dramatic differences in the rules of the game are often for the benefit of their company and themselves and are necessary to succeed. A good expat is worth as much to his company as a top tier quarterback is worth to an NFL team. The company and the NFL team look after their asset as they would any other valuable property they control.

This book is a chronicle about what I dealt with from time-to-time as an American newsmagazine executive on assignment in Latin America. It is not a book about business enterprises and practices. The book will also point out a few of the marked differences of how careers develop and unfold in the United States as compared to the international business arena. Readers can reach their own conclusions as to the morals of each event.

As time took its inevitable toll, my old friend and mentor in the real world and I grew closer. I was in a better physical condition to fly from Dallas, Texas, to his country home in Pawling, New York, so I made the trip a few times before I too was grounded. Proud to be a genuine Russian prince, my friend always had chilled vodka for the asking. We spent enjoyable hours reminiscing about our respective adventures in Latin America and Europe.

" Bobby," he said, "you're a decent wordsmith, why don't you write a book about what you did, what you saw, the unforgettable characters you met and did business with, and all the rest of the hoopla we were involved in?"

Never did I think that writing a book, so easily said, would be such a daunting and difficult task. After open-heart surgery and five bypasses, leukemia, cancer, respiratory arrest, and five years later, I felt I should put the actions to words. Perhaps as a book, those who are still living will come to understand and believe my life and times in a troubling part of the world. Unfortunately, my good friend passed on before I finished writing the book.

AUTHOR'S NOTE

Time constraints were used to limit the storyline by not including the everyday mundane business tasks. The names of persons involved in these events as well as names of companies have been changed or omitted for obvious reasons. I kept a journal to chronicle most of the circumstances as they unfolded and are described in the book for what I hoped would someday be my memoir. These notes also document my conversations and comments and that of others present at the events herewith described. I kept the journals for embassy debriefing purposes that are also an important part of this work. I should point out these episodes are only half the adventure. I left Latin America after the first twenty years for personal reasons later explained and returned after three years in the United States. Had I included the years after my return to Latin America, the book would be as voluminous as *War and Peace*.

I also conducted a search over a period of a year for former colleagues, senior level secretaries, and personnel on various levels of the business and social spectrum that played a small or large part in these events. In all I was able to reach and speak with eighteen former comrades-in-arms. They were able to confirm some of my notes and added some of their own. Without these people who freely shared their memories and notes, I would not have been able to write this book. Some of the events are serious, some are deadly serious, some are humorous, others tragic, but all are true. I hope they are entertaining as well.

In the Trenches:

MEXICO CITY

MEXICO - A SIDEBAR ON CORRUPTION. Since the Constitution of 1917 and for the following seventy years, one party ruled Mexico. The PRI (Partido Revolucionario Institucional) had Mexico in an iron grip. How people fared depended on the whims of whoever was president at the time. Some ruled harshly, others in a "kinder, gentler" way, but all were authoritative, and their word was law. Some foreign heads of state and diplomats considered Mexico as one of the most absolute dictatorships in the world. The PRI controlled and ruled Mexico under the guise of a democracy with voting rights that somehow elected the official PRI candidate time after time

On the positive side, it was the stranglehold of the PRI political party that kept Mexico reasonably stable, unlike the rest of the Latin American countries. If it had not been so easy for corruption on all levels of the socioeconomic hierarchy to take hold, Mexico might have been the shining example of what can be achieved in developing countries. Alas, that was not to be. Corruption in Mexico is not something to be ashamed of by Mexicans, but rather it is the fool who won't take advantage of the opportunity to benefit him.

An example of the mentality of corruption is the case of a fellow who was hired through personal contacts, of course, by PEMEX, the Mexican nationalized oil industry. His position was as a senior level attorney in the legal department. About six months after he had been hired, I enquired about him and how he was doing. I was told he had been fired.

"Why?" I asked stunned.

"Because," replied my friend with a shrug, "he didn't know how to steal quietly and effectively. Then, if he couldn't steal properly, or at all, it made it impossible for his boss to steal as well."

According to many, the Spaniards brought the mentality of corruption to Mexico. That is no different than saying the Europeans brought all the illness to the Americas. I suppose any excuse can be used, but the fact is, from the traffic cop to the presidency, corruption was an established way of life.

PRESIDENT GUSTAVO DIAZ ORDAZ, 1964–1970.

The presidency of Gustavo Diaz Ordaz was successful, but in spite of financially good times with inflation at its lowest level in years and more money being designated for education, the student revolution at universities continued. Many have concluded that much of the turmoil was planned and executed by communist agitators who had infiltrated the student groups. As stated above, whoever was president governed the country according to his own personality, whims, and view of what would be the best course for Mexico. Protests are popular in Mexico. Little is gained by a protest, but the Mexican government tolerates them to show Mexican democracy in action. President Diaz Ordaz had an innate authoritarian manner fueled by the constant attack in which railroad workers, teachers, and doctors took part. Many were unjustly fired from their positions for being active participants. President Diaz Ordaz's cavalier attitude and hatred towards students only created extreme anger by the Marxist students and many who followed the Marcuse theories of the "New Left."

President Diaz Ordaz had an ongoing war with Mexico's students, who constantly criticized his policies and even added personal taunts concerning the president's less than attractive physical appearance. However, as president, he wielded a very big stick. While the students marched on the presidential palace with shouts challenging the president to "come out and fight," President Diaz Ordaz did exactly that. He sent Army troops to occupy the National Autonomous

University of Mexico, headquarters for Marxists, Marcuse followers, dissidents of every stripe, who were simply advocates of the "poor against the rich." Occupying the National Autonomous University of Mexico was intolerable, and no previous government had dared "invade" the university campus with troops.

There began what has been labeled as Mexico's *dirty war*. A week before the Olympics were scheduled to initiate activities, several thousand people gathered at the Plaza of Three Cultures in Tlatelolco for a mass meeting. The president knew what was coming, and with the Olympics only a few days away, he gave orders to Luis Echeverria, Minister of the Interior, to quell the demonstration with whatever means were necessary. Police and soldiers shot down participants in the meeting. When it was over, at least three hundred and possibly as many as four hundred people lay dead. No one really knows the exact amount. The government blamed terrorists who began firing at the police and demonstrators trying to take over the Ministry of Foreign Relations located nearby.

After the Tlatelolco Massacre, Mexico was never the same. Luis Echeverria was the successor to President Diaz Ordaz, and with him Mexico entered into the era of presidential robber barons. Corruption hit an all-time high, and various financial disasters followed.

THE BEGINNING.

It was now several years since I had been hired out of college and had since moved into the newsmagazine business. My career had blossomed, and I was promoted to CEO for all Spanish-speaking countries south of the Rio Grande, including the Caribbean. It was a position I thoroughly enjoyed and took advantage of all the available trappings of the office. I used whatever legitimate opportunity to credit the reputation of my close colleagues, as well as the reputation of our magazines, with journalistic achievements, investigative reports, and other events of merit. My active participation in anything remotely connected to my line of business added to my visibility not only in Mexico, but in the rest of Latin America as well. Obviously, I was making myself available in each country by flying a very heavy travel schedule. My extra efforts paid off handsomely not only for our magazines, but myself as well.

CENSORSHIP IN THE NAME OF MORALITY.

The following account is as ridiculous as it is humorous. It is included to illustrate to the reader the difference in the culture of the United States and Mexico, including the rest of Latin America. It paints a picture of how our neighbors are so close and yet so far culturally, morally, and emotionally. Their lives unfold following their own social and business mores and, in most cases, ignore how the United States and the rest of the world view them.

The president's wife was a devout Catholic, faithful to the church and its traditions and policies. With the power her husband wielded, she felt she could impose a higher standard of morality. She, therefore, decided to take on the press as a first step. At that time there were a number of black and white tabloid weeklies that featured semi-clad female models. Both the models and the tabloids printed on a poor grade of newsprint looked terrible. In spite of the poor quality of the product, it sold well on newsstands. Mrs. Diaz Ordaz had no problem in having those publications removed from the newsstands in Mexico City in twenty-four hours and forty-eight hours in the interior of the country.

PLAYBOY INVADES MEXICO.

There was still a bigger problem. *Playboy Magazine* was coming into Mexico carried by airline passengers. Not to be defeated by a something called freedom of the press, she had congress, with her husband's support issue, a law-declaring *Playboy* a menace to the moral standards of the Mexican people. After that, it was against the law to be in possession of a copy of *Playboy Magazine* anywhere in the Mexican republic.

During this morality furor, it occurred to me to test the new censorship law at the Mexico City airport. Knowing the Mexican mentality in these "holier than thou" laws, I knew that enforcement would break down as the echelon of authority reached lower levels. In order to set up the test, that would be more of a con, I called Eduardo Villegas, our editor, explained the con I wanted to pull off and asked him to send a reporter and a video photographer to the Customs area of the international terminal. They could get in with their press credentials and say they were waiting for some foreign dignitary. I gave him my flight schedule, airline, flight number, and arrival time flying from San Antonio, Texas, to Mexico City. There are six inspection tables in the Customs area as travelers exit Immigration, so I wouldn't be hard to spot. "Eduardo," I said, "please tell the reporter and the photographer to take as much footage as they can and to try to pick as much of the conversation as the video recorder will allow. I won't be hard to spot with the commotion the Customs Officer will make." Eduardo agreed that this "holier than thou" attitude adopted by the Mexican government was out of line and in the end would cause havoc and confrontation among the people. He jumped at the opportunity to work on the con. Eduardo could make a fun, tongue-in-cheek story with all the downside aspects of the new law. He had already initiated a team to work on the subject since complaints about the law had begun to spring up.

Frankly, I didn't care about the censorship squabble, but I thought the whole matter to be ridiculous and invasive of our personal property rights. Still, I thought we could have some fun with a story on the subject and get some licks in on the absurdity of this new law.

I had a copy of the recent issue of *Playboy* clearly visible in my briefcase. It would be easily noticed by the Customs Officer and was the first phase of my test. That would lead to the chain of events for what ultimately would happen to the magazine once it was confiscated. As I moved along the queue and lifted my luggage onto the inspection tables, I carefully opened each bag to show I had nothing to hide other than my dirty underwear. I also opened my briefcase and allowed a partial view of the *Playboy Magazine* cover to be in sight. The Customs Officer rummaged around in each of my bags and wished he could find something he could pull out and label me a smuggler or a black marketer.

He gave up on my luggage, but as he moved on to my briefcase, his eyes lit up like two stadium lights as he pulled out the copy of *Playboy Magazine*. The Customs Officer couldn't hold back. He held up the magazine so that others could see it in my queue, as well at the other inspection tables. What he didn't know was that I had spotted our reporter and the photographer, who was busily filming the whole incident, while the reporter was taking notes.

The Customs Officer now began to speak loudly. While holding the magazine in the air, he began to strongly criticize my indifference for breaking the recently enacted congressional law. He kept on, almost ranting, drawing comparisons between values in the United States and Mexico and would have kept on had it not been for an alert supervisor who rushed over to our table and put a stop to it. By that time, our two secret investigative reporters had gotten most of the tirade. The Customs Officer calmed down and put the magazine in a drawer of the inspection table.

"What is done with the confiscated copies of the magazine?" I asked in my most sincere, non-offensive tone.

"That's none of your business," he replied rather rudely.

No use asking any further questions, I said to myself. I just nodded, picked up my luggage, my briefcase, some goodies from the duty-free store, and walked on. My guess was that they kept the magazines and sold them on the black market, or they burned about half of the magazines they confiscated with photographers present to placate Mrs. Diaz Ordaz.

We published our story on the *Playboy* incident at Mexico City's international airport. It included pictures our photographer was able to take and quotes from the shouting Customs Officer. The story was good for circulation. It created a lot of laughs and brought embarrassment to the administration.

As a result, the censorship law died a quiet death when President Echeverria was elected two years later.

HIGH SOCIETY.

Another equally ridiculous and financially foolish censorship law was passed. This one dealt with our advertising campaign for Scotch whiskey.

Ballantine Scotch was very popular among the genteel community in Mexico and especially in Mexico City at that time. Ballantine was running a four-color, full page, twenty-six time advertising campaign with our magazine. The campaign represented a considerable amount of money twenty-six times a year for us and for Mexico as well.

Out of the blue, I received a call from the office of the Director

General of the Mexican Health and Human Services Department. Eva, my secretary, took the call. The director general wanted to meet with me. I had no idea what he wanted but couldn't decline the invitation, so I had Eva call the director's secretary and set a date for a time and place at the director's convenience.

The director's office was just another hole in the wall in one of Mexico City's older buildings. Dingy as the office might be, it was still the office of someone who had the power to make your life uncomfortable. The director was of Tolteca Indian decent and wore it on his sleeve as a badge of pride. Like many others, he had obviously been the victim of discrimination by the wealthy of European decent existing in Mexico.

Nevertheless, he did get up when I walked in and shook my extended hand. The director pointed to a straight-back chair in front of his desk that had short legs so he could look down on me, and was as uncomfortable as it looked as I sat down. He was playing with a round, metal object about four inches in diameter that, when opened, became a knife in the shape of a scimitar.

No talk about golf, family, or good restaurants, as is usually the case. Mr. Director wanted to make a point before we got to the real reason for the meeting.

"Do you know what this is?" he asked, holding up the object and opening it to form a knife.

"Sorry, no."

"This is what is used to castrate bulls."

I just stared at him.

"It takes a lot of courage to get down between the legs of an untamed bull and cut off his testicles."

I kept staring at him.

He thought he was in control of our so-called meeting, so he continued with his story.

"I was raised at a small ranch near Chilpancingo and learned to do this difficult work. I thought this might be of interest to a foreigner like you."

Chilpancingo is in the state of Guerrero, Mexico's most violent and murderous state. Since he labeled me a "foreigner," I guess he wanted me to know he was a tough guy. Either way, I didn't care.

I thought I would give him a bit of his own medicine.

"I wasn't raised on a ranch, but I was a rodeo cowboy for several years and have even competed in Mexico against the Mexican Charros. We won all three times. If you know anything about American rodeos, you know we ride on two tons of a wild Brahma bull or we ride a wild bareback bronc or a saddle bronc, or we do some steer wrestling, among other things. The animals we ride on all have a "flank": that is a leather strap tied tightly around the animal's hindquarters so that it is squeezing their testicles. The flanks are used to provoke the bull or bronc into a rage and "bucking" stronger and quicker in an effort to lose the bothersome flank. Believe me, the animals go crazy wearing that strap.

"I know about American rodeos," he said, swallowing. "I've been to the Ft. Worth Stock Show."

I just sat there and continued to stare at him. Both of us could play the intimidation game.

"Let's get down to business. Your magazine is publishing certain advertisements for Ballantine Scotch. They show a handsome man and a beautiful woman, each holding a glass of what the reader must assume is Ballantine Scotch. They are casually, but elegantly dressed, posing alongside a Cadillac luxury convertible in front of several world-renowned landmarks. They include the Eiffel Tower, the English Parliament, and Big Ben, the Roman Coliseum and the Ampudia Castle called 'one of the oldest and noblest castles in Castile, Spain' by *Time Magazine*. It was used in the film *El Cid* with Charleston Heston and Sophia Loren."

"Yes," I said, "you're right on target."

"Would you agree that almost all Mexicans are not able to afford Ballantine Scotch, a luxury automobile, or travel to Europe?"

"I suppose so, but what does that have to do with the advertisements?"

"I have concluded," he said, "that the message in those images will convey some troubling consequences."

"What kind of consequences?" I asked puzzled.

"People will be upset to the point of rebelliousness when they see that there are Mexican citizens who can enjoy those worldly goods; otherwise, why advertise in journals that circulate in Mexico. They are smart enough to know they cannot ever see Paris or Rome or Spain or own a fancy car. This will feed class envy, a difficult emotion that is hard to control."

"Our magazine only goes to a very upscale target audience, so the majority of the population never reads our editorial content, let alone sees advertisements."

"Nevertheless, I must consider the likelihood of an outcry against our government."

I was at a dead end.

"What would you have us do?"

"You can change the advertisements. Make them more appealing. For example, take out the snobby couple, the car, and the world landmarks. Put a bottle of Ballantine in the center of the page and use text that simply says 'Ballantine is a good quality Scotch,' and in this manner you show the public at large they too might buy a bottle of Scotch for special occasions. Frankly, I think most of them will prefer tequila."

"First of all, Mr. Director, it cost thousands of dollars to produce these advertisements. For authenticity, they were shot on location. Secondly, the male and female are professional models and also represent a considerable investment. In short, a large financial loss for Ballantine and a public relations disaster for Mexico that would cause headlines in the United States and Europe." I thought the latter might move him.

For a while I had thought the director meant what he was saying, but true to the values of anyone in his position, he came up with an option to solve the problem negative headlines in the United States and Europe notwithstanding.

"You can, of course," he said with the most sincere expression he could muster, "pay the fine."

Here it is. Making me sweat like the bull about to be dragged from the bullring to be sliced, diced, and sold to a gathering of men and women anxious to get home and start dinner.

The scimitar-looking knife was just to show me he was going to be tough and difficult to negotiate with. The advertisements and the offense they may cause was just part of the show. He was good. No doubt about it, it was a way to soften me up for the kill.

"So what is the fine for an infringement of this kind?"

He reached in his desk and pulled out an official book. I couldn't read the title, but I knew it was a fake.

"It says here that a fine of this kind will cost three cases of Ballantine Scotch and one hundred thousand pesos."

That was about eight thousand dollars at the exchange of that time.

"Done," I said.

"My secretary will give you my address on your way out. The 'fine' can be delivered there anytime this week."

I got up and walked out. What a waste of time for what was going to be the end result anyway but they just had to go through a song and dance to make it sound legitimate. Everything had a way of being fixed. It was a disagreeable way of doing business, but you go along with it or get out.

A FRAMEWORK FOR TRAGEDY.

Luis Echeverria was Secretary of the Interior prior to becoming president. In that position he was in charge of keeping law and order and internal security in Mexico with whatever means necessary. In addition to the police force and an able SWAT team, he formed a commando type group known as the "Halcones" (Falcons). This so-called task force was comprised of thugs and criminals responsible for assaults, kidnappings, holdups, and murder. The "Halcones" were brought in to quell civil disturbances such as demonstrations, riots, or individuals who were a voice of opposition. They were brutal and dealt with women and children as they did with men. They had carte blanche to mete out whatever punishment was necessary according to their own code.

THE TLATELOLCO MASSACRE.

In 1968, Mexico was to be the host of the 1968 Olympics. The incumbent President of Mexico, Gustavo Diaz Ordaz, gave Luis Echeverria his marching orders: Put down any and all demonstrations that could disturb the Olympics and have a negative impact on Mexico's image worldwide. Luis Echeverria, seeking the presidency in 1970, followed his boss's order to a tee. In Mexico, the sitting PRI president would choose his successor, no questions asked. It was called the *dedaso*, meaning, "I anoint you for president." So Echeverria went about the business of quelling any kind of civil disobedience or demonstration with no holds barred.

Protests in the form of public demonstrations are not unusual in Mexico. Protests and the demonstrations go hand-in-glove, covering a variety of subjects, many ridiculous and frivolous. For example, students have protested an increase of the National University tuition from less than one dollar per semester to forty dollars. Elementary, secondary, and high school teachers protest salaries, vacation time, holidays, and school hours. Others protest the price of milk, electric power rates, crime, and so on. Mexico does not have a designated area for the demonstrations, so they take to the streets, especially the major thoroughfares, and block traffic for hours and sometimes days. They are not easily dispersed. The government allows the demonstrators to cause this mayhem to let the groups cool their heels and show democracy at work to their own citizens and the world. In fact, the bottom line is that nothing changes.

THE BEGINNING OF THE END.

Student demonstrations had been going on for months all over the country, and the response from President Diaz Ordaz was a hard-line stand when it finally appeared as though Mexico City might be under siege with the world looking on during the Olympics. The night of October 2, 1968, brought the violence to a head. Mexican "Security Forces" using automatic weapons massacred student demonstrators in *La Plaza de las Tres Culturas* at Tlatelolco, Mexico City, and even used fifty-caliber machine guns, a particularly lethal weapon mostly used in the Second World War and Korea. When it was over, hundreds of people lay dead or wounded. The survivors were rounded up and hauled away. The country was shocked but not surprised. It was nothing new; strong-arm tactics was how the government kept the country in line and under control.

The Cover-up:

MEXICO CITY

THE DISAPPEARANCE OF NICO'S SON. A few days after the Tlatelolco Massacre, Nico, our company coffee girl, asked to see me in my office. Nico was a chubby, jolly lady of indiscriminate age and served coffee to anyone who asked for it on our executive floor. She had other chores, but serving coffee was her main responsibility.

I ushered her into my office and asked her to take a seat, which she did with hesitation. Nico was of mixed Indian blood and not comfortable in what she perceived to be the seat of power and with a member of the "ruling class." She was holding back tears but would soon let them flow. She told me her son had been one of the student demonstrators, but by the Grace of God, he was alive when he was taken away by the security forces. Her son had managed to get a message to Nico through a female bystander. He was being taken but did not know where. Nico said she had not heard from her son and wanted to know if there was any way that I could help locate him. Again, to Nico, the seat of power could make anything happen. I was not looking forward to dealing with the security forces and the military that also participated in the massacre, but I couldn't turn Nico down.

The title of Chief Executive Officer and Publisher is not used in Latin America. Instead, I also had the title of director general and used it as the circumstances required. Armed with my lofty title and my press card, I set out with Nico to initiate our investigation as to the whereabouts of her son. As a first step, I had my driver get the addresses of all the police stations in the Tlatelolco area. There were four. After thinking about it, I decided the best way to approach the investigation was to tell the truth. We would say we were looking for Nico's son, Octavio Gomez Palacios, and I would hand over my impressive credentials.

NO HELP FROM ABOVE.

Mexico City was in the middle of the rainy season. Automobile traffic in the city, at best, requires a great deal of effort and, above all, patience. If I was invited to a dinner party in the Pedregal residential area of the city, which is south, and I live in Lomas, north of the city, I could count on an hour and a half drive. Of course, I had a driver, and I would generally take something to drink and listen to my favorite music. Under the worst of circumstances, you are faced with traffic accidents, traffic congestions caused by traffic light malfunctions, impatient drivers trying to move ahead and causing a snarl of one kind or another, or mobs demonstrating for whatever reason. Throw rain in to the equation and you have a traffic nightmare worse than Dante's *Inferno*. Our bad luck was it was raining cats and dogs, and we were not going to one destination, but several.

This was not going to be a fun evening. My driver brought the car to the front entrance, and we climbed in. Nico sat in the backseat. She would be more comfortable riding alone then the possibility of having to make small talk with me. I rode shotgun along with Benito, my driver. I didn't expect that we would be able to discover anything about Nico's son or his whereabouts. I had a feeling that her son was no longer of this world. The police officers I would be interviewing were not exactly British gentlemen or any other kind of gentlemen either. These were people not long from the meanest poverty existence that had made it to a police officer level, clawing and fighting their way in, so I didn't expect kindly cooperation or any cooperation for that matter.

Our first stop was at the police station closest to the site of the massacre at the *Plaza de Tres Culturas* in Tlatelolco. With my umbrella, I went in alone, flashing my press card and my business card with my fancy title to the desk sergeant. I asked to see the captain. All police stations had a captain in charge. The office was seedy and dingy, full of cigarette smoke, and not so different from other police precincts in the world. The desk sergeant was smoking a *Delicado* cigarette, which smelled like it was made from cow manure and locoweed. He was a very dark-skinned individual with straight black hair that pointed in different directions, and he resembled one of the many Aztec idols. He spent about fifteen minutes quizzing me on a variety of topics, which had little to do with the reason I was there. Finally, he used the phone on his desk to announce me to the captain's office. Mexico is at the top of the list for countries with the most red tape in any city, state, or federal office or department. If you have no patience for the way the process is purposely entangled in red tape, you better pack your bags and go home.

I was finally ushered in to the captain's office. It was a bit better decorated, and he had a wooden desk unlike the metal ones in the other offices. He also had an executive chair of sorts. Our initial conversation, as usual, covered several topics that had nothing to do with my reason for being there.

He was a soccer fan, and we talked about the rivalry of the competition between the Necaxa Soccer Club and the Atlante Soccer Club. The Necaxa was his team. I said it was mine as well. I hate soccer. Then we talked about American Football, especially the Dallas Cowboys. He was a fan of American football, the Cowboys in particular.

Fifteen or twenty minutes into the conversation, we finally got to the matter of Octavio Gomez Palacios and his disappearance. The captain had not seen him or knew of him and added that none of the Tlatelolco survivors were booked into his facility. We checked the booking journal, and Octavio's name didn't appear on the October 2 page or any of the subsequent pages. His only suggestion was for me to check with the other stations in the Tlatelolco precinct area.

Thanks for nothing, Captain. I expected the other stations would have the same story. Each time I returned to the car with the sad news, Nico would burst into tears. At this point I smelled cover-up. I was wondering what I would do if one day my son turned up missing. I knew Nico well, and my heart went out to her. I could only imagine the grief she had to be feeling. Deep down, I knew Nico's son was gone forever.

Although the massacre was reported in the newspapers, radio, and TV, it was given a spin. I didn't think much about it at the time when *Los Pinos*, the Mexican White House, blamed professional agitators, communists, and gangs paid by foreign interests with the intention of embarrassing the Mexican government. A cover-up didn't cross my mind until I heard the same story over and over from the police captains. Cover-up or no cover-up, where was Octavio Gomez Palacios?

I had one card left. One of my uncles was a friend of the *Comandante* of the entire Mexico City Police Force, the SWAT team, and the Security Force. I told Nico not to get her hopes high and explained what I was about to do.

"The *Comandante* may not even see me," I said.

Again, armed with my trusty, fancy title, my press card, and my Ampudia surname, I called on the *Comandante*. I was quickly ushered in to his office. Whether it was my surname, my press card, or my fancy title, I did not have to do reception area time. His office was decorated with awards and pictures with senior political figures, including the President of Mexico. All pictures were signed.

The *Comandante* was a big man for a Mexican. He stood over six feet tall and weighed at least 250 pounds. He was handsome, but it didn't hide the fact that his reputation was as a hard top cop who dealt harshly with criminals on whatever socioeconomic level— blue collar to white collar, Indian, Meztizo, European, or American. Suddenly, I recognized him. He had been a defensive lineman for the *Universidad* (UNAM) football team when I was playing for the University of the Americas. He was the player who knocked out one of my front teeth, and at the same time knocking me out for about twenty minutes.

I can't lose anything, I thought, *by reminding him of the incident wherein he knocked me senseless, even though we won.*

That did it. We were suddenly comrades-in-arms. He was all smiles and offered me a shot of that tequila. I decided to have the drink and a cigarette with him, hoping it would surely cement our newly formed friendship. In Mexican political circles, a visiting individual may be offered an alcoholic drink by the host. The offer of the drink is serious, deliberate, and to demonstrate to the guest he is considered a valued visitor. It is not the start of a drinking bout but simply establishing a bond between the two gentlemen. There is no turning down the drink; that would provoke an affront and lose the favor of the host forever.

The conversation took longer than I had wished for, and after football war stories and explaining my relationship with my uncle, I got to the reason for coming to see him. At this point he became quite serious, hardly speaking at all. I knew a cover-up was well in place. He repeated the party line that all the demonstrators had been released, and that most of them had been seen going up in the mountains. I thanked him for the tequila, we embraced, and he showed me to the door of his office. He handed me a small brass sculpture of an elephant that is considered good luck in some quarters. He lowered his voice and said, "Roberto, leave this alone. Walk away from it. By the end of the week it will be known that you have visited the police stations and that you came to see me. It isn't healthy." With that, he turned and walked back to his desk. There went our short-lived comrades-in-arms special friendship.

END OF THE LINE.

I hated to back down on the investigation, but I was convinced it would go nowhere. People in very high places would see to that. There was the implied warning from the *Comandante*. Any further intrusion into this matter could be hazardous for my health. Sadly, I would have to tell Nico that I had failed, and she would never see her son again. It hurt me because it had become personal. It wasn't that my investigation failed, it was my fondness and respect for Nico and the grief I shared with her that made me feel as if I had lost a member of my own family.

Not long after the tragedy of Nico's son, I had lunch with one of my Ampudia uncles. I described the events that took place in my search for Nico's son. He just shook his head and took a sip from his single malt Scotch.

"Bobby," he said, "that young man will never be found. What's more, there will not be any trace of his remains either. You got about as close as you can get to Echeverria's goon squad and walk away in one piece and, for that matter, still breathing.

My uncle was friendly with the president and other chief executives before Echeverria. He wined and dined with senior political figures as well as those in the movie and entertainment industry. He was very well known and highly regarded as a friend by many and was privy to most of the scandals, political corruption, and downright underhanded manipulations of the country's laws. He was one of my mentors in Mexico and my source of hard-to-get information. He explained that the goon squad had lye pits in the mountains where they put their victims, dead or alive, when they didn't have time or desire to bury them.

"No one will ever see that young man again. Just pray that he didn't suffer at the hands of the Halcones."

Why was I surprised? I had been around here long enough to know how things work in Mexico for those not able to defend themselves legally or with power or with money. In Mexico that means most of the population. I sat there sipping my drink and staring about me at the opulence. There was always plenty of food and drink by the ruling class that could afford it. The patrons were mostly well-dressed men, and I wondered what any of them would do if they were caught protesting in the streets. Of course, that thought was ludicrous. They would never be caught in a similar situation, because they were part of the establishment, even if they didn't like it. Those protesting had no recourse but to take to the streets as a way to demonstrate their anger at whatever egregious position the government had taken that affected the populace. Of course, nothing was ever solved by the protests except to disrupt the daily traffic routine.

I chatted a bit more with my uncle, finished my Brandy & Benectine, and thanked him for his advice and lunch.

"Let's get together again soon," I said and walked out into a very bright sunny afternoon. *Life goes on,* I said to myself.

After the incident of Nico's son, my life went back to normal, if normal is what it can be called. Nico came back to work, although she was no longer the same bubbly, happy, smiling self. The Olympics came and went without any trouble. The tragedy at Tlatelolco was topic of conversation in restaurants, at cocktail parties, and other gatherings. About half the people accepted the party line that it was a Communist plot, and the other half-blamed Echeverria, Diaz Ordaz, the *Halcones*, and even the United States.

Six months or so later, Tlatelolco and all the theories about what *really* happened began to fade into the background. The Halcones security force was disbanded, along with their strong-arm tactics. Mexicans returned to their happy-go-lucky life. The restaurants and bars continued to do a thriving business and the baseball games, soccer matches, boxing, and bullfights were all on schedule.

Nevertheless, Tlatelolco ushered in what is now known as the Lost Generation, Mexico's *desaparecidos*, those who disappeared.

Brutal Justice:

MEXICO CITY

PRESIDENT LUIS ECHEVERRIA ALVAREZ, 1970-1976.

In 1970, Luis Echeverria began his reign as President of Mexico. He had no opposition, either before or after the election. In fact, he campaigned vigorously in an effort to show the world that in Mexico, democracy and free elections were a matter of national policy. It was all for show because he would become president, and that was a forgone conclusion. The Mexican people shrugged their shoulders and went on about their own business. No one ever thought that the PRI would ever lose an election. They knew and tolerated that all sitting presidents would become robber barons, illegally acquiring property and other national resources, including domestic and international hard currency. Luis Echeverria turned out to be the king of the presidential looters.

It was during Echeverria's worldwide public relations campaign that a unique opportunity fell into our hands. All media is flooded with letters praising or complaining a particular article or editorial position, suggestions for topics, threats of bodily harm, or serious damage to your establishment, requests for interviews, and even pleas for employment. Pictures accompany many of these overtures. Most are black and white amateur shots.

We had two junior editorial trainees go through the daily stack of press releases and pick out those that seemed interesting. One of the trainees selected a picture with writing on the back and took it to

51

our editor. The picture would not change the course of history, but it would cause anger and embarrassment by the president's administration and ridicule from many of the countries in Latin America.

EL RUTAS, FAMOUS MEXICAN HIGHWAYMAN.

The photograph was of *El Rutas*, a famous Mexican highwayman who had eluded the local gendarmes and federal law enforcement agencies for more than ten years. He was dubbed *El Rutas* (which means The Routes or The Highways) because his specialty was to hijack cars and trucks on a variety of highways in the country. He was responsible for murdering men and women occupants of the vehicles and even children if they were traveling with adults. Law enforcement agencies came close to capturing him several times, but he always made good his escape. The result was that the local police, state troopers, and even the federal special task force became fair game for the press. There was ridicule enough to go around.

As quickly as our editor was handed the picture, he walked over to my office and handed it to me. Eduardo Villegas, our editor, was a Cuban exile. I knew him by reputation to be a first-rate editor. He had taken strong stances against the Castro takeover of Cuba while there was still relative freedom of the press. Soon thereafter, running from the police, he was able to escape with nothing more than the shirt on his back. When he arrived in Mexico, he came straight to our office, and half an hour later he had a job.

I couldn't believe my eyes. On the back of the picture, written in rather childish block letters, were the words *El Rutas*. The black and white picture showed two policemen sitting on a bench holding up a body that was propped up between them. There were several other uniformed officers standing on each side. All looked to be laughing and pointing at the body, but the body was what took your breath away.

El Rutas was beaten to a bloody pulp and very dead. He was shirtless and had cuts and cigarette burns all over his upper body. The end of his fingers looked like the nails had been pulled off. One ear was missing, an eye had been gouged out, and his face resembled chopped meat. He was barefoot but had on a pair of torn cotton trousers. The blood seemed to be seeping through the soft cotton fabric.

El Rutas was a grotesque mess. The picture was obscene. Man's inhumanity to man.

Eduardo was still smiling.

"So what do we do with the picture?"

"Something dramatic," I said, "but we better decide now, because if we put if off, we won't do anything." I sat in my chair knowing what I wanted to do but weighing the trouble I would create for the magazine by bringing the administration into a fit of anger and embarrassment that could damage our relationship with the government permanently. On the other hand, I felt it was my duty as the publisher to report the news accurately and without fear of reprisals. After all, *El Rutas* had received a considerable amount of press through the years, and it wasn't as if he wasn't a well-known and feared criminal. The Mexican people deserved to know about his final days and would likely breathe a sigh of relief. So be it.

"We're going to publish the picture," I said with a serious face but then broke into a smile and then started laughing. Eduardo joined me and we both laughed for several minutes. Nervous laughter? Possibly. Laughing at our macabre intentions? Definitely.

Our flagship magazine was distributed throughout the Americas and the Caribbean. Foreign embassies in Washington had bulk subscriptions, as did universities and libraries. Complementary copies were sent to all corporations big and small in the United States, Europe, Asia, Australia, and Africa. Although the editorial content was in Spanish, the magazine was seen and read around the world. Our magazine was a successful publication with advertising from most corners of the globe. Strong clout. We were going to make *El Rutas* an international star.

For our advertisers who were interested in only running their ads in specific countries for specific product lines, we had what we called split editions. For example: We called Mexico and Central America the Mexico edition. Venezuela, Colombia, and Ecuador were called the Gran Colombiana edition. The Southern Cone edition consisted of Bolivia, Peru, and Chile. The River Plate edition was Argentina, Paraguay, and Uruguay. Many of our big corporate advertisers from the U.S., Europe, and Asia ran in all four editions. It was in the four editions that we would publish the picture of *El Rutas*, Master Highwayman.

Our magazine was fortnightly, and we were, at that moment, closing the next edition. Eduardo did an excellent piece, writing about the younger days of El Rutas in time to make the closing deadline. As a boy, he was taught to steal anything that wasn't nailed to the floor. Like any good journalist, Eduardo wrote an objective piece. He described the more than two hundred known crimes and the murder and torture of innocent men, women, and children. Still, there were probably more victims that had never come to light. *El Rutas* was twenty-eight years of age when he was captured, but he had terrorized the highways and byways in Mexico for ten years.

Eduardo took it easy on the law enforcement individuals in the picture without charging them with the physical atrocities heaped on the infamous Master Highwayman. Nevertheless, it was perfectly clear that the gendarmes had fingerprints all over El Rutas.

Coincidentally, the President of Mexico was in Brazil at the same time our magazine hit the newsstands. He was speaking on civil and human rights and that he intended for Mexico to be the standard bearer in Latin America for both of these causes. Brazil is not a Spanish-speaking country. Their native tongue is Portuguese. However, Brazil was a notorious violator of human rights with a gruesome reputation for their torture chambers. The President of Mexico was delivering his speech to the Brazilian Chamber of Deputies. What the president didn't know was that the *El Rutas* story and picture was now circulating all over Latin America. To add insult to injury, the Brazilian press picked up the story from a wire service and published it in their local press precisely because Mexico's president was chastising Brazil's abuse of human rights.

I felt very righteous in the stand we had taken. Whatever goody-good feeling I was having, I knew I would have to pay some government bullyboy for my strong but indirect attack of the president and his administration for the Mexican image of human rights abuses. I also knew our headquarters office in New York would have something to say about the story and its implications.

We sent our advance copies to New York via our express press pouch. In those days, the press pouch was a counter-to-counter exercise. We delivered the pouch to the airline airport counter for a particular flight, and the pouch was picked up at its airport/airline destination by one of our couriers. Advance copies were in the hands of our New York office in twenty-four hours or less. A small group of senior management executives, including the company president, scrutinized the magazine. A sound verbal thrashing followed any mistake or misstep in the editorial content or advertising.

The day after our advance copies arrived at our New York office, my secretary (we did not call secretaries "assistants" in those days) called me on the interphone and said in a half-frightened voice, "Mr. Fielden is on the line." Mr. Roger Fielden was our peerless leader, the president of our publishing company. He was a WASP through and through. In addition to his New York City townhouse, he had a second home in Garrison, New York, a very chic residential area populated by old money only. He was a man with a mission that included the success of his publishing empire and money. In later years, I learned from Roger that money in and of itself was not the ultimate goal; it was the only way to keep score.

I got on the line, said hello, and held the phone away from ear. Roger was fuming.

"What makes you think you set editorial policy?" he shouted into the phone. "Do you realize what you've done with the *El Rutas* story? The whole of the Mexican government may come down on us. We may get fined or sued or worse, banned from Mexico altogether." He went on non-stop for five minutes.

"Let me remind you that you are the CEO for Latin America as long as you follow the rules, and I set the rules."

Roger was right. The Mexican government might do something to hurt the magazine, but that something had nothing to do with a lawsuit, a fine, or a distribution ban. What might happen was that some of our sources in high places would shut down, and we had a way to get around that possibility. Our magazine was well known worldwide, and any attempt to stop its distribution in Mexico would be more of a blow to Mexico than the *El Rutas* story. On the other hand, I could come to bodily harm. It had happened before to a few writers and reporters publishing critical stories about the administration. At that stage of my life, I had the mistaken idea that I was bulletproof and the administration could shove it.

As it turned out, the *El Rutas* exposé turned out to be a windfall of favorable publicity mainly from Latin America. I was told our New York office received numerous calls of praise from embassies and consulates and private citizens whose mother country was in Latin America. In our Mexico office, our telex began to print non-stop with messages from our principle offices in the major cities in Central and South America. The gist of the messages was that they were receiving calls complimenting our magazine for the courage and bold stand we had taken in tackling such an outrageous human rights violation. I made copies of all the messages, put them in a press pouch, and sent them on to the president in our New York office. Circulation jumped almost thirty percent for that issue, and overall circulation in the following months grew by almost twenty percent. I never heard another word from our peerless leader about *El Rutas*.

Dangerous Ground:

MEXICO CITY

SCARE TACTICS. Less than a week after the magazine had been on sale, I received a call from Oscar Carral, Press Secretary to the President. Oscar was suave, handsome, very well spoken, but he also carried a big stick that he used in a most subtle manner to make a point. He was a powerful man in the administration who could make or break most men and have a company's government relations policy change with just a suggestion.

"Hola, Roberto," he said in a low and silky voice. Most people who knew me well in Mexico and Latin America called me Bobby or Bob except Carral and President Echeverria, who considered those two nicknames to be American and did not fit in with their nationalistic state of mind.

"Hola, Oscar," I said knowing what was coming and trying to guess what kind of strategy he would use in strongly explaining their displeasure about the *El Rutas* story.

Oscar and I had met for lunch a few times. We spoke on the telephone more frequently but we were always very cordial on both our parts and had established a sort of pretended friendly relationship. This time began no different. He asked about my family, I asked about his. He asked about my health, I asked about his. He asked about my tennis game, I asked about his. We spent several more minutes discussing the best and worst of the Dallas Cowboys, the Guadalajara Soccer team, and other mundane topics. We had discussed nothing of interest to either of us and were beginning to say our good-byes. I was puzzled but pleased that he had not dealt the *El Rutas* card.

It was too good to be true. Oscar stopped in mid-sentence and said, "Roberto," again his soft, silky voice, "I enjoy our conversations so much, I forgot to bring a matter of some importance to your attention."

Here it comes, I thought. *Let's see how I can field this one.*

"I hope you haven't had problems with your paper shipments," he said with a soft and silky voice. "Some shipments have not reached a few of the media."

In Mexico, the paper industry is almost non-existent, so they must rely on the importation of paper that is controlled by the government. All newspapers and magazines in the country have allotments based on current and projected circulation. Generally speaking, all publications receive their paper allotments on time and with little or no problems, but the government uses this as a stick to keep the media in line. A few months before, a small newspaper decided to publish articles attacking the administration for corruption, violence, human rights abuses, and other crimes against the citizens. It didn't take long for the administration to retaliate. A few weeks after the initial story, the newspaper was told that the ship carrying their allotment of paper had sunk. No paper, no newspaper.

In our case, Oscar couldn't get away with the "ship sunk" story about a ship transporting our paper allotment. We were too big and too well known around the world. It was his way of telling me that some sort of retaliation would take place if we were not careful what we published about the administration in the future.

A SHOT IN THE DARK.

It was not unusual for our editorial meetings to last well into the night. I didn't always sit in on the meetings since editorial was not my direct responsibility. In all good magazine publications, a sort of "church and state," a written, or unwritten law, exists between the editorial department, the administration, and advertising departments in order to preserve editorial integrity. It simply means that the advertising department doesn't tell the editorial department what to write, and the editorial department doesn't tell the advertising department what advertising clients they should sell. Call it a separation of "Church and State."

I only came into the picture in cases such as the *El Rutas* story when the editorial content required an executive decision. In other words, I would be a scapegoat if anything went wrong, and for a short while, I paid a price for the *El Rutas* story.

I sat in on the editorial meeting for the next issue of the magazine. I had a feeling of ambivalence about having editorial go to bed without scrutinizing the whole line-up, so I stayed with them until the end. The editorial stories, articles, and commentary were good, thorough journalism—no reason for another round of verbal thrashing from my peerless leader and no threats from the Mexican seat of power.

It was then about 1:00 a.m. on a Monday night when I drove out of the office parking lot. Our offices were located in the *Zona Rosa* a couple of blocks from the *Paseo de la Reforma*. Once on *Reforma*, it was a straight shot to *Lomas de Chapultepec* and home. I arrived about 1:30 a.m. No matter the socioeconomic level of the residents, high walls and huge garage gates surround homes in Mexico. I would generally honk the horn in a special way, and one or more servants would come out to open the garage gates.

No need to wake up the servants and the neighborhood by honking the horn tonight, I thought. I got out of the car, keys in hand, and walked to the gate. At the same time, I heard a car coming around the corner and then saw it heading in my direction. I was puzzled. My street is very quiet. No need to turn on the street unless you live in one of the homes in the neighborhood.

As the car approached me at a more than necessary speed for a residential area, I saw a man hanging out of the rear window, but it all happened so fast I wasn't sure what to make of it. The first shot was fired about twenty feet away. By the time the car was even with me, the shooter had fired three more rounds. I ducked in front of the hood of the car, but by then they were pulling away and turning the corner at the end of the street. I stayed down for a while longer hoping they wouldn't double back. They didn't. I was reasonably certain they were not trying to use me as target practice but rather sending me a message.

Take it easy, Roberto. You'll live longer.

A Spy Temp:

MEXICO CITY

BACK ON THE MLR (MAIN LINE OF RESISTANCE). After that incident, I stayed close to the business side of business. Oscar Carral had made his point. *Think twice before you take on the full force of the Mexican government again.* On the other hand, reporting the truth, whatever the cost, is our responsibility.

We had to prepare for a circulation audit that was coming up in a few weeks. A circulation audit of our magazine was especially complicated, as we had subscribers and newsstand sales in eighteen Spanish-speaking countries and were the base for our circulation guarantee. Circulation audits are no different than financial audits in that you better have your numbers correct because if you fail the audit, you do not meet your circulation guarantee. If you do not meet your circulation guarantee, the magazine will lose advertisers and those are the lifeblood of a publication.

Production of our magazine was also a complicated exercise. The magazine was produced in Mexico City for the Mexico, Central American, and Caribbean editions. In Bogota, Colombia, we produced the magazine for Colombia, Venezuela, and Ecuador editions. In Santiago, Chile, we produced the Chile, Peru, and Bolivia editions. Finally, in Buenos Aires, Argentina, the magazine was produced for the Argentina, Uruguay, and Paraguay editions.

Getting the magazine ready for production in four printing plants in Mexico City, Bogotá, Colombia, Santiago, Chile, and

Buenos Aires, Argentina, was a veritable logistics nightmare handled by a wild bunch who were experts in the art of red tape, locating lost documents, bribing Customs agents in various countries, and more all on a fortnightly basis. The bribes were necessary to keep the wheels of what we called "press pouches" well oiled and to avoid delays that would affect production schedules. For a couple of days after closing the magazine, each production team would disappear into whatever world of reality they came from before preparing for the next press pouch.

For example, in the days of four-color film, each advertiser from a dozen countries would send their film and color guide to our New York production office. These were then sent to each production center in Latin America. Black and white editorial film and layout were produced and concentrated in Mexico City. Editorial was written and proofread in the Mexico office with information from our regional bureau chiefs, stringers, local sources, and stories from all over the world. I selected each regional production team using a profile of a non-conformist, unconventional, and with more than a touch of a "free spirit." Of course, they knew magazine production better than they knew how to spell their names, and even more, they spoke English and Spanish. They were handsomely compensated. We rarely lost one.

USIA (READ CIA).

I had a few friends at the U.S. Embassy in Mexico City who were always good for a commissary cut-rate price of a bottle of French wine. It wasn't all a one-way street. I helped them opening the doors with contacts they didn't or couldn't have. We did lunches, dinners, and parties together and praised or badmouthed the Washington establishment depending on the subject matter.

James Warren, one of my embassy friends, was in charge of the USIA publishing program in Spanish for Latin America. The program dealt with books on free enterprise, books disguised as journals for assistance in agriculture, economics, free market advantages, education, and even population control. Although helpful, the books were subtle American propaganda. The Latin American book distribution agreement was set-up by our New York office and the USIA headquarters in Washington, so I didn't have a choice. We had office and warehouse facilities in all of the Latin American capitals, but I didn't like the additional risk and responsibility.

Jimmy had his hands full with book titles, translations, sales, distribution reports, and traveling to many of the countries to check on the sales staff. After one of his trips, he invited me to lunch, and after a cool glass of *Sangria*, the Spanish fruit, wine, and seltzer water drink, he got right to the point. It had been strongly suggested to Jimmy by his colleagues to ask for my help in gathering intelligence on my trips to Latin America. Before I could answer an emphatic *no*, he continued to explain.

"In your travels, we would like for you to keep your eyes and ears open and bring back any Intel you feel could be of benefit for us to know."

As the senior person on our magazine masthead, I was in the unique position of being able to gain entrance to most seats of power in both the private and public sector. For example, I was frequently invited to embassy parties, met with and interviewed heads of state, had meetings with chief executive officers of local, Asian, European, and American companies located in Latin America, and was generally able to eavesdrop on conversations and gossip that might have value for our government. I didn't like the idea and told him my job description did not include being a spy temp.

It was obvious why they wanted me to take on the job. I spoke Spanish, my press credentials allowed me to gain entrance to just about any office in the private and public sectors, and I had reasonable manners. Jimmy assured me all they wanted was to "debrief" me on my return to Mexico City. What they wanted was for me to talk about whom I met with and what was said or done. They said not to worry if I felt the information was trivial, they wanted to know about it anyway. Jimmy said gathering intelligence was a matter of putting bits and pieces together until they formed a big picture. There began my career sideline as a CIA informant (at least that's the way I felt about it).

A few months after I began my CIA "assignment," I realized I was learning interesting details about matters most often overlooked in my travels before. Some I considered valuable, others boring, but with enough meat to pass on and trivial ones, which had no particular value but were deliciously amusing. I learned one head of state had three mistresses, I was privy to conversation of a possible coup of the Peruvian president, and I was invited to a private meeting on the forces against the Alliance for Progress and the *Punta del Este* Charter. I overheard senior Latin American diplomats discussing the possibility of a Marxist president coming to power in a neighboring country and trivial things such as political and diplomatic trysts, senior management comings and goings, and likewise trysts among the captains of industry. In all, it was a learning experience. I passed everything on to my "handlers" at the embassy and enjoyed a good lunch and some juicy embassy gossip.

The irony of it all was that about two years after I had become the CIA "informant," Jimmy Warren was recalled to Washington. I was offered his position as Director of the USIA Publishing Group for Latin America. In a way, I was flattered and sat through the interviews and even prepared an extensive biography. In the meantime, I was the subject of a complete background check by the CIA going all the way back to the sixth grade and right up to my current next door neighbors. That exercise took three months. Outside of some barroom brawls and drunk and disorderly conduct in my rodeo days, I was clean. It was time to fish or cut bait. The benefits included having the rank equivalent of a full Colonel, access to the commissary that provided cut-rate groceries, healthcare forever, and automatic raises no matter what kind of job performance I made. I didn't like this last one, thinking that it didn't matter if I did an exceptional job, there would be no merit raises or bonuses.

I almost went for it when I learned that the director of worldwide operations of the publishing program was a twenty-four year-old presidential appointee whose only experience was a two-year tour with the Peace Corp in Honduras. That did it. I just couldn't handle reporting to a barely-out-of-college son of a friend to the president with no experience. I had enough of those second lieutenant ROTC geniuses who didn't know the difference between a BAR (Browning Automatic Rifle) and a bar serving martinis. I turned down the offer but continued on as their Latin American pseudo-spy.

Tragic but True:

LIMA, PERU

A TELEPHONE TÊTE-À-TÊTE. I had a direct telephone line that was nothing less than a miracle considering that telephone lines were only available for the right price and a purchase of telephone company stock. Still, our company's peerless leader wanted me to have a direct line so he could call me without going through the bureaucratic Mexico system of receptionists and several other levels of red tape. When someone called the director general, the person was required to answer several questions before being passed along to the next level and so on. With my direct line, either I answered the phone, or my secretary took messages if I was out. No such thing as being in a meeting as an excuse not to take the call when Roger Fielden, chairman and president of our publishing empire, was on the line.

The phone rang, and I answered after the first ring. It was good old Roger. He didn't call often. He generally relegated the duty to whatever or whomever the message was about: production, circulation, advertising, whatever.

"How are you, Bobby?"

Uh oh, I thought to myself, *he didn't call me Bob, Robert, Roberto, but spoke to me in that low, smooth voice and addressed me as Bobby. I probably won't like what he's calling about but, as usual, I'll have no choice.*

"We have an invitation from the People of Peru to visit Lima for a couple of days next week."

"The People of Peru," I said repeating his words, "what in the world is 'The People of Peru'? It sounds fishy to me. What's going on, Roger?" I said, trying not to sound sarcastic.

"Look, Bobby, we have a certified check for five thousand dollars to cover travel expenses to Lima. Other major publications in the U.S. and Europe are also being 'invited,' if that's the word. We can't afford not to make our presence felt in whatever will take place. Your safety is guaranteed and you will be picked up by a military—"

I didn't let Roger finish the sentence. The word "military" triggered my response.

"It's a military coup they're planning," I said shouting into the phone. "You want me to go down there and put myself in a vulnerable and potentially dangerous situation in order to 'make our presence felt'? No thanks, Roger. Been there, done that."

"You, first of all, should understand, Bobby, that it is your direct responsibility to cover these kinds of events. You are very well paid; you have an envious position at an early age in your career, a position and title that allow you to rub shoulders with senior individuals in the public and private business and social arenas. It's like this, Bobby. If you refuse to go, I'll have to send someone else in your place, and our board and I will be very appreciative of this individual."

I sat in silence for a few seconds knowing that Roger wouldn't fire me, and a demotion was out of the question. I coughed into the phone to let him know I was still on the line.

"If you want, I can help you find my replacement. Let's see. He should be not too old, he should have some social graces, like not eating with his hands, be properly packaged, and willing to live life with ongoing risks. He should have some experience in periodical publishing, he should have native fluency in English and Spanish with a bit of Portuguese thrown in, and he should be intelligent. Not book-smart but quick on his feet, street smart, clever, sharp, articulate, sincere, and well spoken. I can go on."

"No need for that," he said.

"It's like this, Roger. I don't like to be threatened, and if push comes to shove, I'll leave the company. If that happens, it will be a mini logistical disaster for our five publications, including our flagship business and news magazine that would take much time to repair. My qualifications more than justify the title, compensation, and benefits, but that isn't the point. The point is I know more about Latin America and what it takes to live and work and survive in this environment than anyone in or out of our company. What 'The People of Peru' want is legitimate and bona fide witnesses to what they hope will be a bloodless coup so I believe I know what I'm talking about."

"I have the highest regard—"

Again I didn't let him finish the sentence.

"Okay Roger, I'll do it. Send me the check and the particulars in a special press pouch."

Actually, Roger was a very decent person. He treated everyone fairly and was well liked by most of the staff, but the magazines were his first priority, and nothing stood in the way of moving them forward.

LIMA, PERU.

I arrived at Jorge Chavez International Airport in Lima in the early morning. It had been a red-eye flight, and I wasn't in the best frame of mind when we landed. First of all, I had practically been pushed to make this trip against my better judgment. Secondly, all the hush-hush that the trip was wrapped in appeared like something out of a "B" movie that could have me end up in a world of hurt. Yet, here I was.

Two men in civilian clothes picked me up as I deplaned. It was easy to tell they were military men. Short haircuts, perfect posture, and they walked as if they were marching. They ushered me away from the administrative building so that I wouldn't go through Customs and Immigration and was quickly taken to a civilian limousine parked inside a hanger. The limo had dark-tinted windows impossible to see through from the outside. My "bodyguards" didn't talk, and neither did I. In the car was a driver who looked and acted just like the other two. One of the men rode shotgun, and the other sat next to me in the backseat. Both were armed. The scene was making me a bit nervous so I began singing my college football fight song in a low voice that had a calming effect on me most of the time.

Thirty minutes later we arrived at the Country Club, Lima Hotel, a very exclusive five-star luxury hotel located in *San Isidro*, the most chic and elite residential and commercial district in Lima.

The two men disappeared, and a bellboy led me to my suite. No registration, no checking my passport, no indication I was in the hotel. I asked myself if that was good or bad. No record of entering the country and no record I was in this hotel. As far as the world was concerned, I was the man who wasn't there. On the coffee table leaning against an ice bucket with a bottle of chilled Veuve Cliquot champagne was an envelope addressed to me that simply said,

> Welcome, Sir,
>
> We will meet with you and your colleagues, this evening at six o'clock in the Presidential Suite. Please enjoy your short stay and anything you would like from Room Service just ask. We prefer you stay in your suite until this evening.
>
> Signed: The People of Peru

Just follow the instructions, I said to myself.

The suite was lavish with several rooms, a fully stocked bar, and a bed that beckoned me after the long flight from Mexico City. It didn't take me long to fall asleep. I slept non-stop for three hours, got up, called room service for a sandwich and chips, and later took a long, hot shower, wondering all the time what or how I would be party to whatever was being planned.

Surely it had to be a coup, but how was it being handled? Would I be put in a compromising position? Would I be required to testify in an international tribunal? The more I thought about it, the less I liked it, but here I was, and I had to go through with the program. Promptly at six o'clock the doorbell to my suite rang. Not to my surprise, the two men who picked me up at the airport, still in civilian clothes, were standing there with the same stoic look on their faces.

"Come with us," one said, his voice dry and throaty. As I walked out of the suite, my two companions, bodyguards, or whatever, took their place along side of me. We actually marched through the halls to the Presidential Suite. We entered without knocking, and I immediately scanned the room. On one side there were five other men in casual attire having a drink and making small talk with one another. On the other side of the room were three older gentlemen in their late fifties or early sixties sitting at a small table. They were chatting and sipping wine. Behind them were my two "bodyguards" and eight other men who had the same appearance of short haircuts and a military bearing. All were carefully scrutinizing the group of five, including me. I later learned that they were paratroopers, the equivalent of our Rangers.

I recognized two of the men standing in a small group as expats and representatives of two of the major U.S. Publications. Walking over, I said hello, shaking their hands, and they, in turn introduced me to the other three: a German, a Frenchman, and a Spaniard. As we all shook hands, they repeated the names of their respective publications, and I did the same. The publications in this room, tonight, were the big leagues of magazine journals. I was impressed.

One of the older gentlemen in the middle of the three rang a small bell on the table to get our attention. He was obviously the Master of Ceremonies.

"Gentlemen," he began, "we are sure you are wondering exactly what you are here for, although we are certain you have entertained a variety of possibilities. The People of Peru have asked for a change in government in order to take our country in the proper direction. However, we are not here to explain our politics to anyone or any country. You are here to witness a 'changing of the guard,' if you will, in a most civilized, calm, and bloodless manner. You may write about it or not. That is your choice. Anyone of you who prefers not to be present may return home tomorrow morning. Those who will join us will return to their respective suites now and will be escorted to our destination at eleven-thirty tonight. Forgive us, but we're sure you understand that you do not have telephone service in your suites. Of course, you may order dinner, but again, please remain in your suites until your escorts come for you."

SHOWTIME.

My two bodyguards now dressed in formal military uniforms with the rank of major and a chest full of ribbons came for me precisely at eleven-thirty. Without much ado, we marched to the front entrance of the hotel and into a waiting limousine. Minutes later, my two American colleagues joined me in the backseat of the car. Our driver was leading the three-car parade that included our three European pals in the second car, and the third car was surely filled with more paratroopers, as a safeguard should the need arise. I was having a bad feeling about the whole program and silently prayed that I would survive the affair with my body and mind intact.

Along the way, four more black color cars with tinted windows fell in behind us. We could be called a mobile caravan of seven automobiles. There were seven black automobiles with tinted windows, loaded with senior staff officers, several foreign journalists, and a complement of paratroopers. It was enough for a small war that just might be what we were walking into. Twenty minutes later we arrived at our destination. It was a lovely residence fit for a president and, in fact, it turned out to be the home of the current president of Peru. Immediately, the front entrance was flooded with powerful lights coming from the seven cars.

"Why all the lights?" asked one of my companions.

"To prevent whoever answers the door from seeing beyond the immediate periphery," I answered. This was a technique often used when interrogating a POW.

The three older men approaching the entrance to the residence were the same three who had interviewed us in the hotel, only this time they were decked out in their military uniforms with all due medals and decorations. Two were generals, and the third was an admiral. We exited the cars, and I was able to identify two more generals and two admirals. One of the officers appeared to be a general of the Air Force. He wore wings on his tunic, and his uniform was more flamboyant. In all there were eight senior staff officers for whatever was to come next. They approached the entrance, and the leader knocked vigorously on the door. Then he knocked a second time and a third time. The door was opened by a sleepily and out-of-sorts aide. The general didn't give him time to speak.

"Inform the president he has visitors. Do it immediately."

"The president has retired for the evening and does not wish to be disturbed."

"Wake the president and tell him he is needed at once. Not in his study, not in the living room, not anywhere in the house but right here at the door. Do it *now!*"

Ten minutes later the president, soon to be addressed as mister, was standing in front of the senior military staff. He was visibly shaken and pale but made a strong effort to hide his condition by speaking with a strong and commanding voice. Knowing full well what was coming, he said, "I find it impertinent on your part to wake me at this hour. Whatever you have to say, get it over with. This is hardly the place to do business, and I need my sleep."

THE COUP.

It was obvious the president was making an effort to sound strong and buy time to organize his thoughts and hopefully head off the coming train wreck, but the general didn't give him a chance to get off the hook.

"The Peruvian Armed Forces is here to take over the government of our country as mandated by 'The People of Peru' for the purpose of giving our nation its proper position in the community of nations beholden to no one country or enterprise in the public or private sectors."

The general was obviously referring to an agreement made by the president, whereby Standard Oil of New Jersey would receive compensation for handing over the installation over claims to rich oil fields, including the document of agreement. The president's entire cabinet resigned over this matter and a serious devaluation of the country's currency ensued. The former president, now a civilian, looked the general straight in the eyes and said evenly, "I would never expect this of you, General; you and I are friends. Our families visit and party together. You are the godfather to my granddaughter—"

The general ignored his plea and cut him off, "Come with us, sir. You will not be harmed while under our care."

"You mean come with you in my pajamas, robe, and house slippers?" His voice was low and almost toneless.

"That's right. Let's do it."

The general moved to one side, as did the other senior officers, to allow the former "president" to walk through, seeing he had no choice, and get into still another black limo with tinted windows. All guards who were standing jumped to their assigned cars, and we all played "follow the leader."

"Now where are we going?" I asked no one in particular. No answer from either the driver or the one paratrooper riding shotgun.

"Okay, have it your way." One of my companions opened the bar in the limo and both served themselves. I was not interested in a drink at this point. I needed a clear head to see and hear what was about to happen next. Most military coups are violent, and those that are not are because the individual about to be "dethroned" has agreed to step down. In this case, the president did not want to give up his position and power and tried to argue his way out his removal. However, he had no choice, and he had no Army or Navy or Air Force to rally behind him. Even the aide was nowhere to be seen. I was not eager to see what was going to happen next but I too had no choice.

Forty minutes later we arrived at Jorge Chavez International Airport. Our caravan drove right on to the tarmac. The former president's limo was parked directly in front of the boarding staircase. It was a Braniff flight with Buenos Aires, Argentina, as a final destination. One of three generals who interviewed us came over to our car and asked me to follow him. The other general went to the second car and motioned to one of the three European media representatives to follow him. We started walking towards the plane and he explained, "We can't have a crowd to see this individual leave for exile from the motherland, but you and your other colleague can fill in your companions."

There were three generals, two admirals, the Spaniard, and I. There was no one else. No drivers and no paratrooper bodyguards. The general who did all the talking at the hotel and at the president's residence continued as the all-knowing, all-seeing speaker for the group.

"We brought you two media representatives to witness this person's departure alive and in good health, or at least in the health he was in when we met him at his residence."

One of the generals and one of the admirals who were standing by the limo opened the door and asked the passenger to step out. There he was, standing tall, his shoulders squared, looking as defiant as he could muster under the circumstances.

"Sir, you will now leave Lima and the country of Peru to live in exile. As long as this Military Junta is in command, you will not be welcome. We have held up this commercial flight for Buenos Aires, Argentina, in order not to use a military aircraft and risk the allegations that you would never arrive at your destination alive. The entire first-class cabin is reserved for you. There will be an armed guard in front of the curtain separating first class and coach. You will be allowed to deplane first. Our ambassador has handled all your paperwork. A car from our embassy with a driver and two bodyguards will pick you up at the airport and take you to the ambassador's home, where you will be sequestered until you contact friends or family and you get appropriate clothing and funds. You will see or talk to no one of the embassy, with the exception of the ambassador when needed. You may be assured your estate, properties, securities, and funds on deposit in banks will be not be confiscated and will be available to your family. You may now board."

A devastated man, he turned and began climbing the stairs. No waves, no salutes, no goodbyes. We stood there watching him reach the cabin door and enter the plane. We remained until the door to the plane was closed and continued to stand there transfixed to what we had seen. It was a sad and frightening case of usurping power and the closing of another page in history.

In the limo on the way back to the hotel, very little was said between the three of us. We had all had seen our share of international intrigue, conspiracies, plots, and counterplots, but never had a ringside seat to a coup and much less a bloodless coup. I felt sorry for the former President of Peru. Whatever bad judgment calls he made, one was going up against an American oil company—a favorite of the United States government no matter what party was in power in Peru or any other country. He also had to face the anger of the Peruvian people for bowing to the American oil company for putting the sovereignty of his country in the hands of foreigners.

I reflected on the series of events. First, a stranger with Diplomatic credentials walked into our New York office, including an invitation to visit his country for a brief visit. Then I got a telephone call from New York to Mexico City, giving me my marching orders. Next, I took a red-eye to Lima, Peru, and was picked up by bodyguards and driven to a super luxury hotel. We met with the making of a Military Junta and received our guest instructions. Finally, we took a ride to the airport and bid Bon Voyage to the former president of a legally constituted and sovereign nation. It was sad, but true, and I had been a party to a bloodless coup.

STATESIDE FAMILY AND FRIENDS.

Periodically, I would call home to enquire about the health, fame, and fortune of my family and friends. For the most part my family was in good health. None of my friends had been shot at as a warning about anything. None were pseudo-spies or had been a witness to the bloodless coup of the Texas Governor. They were raising their children, making money, and being good citizens. Theirs were good lives.

The Political-Military Evolution of Latin America

During the early 19th century in revolutionary Latin America private armies headed by leaders known as "Caudillos" took it upon themselves to control as much of the population as their forces could command. Their leaders were magnetic and charming individuals who kept their band of mercenaries in the best weaponry and cared for their personal needs. Some "Caudillos" simply sought to secure their private interests and become wealthy by any means possible. Others, with a kind of "Robin Hood" image, even became famous for their generic populist programs.

It was the "Caudillo" mentality that led to the era of modern-day dictators who used the country's armed forces to overthrow vulnerable independent states in Latin America. Some would argue that were it not for the political role of the militaries, Latin America would have descended into regional fiefdoms in some areas and anarchy in others. Most country's legally elected presidents have also had the backing and strong support of the military in order to stay in power. Nevertheless, greed, avarice, and lust for power led those in command of the armed forces to take possession of a government and install themselves as dictators.

A Rogue's Gallery of Latin American Dictators

MAXIMILIANO HERNANDEZ MARTINEZ
General of El Salvador

General Hernandez came to power by way of a coup attacking "communists" throughout the country. His anti-communist programs left 40,000 peasants massacred in the highways and ditches, eliminating at least half of the country's Indian culture. Farabundo Marti, founder of the Communist Party, attempted to retake the country but failed. With communists as a target, a violent assault was launched on anyone with blond hair and staying in a hotel. They were then taken and summarily executed as Russian spies and communist agitators.

VINICIO CEREZO
President of Guatemala

Shortly after the inauguration as president, strong opponents to his power takeover claimed there were fifty-six murders by security forces and death squads. The press in Guatemala reported there were at least 100 killings per month. According to Amnesty International, "arbitrary arrest, torture, disappearance, and political killings were everyday realities" for Guatemalans.

ANASTASIO SOMOSA, SR. & JR.
Presidents of Nicaragua

With the help of the Nicaragua National Guard, Anastasio Somoza, Sr. became president. In the early days of his presidency, he battled with Augusto Sandino, who finally signed a truce and put down his arms. Shortly thereafter, Somoza assassinated Sandino. The Somozas became millionaires, profiting from a variety of questionable international banking maneuvers and plundering the country according to leftist sources. The elder Somoza was gunned down in the streets and was replaced by his son, Anastasio Somoza, Jr.

GENERAL JORGE RAFAEL VIDELA
President of Argentina

General Videla became president of Argentina by a military coup. One year after the coup, Amnesty International estimated at least fifteen thousand people had disappeared and others were in detention camps. The World Anti-Communist League funneled aid to Videla using its affiliate CAL (Confederacion Anticomunista Latino Americana) in support of his so-called "moderate" position revitalizing his nation's economy. He left office in 1981after the disaster of the Falklands War with England of 1982 and was tried for human rights abuses.

GENERAL HUMBERTO BRANCO
President of Brazil

General Humberto de Alencar Castello Branco initiated a military coup that overthrew the Brazilian president and put him in power. He had a short presidency, continuously fighting suspected communists and labor unions. Based on national security interests, drug dealers were protected. The World Anti-Communist League joined in supporting the Branco administration and together assisted General Videla in his takeover of Argentina. When General Branco stepped down, he had managed to substantially increase military and executive powers, making it difficult for Brazil to restore democracy.

COLONEL HUGO BANZER
President of Bolivia

By nationalizing American business interests in the country, attempting to make trade agreements with communist nations, and establish relations with Cuba, President Juan Jose Torres paved the way for a military coup by Hugo Banzer. Banzer ruled with an iron fist, closing schools as political subversive agitation centers and raised a loan to pay Gulf Oil compensation and other U.S. business interests. The Soviet Embassy was closed, and the "Banzar Plan" for anti-Catholic actions became a model.

ALFREDO STROESSNER
President-for-life of Paraguay

Alfredo Stroessner came to power in 1954. During Stroessner's presidency, Paraguay was labeled "the poor man's Nazi regime," and many war criminals, including Joseph Mengele, settled there. In 1971, several top Stroessner administration officials were implicated in a French drug ring. Paraguay was used as a "way station" for shipments en route to the United States. The combination of human rights abuses of Indians and drug trafficking were finally condemned by the United States. In 1988, General Andres Rodriguez took over after a coup in spite of being a known drug dealer, and his 1989 election as president was call a massive fraud.

GENERAL EFRAIN RIOS MONT
President of Guatemala

As military ruler of Guatemala, General Rios Mont was one in a long series of dictators who held Guatemala in an iron grip for personal gain. Dictators ran the country for thirty years based on strong anti-communist policies. Although highly criticized by human rights groups, General Rios Mont supported a reign of terror by Mario Sandoval Alarcon, the "Godfather" of Central American death squads who carried on a dirty war in urban centers and later against "communist subversives" in the countryside through mass killings.

ROBERTO SUAZO CORDOVA
President of Honduras

President Suazo Cordova disliked having Honduras being called the original "Banana Republic," but the connection with United Fruit Company represented considerable money for the president's coffers. Honduras became a training center for Nicaraguan "contras" and was led by Honduran General Gustavo Alvarez, a virulent anti-communist. His own men overthrew General Alvarez for pocketing U.S. aid and because he belonged to a religious cult know as the "Moonies". Suazo's ties to Alvarez cost him reelection.

GENERAL MANUEL NORIEGA
Chief of Defense forces, Panama

General Noriega has backed most figurehead presidents of Panama. He was never president of Panama but was the de facto military leader of the country for many years. He was considered an asset by U.S. intelligence operations, but in the late 1980s, relations between Noriega and the United States Government had cooled. In 1989, the General was overthrown. He was indicted by a Miami grand jury for drug trafficking and convicted. He remains in a federal prison in Miami, Florida.

OTHER LATIN AMERICAN DICTATORS LISTED BELOW EXERCISED THEIR POWER IN A MOST CRUEL AND INHUMANE MANNER, PILLAGING AND KILLING THEIR WAY TO UNTOLD WEALTH (NOT PICTURED ON PREVIOUS PAGES).

Complex Politics:

MEXICO CITY

RETURN TO HOME BASE. The next day, I flew back to Mexico City non-stop. I was exhausted, and I slept from four in the afternoon then overnight until eight in the morning. After a late breakfast of *huevos rancheros*, scrambled eggs Mexican ranch style, I walked into our building at noon. After the usual "hellos" and shaking of hands, I made it to my office. There is a certain protocol that must be followed when leaving or arriving at your office, even if it was just for one day or one week or longer, or you will be taken for a snob or angry at the workforce or that business is going badly or simply something else.

First order of business was to call Roger. He was pleased with my oral report and asked that I turn over my notes to our editor right away but to be certain I reviewed the article for accuracies. It would be our cover story in the next edition. It had to be an in-depth story since the news about the coup was already in the newspapers, radio, and television. Then I returned calls and looked over my mail. There was nothing earth shaking that needed my immediate attention. I asked Nico for a cup of coffee, leaned back in my chair, and began smoking a cigarette. On the return trip I was so tired I slept most of the way back to Mexico. Now sitting in my office relaxed, I reflected on the events of the last few days. I had taken part in a tragic drama. I didn't like it, and I didn't feel good about it, but it wasn't my ball, my field, or my game. I was just an "innocent" bystander. The actions I had just witnessed were "Machiavellian" in every sense of the word, and I had been used to give the bloodless coup legitimacy as a foreign journalist participant.

BACK IN THE SADDLE.

Meanwhile, I went about the business of the magazines and tried to keep a low profile. I also called the embassy and walked over for a debriefing from my "handlers." There wasn't much to tell that had not already been covered in the press. The reports included the names of all the major players in the coup, so I added nothing new. Still, they wanted to know everything I saw and heard although I really didn't want to talk about it.

Some people were still debating the Tlatelolco Massacre and were trying to put it behind them. There was a cover-up by the government pointing its finger to Communist agitators and radical extremists, claiming these groups to be responsible for initiating the violence. There was no official explanation of who was responsible for the Tlatelolco Massacre and the Federal Government continued to deny the people of Mexico the basic facts of what had happened. This was the beginning of Mexico's extended political crisis.

Politics in Mexico and other Latin American countries are complex, and to understand what is really taking place, you have to spend a good deal of time researching the subject and include a period of total immersion in the country or countries you are targeting. I have spent more than forty years living and working in all eighteen Spanish-speaking countries. Due to the constant change in politics and governments, I still have a difficult time trying to fathom the reality of their social, business, and political nuances. I am really quite amused that Joan Didion, a well-known writer and author spent only two weeks in El Salvador and returned to write a book detailing what she saw and heard and her conclusions about the violence, the poverty, and the military abuses. Ms. Didion, the author of the book titled *Salvador*, was there in the midst of a civil war and wants us to believe the book to be fact and the last authoritative word on the subject. Even more, she reported how our government was involved in the disappearance of dissenters. Ms. Didion became an expert on the Central American country in only two weeks.

No matter your experience, understanding all facets of any

country's behind-the-scenes manipulations is a difficult task. For example, I always pay attention to political affairs in Mexico when a new administration comes into power. A change of administration generally provoked currency devaluation whether or not there was any reason for it to begin with. Devaluations benefit the "in group" in Mexico to the tune of billons of dollars. The corruption that has taken place by each administration reached its peak with President Luis Echeverria. He was known as "Ali Baba," and his henchmen were labeled "the Forty Thieves."

SIDEBAR ON BRIBES AND THE PRESS.

It was always a bit suspicious when a government spokesman called a press conference. The press conference usually had to do with some matter of importance that had transcended the usual course of events. For example, the massacre at *Tlatelolco* or *El Rutas* were two that merited the attention of the government hierarchy sufficiently to call a press conference. Special invitations were sent to reporters representing the newspapers and local magazines and were held at the government offices in question. Our magazines were never invited. At the press conference, the government spokesman would give a brief ten or fifteen minute talk about the event to be covered. He would hand out a preprinted press release together with a white envelope to each reporter. The envelope contained money. The amount depended on the seriousness of the event, and it was expected that, on acceptance of the envelope, the reporter would file a story in accordance with the press release guidelines. For reporters it was like finding money and helped to augment their paltry income. In a way, I always felt that the root of corruption in the middle and lower classes in Latin America was poor compensation to handle everyday cost of living expenses.

A Marxist President:

SANTIAGO, CHILE

CHILE - PRESIDENT SALVADOR ALLENDE, 1970-1973

SQUARE ONE. Prior to the election of Allende, Chile, had been known to be the most democratic nation of the Americas. By the late 60s, the polarization of Chilean politics made it very difficult to attain compromise and conciliation. Although Allende was a card-carrying Marxist, he was elected with only thirty-six percent of the vote, mostly women, with little or no knowledge of where he would take the country. The three other political parties refused to form a coalition and launched their own candidates in the mistaken hope of obtaining a majority. They were wrong, and they lost.

Allende's first year was a piece of cake. Everything went well, and Allende was congratulating himself and his staff for outstanding accomplishments. The president and his entourage wanted to tell the world about their socialist successes. They didn't trust American or European magazines, although all of them had tried in vain to interview President Allende. Major international publications were blacklisted. On the other hand, we had the advantage since our magazine was published in Spanish and was the leading business and newsmagazine in Latin America. The magazine was well known around the world. Finally, halfway through President Allende's first year in office, we were invited to interview the president. It was not the first time we had interviewed heads of state, dictators, pretenders, and "wannabes," but to interview Allende was going to be a unique opportunity. While other countries in Latin America had varied political leadership, Chile elected a bona fide socialist. Still, a person-to-person interview with *El Presidente* would get us a lot of good public relations mileage not only in the Americas but in Europe and Asia as well.

Allende's press secretary considered the interview important enough to fly to Mexico City for a meeting with us. Our first encounter was at the Chilean Embassy. The press secretary appeared to be a serious and stiff-necked individual by the name of Guillermo Prieto. In spite of his quiet demeanor, he was a semi-tough negotiator. Eduardo Villegas, our editor, would be with me for the editorial side of the meeting with Dr. Allende. After settling on a time and schedule over a three-day period, we got down to the "nitty gritty" of what questions the interview would cover. For starters, Prieto handed us a list of questions he wanted us to ask. Prieto thought he was holding a winning hand, but we were the only Spanish language magazine with an international reputation that would interview the president, so we had a few trump cards ourselves.

Eduardo brought along our own list of questions that we wanted covered in the interview. We spent several hours going back and forth on both lists. Delete one, add one, back and forth and so on, negotiating questions on each list. We finally settled on a mutually acceptable master list.

Our first meeting with President Allende was to take place in *La Moneda* Presidential Palace that also housed the Party's administrative group. On the west side, the building faced the *Plaza de Armas*. On the north side, the *Hotel Carrera* also faced the *Plaza de Armas*. The *Hotel Carrera* was our hotel when we traveled to Santiago, so it was going to be a short walk from there to Allende's office. Having a drink with Eduardo in the *Carrera* bar, we both sat without speaking wondering where tomorrow would take us.

The next morning at 10:00, Guillermo Prieto came to the hotel to pick us up. He seemed to be in a jovial mood, so we kept our mouth shut for the most part. Although the entrance to the president's office was no more than a block away, Prieto's driver drove us the short distance. It appeared to me that Prieto only wanted to impress us with his car and driver, so Eduardo and I winked at each other and acted impressed. We were met curbside by armed guards who ushered us to the front gate. Just inside the entrance hall, Eduardo and I were body searched very thoroughly and very carefully. With only thirty-six percent of the vote, I assumed *El Presidente* and his advisors were taking security measures seriously. He had not wanted to form coalitions, so it was like looking down the barrel of a gun in the hands of parties from the left, center, and the right.

We made our way through several halls and finally to the president's reception area. There were about a dozen well-dressed men sitting stiffly in what looked to be uncomfortable reception chairs. The receptionist asked us to wait and used his phone. A moment later, a heavyset man in a tight-fitting suit opened the door to the president's private office and said, *"Adelante."*

FACE-TO-FACE.

Finally, we were in the presence of his Excellency Dr. Salvador Allende Ugarte, the first Marxist President of the Republic of Chile. He was a robust individual, medium height, slightly overweight, with a well-trimmed mustache and piercing dark eyes. He stared at us for a minute or so, giving us the once over from head to toe. Finally, he stood from his large desk and moved towards us to shake our hands. It was easy to tell he was physically strong by his firm handshake, and he wanted us to know it. He was immaculately dressed in an expensive, custom-tailored Savile Row suit with a shirt and tie that had Turnbull and Asher written all over it. He had made a point of making his ego be in concert with the trappings of the office and his excellent taste in clothing. Obviously, he wanted us know he was no revolutionary peasant.

"Welcome to Santiago," he said smiling. "Please have a seat and be comfortable." He motioned over to several deep leather chairs that surrounded a large coffee table with several issues of our magazine prominently displayed. A young boy suddenly appeared, and Allende asked if we would like water, coffee, or wine. Eduardo and I asked for coffee. Allende asked for a glass of white wine. Prieto, sitting behind and to the side of the president was left out of the drink orders. Allende made some small talk, mostly about a French journalist who interviewed him early on. The interview was less than acceptable, so he decided to come to us inasmuch as our magazine was in Spanish, and the magazine's management spoke Spanish as well. I didn't want to tell him we were owned by a bunch of New York and Philadelphia mainliners, had the support of the U.S. State Department, and worked with the USIA.

Each of us had our watered down list of questions to be asked in the interview. Here we were, an ardent Marxist in one corner, facing off with Capitalists in the other corner. As we moved down the interview list, Allende kept wandering off, bringing up topics that had nothing to do with our reason for having the interview. He advocated far-reaching socialist reforms and other Marxist doctrines. We crept along slowly, moving from one question to another, enduring his sidebars. At that rate, it was going to be difficult to finish the interview in three days. Two hours after we were introduced, he suddenly rose from his chair, thanked us, smiled, and walked away

We were left with the self-important Mr. Prieto, who ushered us to the reception area. He scheduled the next day's meeting for two o'clock. Once outside the Presidential Palace, Prieto insisted his driver take us back to the hotel. We didn't have a choice. We accepted. For about a three-minute drive, we sat in comfort in the limo with two motorcycle special security officers as escorts. Latin social protocol. You can't beat it, so join it.

OUT AND ABOUT.

The next morning, Eduardo and I had breakfast and took a walk around the downtown of the city. There was a lot of activity. Shops were open, people walked back and forth with purpose, pairs talking to one another cheerfully, and well dressed for the most part. They were shopping and buying, which was no different from what you see in the downtown areas of most large cities in the world.

"I don't think this Marxist thing will work," I said to Eduardo, who was impressed by what he saw, but he agreed. It all seemed too hot and too fast moving. It appeared like consumers were eager to spend and vendors anxious to sell as if they were living in a fantasy world. We stopped at a man's boutique named "Brit." They had a full line of men's clothing, including Hacking Jackets, sports coats with double vents, peak lapels, some Harris tweeds, trousers, and other British snob appeal trappings. The price was right on all items I checked. There were a couple of items, like their Harris Tweeds, that I might drop in and buy before we left if there was time. The frenzy to buy and sell was artificial, but as long as the economy kept humming along, shopkeepers didn't complain.

For lunch, we stopped at a restaurant famous for their seafood dishes and highly regarded by those who could afford it. The restaurant had been the main dining room of a colonial-style hotel that was very fashionable in its time but was overtaken by progress, plastic, and chrome. Nevertheless, the restaurant remained with five-star dishes and service. The maitre d'hotel ushered us to a table with a white linen tablecloth, real silverware, and crystal wine goblets and handed us the menus. As in Europe, Latin American countries frown on serving cocktails before lunch since hard liquor will dull your taste buds. That was acceptable to us, and after some deliberation, I chose Chilean Sea Bass, broiled and just a splash of lemon. Eduardo selected an international mixed grill that included salmon fillets, Chilean sea bass, and tilapia fillets. We both ordered fresh sea scallops as appetizers. I ordered a bottle of Cousino Macul white wine to accompany our delightful meal. How can you be in Chile and not eat delicacies from the sea and accompany your meal with some of the best wines in the world?

Allende: Ego or Conviction:
SANTIAGO, CHILE

THE INNER SANCTUM. After a brief stop at our hotel, we came down at one-thirty, and sure enough, there was our driver waiting for us in the lobby.

"Here we go," said Eduardo, and we slipped into the backseat of the long, black limo. This time Mr. Prieto met us at the door of the Presidential Palace. We went through the frisking drill at each of the various halls and entered the president's office. He was not there, so we stood waiting for him along with Mr. Prieto. We didn't utter a word. I felt like I was in formation and at attention back in the paratroopers waiting to be dismissed.

About ten minutes later, President Allende finally appeared through a door at back of his desk. He had a half smile as he came around the desk and shook each of our hands, excluding Mr. Prieto.

"Buenos dias, caballeros," he said in a somewhat jovial manner. "Tomen asiento, take a seat," he added. He was impeccably dressed: different suit, different tie, different shirt, and different shoes, giving the impression of a capitalist preaching Marxism.

It appeared he had read our draft from the previous day and approved of what had been written. Eduardo was giving the story a different slant basically saying that Allende appeared to be a true Marxist and his policies were working. Nevertheless, Eduardo hedged saying that time would tell. The interview began going down the list of questions and with party-line responses. I knew Eduardo was having a hard time trying to write an unbiased story. Once again, President Allende would ramble on about topics that had nothing to do with the interview. It was easy to see he was an unabashed critic of capitalism and believed strongly in Marxism. He had joined the Socialist party of Chile when he was in his twenties and rose to the most senior position of the party. Obviously, he was not making friends with the United States. In that regard, he was either fearless or a fool and never thought about the consequences of trying to face down Uncle Sam. He would eventually pay the price for this bravado.

We ended the interview day at four o'clock as usual. Again he offered us a drink and a cigar as we wrapped up the meeting. As graciously as possible, we turned him down with the excuse that we wanted to get back to the hotel and work on our notes. Eduardo did the note taking, but I took notes as well for accuracy of dates. Together we would be able to show the president a very good idea as to the final gist of the story when we met again the next day. It was nearing four o'clock, and the interview session was winding down.

Suddenly, President Allende stood. We dropped our notes and pads as we quickly jumped to our feet.

"I would like to invite you both to my home tomorrow for the final interview," he said. "Two o'clock sharp, as usual," he added.

Eduardo and I were stunned. I looked over at Señor Prieto, who was white as a sheet. Although I stood there like a Wooden Indian for a few seconds, I managed to gain composure and accepted his invitation with as much assurance as I could muster.

THE LION'S DEN.

The visit to President Allende's home was memorable. I had imagined that a true Marxist would be living in dark, dank, and gloomy furnished quarters. Eduardo and I were surprised to see a white, rambling, California style stucco building with arched windows. The interior was elegant with impressive pieces from chairs to paintings. On the other hand, the president's study was somewhat sparingly decorated, giving the allusion of a hard-working man of the people.

So here he was, Dr. Salvador Allende, former pretender to the "throne" for many years and now president of the country of Chile.

As he sat there smiling and looking very self-satisfied, I couldn't help but wonder what kind of a Marxist this man was. He had on a custom-tailored suit, a Rolex watch on his wrist, a large Mont Blanc fountain pen he constantly fidgeted with, and he was sitting in a home that oozed elegance and status. It was obviously an expensive lifestyle that appeared to be more capitalist than socialist.

We went through what was left of the list of questions in about half an hour. For the next hour and a half President Allende told us about joining the Socialist Party at a very young age and later becoming its leader. He explained how he served in a variety of government posts and finally ran for the presidency... and lost! He chuckled when he said he had lost three times before he was finally elected president.

Through it all and knowing there was a story in what he was saying, Eduardo and I furiously took notes. Allende then slipped into a diatribe denouncing capitalism and, of course, the United States. As a result, knowingly or unknowingly, he had become very unpopular with U.S. administrations from Kennedy to Nixon. In turn, the White House felt that Chile could become a communist state and may join the Soviet Union sphere of influence.

Promptly at four o'clock one of the resident's aides came into the study pushing a small mobile bar with two bottles of wine: one white and chilled in an ice bucket and one red, already unstopped to allow it to breathe." Also on the bar were canapés and other finger morsels. This time there was no refusing the offer of a glass of wine. We toasted Chile, President Allende, Mexico, our upcoming article, and world peace. We did not mention the United States. I was impressed with myself. The Dean of Boys of my high school was sure I would fail at anything I tried, and here I was, a kid born and raised in San Antonio, Texas, interviewing the first Marxist President of a Latin American country. It felt good.

So ended our three-day interview of President Salvador Allende. We flew home via Bogotá, Colombia, and on to Mexico City. We were satisfied with the information we had gathered but even more pleased we were able to get his thoughts and philosophical position as to where he would take Chile and his relations with the United States. In many ways, his heart was in the right place in thinking that socialism was best for his country. However, the majority of his fellow countrymen didn't agree, and Allende just didn't know, or want to face, reality. He was an outspoken critic of capitalism and would not accept that there are no free lunches.

Our story on Allende and Allende's Chile was straightforward and pulled no punches. We gave President Allende high marks for his strong ideology but poor marks for his self-centered approach to what was best for his country without a plebiscite. Eduardo and I agreed that Chile was a ticking time bomb with a clash of cultures.

DOWNFALL.

Then came the disasters of the next two years. According to Allende's party, leaders of Unidad Popular party were certain foreign interests were exploiting Chile. They had no trouble in convincing the president to take the next step in freeing Chile from the imperialists, mainly the United States. Without much thought to the outcome of the step he was about to take, he gave the go ahead to socialize the economy.

In 1971, the government totally nationalized the copper companies that were largely owned by two American companies. The takeover of great estates and companies followed. By 1972 Allende's socialist experiment began to crumble to the delight of the CIA and the Nixon White House. Since the election of Allende in 1970, Nixon had given orders to the CIA and others to make the Chilean economy scream. The orders were carried out and more.

The 342% increase

BAD NEWS. During these troubled times, we were still printing our magazine for the Chile, Peru, and Bolivia editions in Santiago with no unusual problems. Early in 1971 Hector Treviño, our CFO, came rushing into my office. He was clearly out of sorts and looked it. Without saying a word, he handed me a telex (I had set-up telexes in all our principle offices as our form of communication). The telex was advising us that the printing company where our magazine was produced was nationalized. Even worse, they were increasing our production costs by 342%. We both stood there speechless.

"Pack your bag," I said to Hector. "We're flying to Santiago, Chile."

Hector and I were close personal friends. He was from the border town of Reynosa and was a graduate of SMU in Dallas, Texas. He was bilingual with native fluency in English and a quick sense of humor. When we traveled together, it was an ongoing barrel of laughs on the flight, at the hotel, restaurants, saloons, and any other place we might go for a bit of R&R. However, when it was time for business, we were dead serious: stand up, hook up, shuffle, and stand in the door serious. On this occasion the jokes were at a minimum. We flew Avianca to Bogotá, Colombia, then Air France to Santiago, Chile. Air France was far and away my favorite airline. I learned to drink chilled vodka neat and eat caviar on one of many, many trips aboard Air France. In spite of the good drinks and good food, our mood was somber. We had no idea what to expect from the new government owners. New owners or not, there was no way we could accept, or afford, the 342% increase in production costs.

We landed at Santiago's Arturo Merino Benitez International Airport on time and made our way through Immigration and Customs without problems, although the officers looked at us suspiciously. Not only were we *periodistas*, the press, as our entry forms declared, we were also Americans. I was reminded of entering Cuba in the early days of Castro. Perhaps this was a first step in what was to come under the new regime.

Federico de la Vega, our attorney for many years, was a quiet, levelheaded man. He had been alerted to meet us at the airport. As we approached him outside the building, he put a finger to his lips indicating we should not speak. I shook my head in disbelief but followed his orders as we walked silently to his car.

"What is going on?" I asked once safely in the car.

He didn't respond right away. He kept on driving well within the speed limit looking from one side to another as if he was in a speed trap zone. Finally, he said, "You won't recognize Santiago, or Chile, for that matter. We are close to anarchy. There is an 8:00 p.m. curfew. Most retail stores are closed, including grocery stores. The only stores that are open belong to the government. You can't even get a bottle of wine, and when you can't buy a bottle of wine in Chile, it's a disaster. Everything is a disaster."

Federico kept up his tirade all the way to the hotel about everything that was now wrong in Chile. Hector and I kept quiet, but I was thinking about our meeting with the printing company management the next morning. It sounded like we would be walking into a stacked deck against us.

We finally arrived at the Hotel Carrera and were greeted by the hotel staff from the doorman to the registration clerks, who used our surnames just to let us know we were not forgotten. However, all the staff had very dour-looking faces. I could understand why. Also greeting us at the hotel was Gabriel Vidal, our office manager, and Rodrigo Valenzuela, our production manager for the magazine's southern cone editions. Both were good, hard-working family men. They came from humble origins, and, in Latin America, that group of people are always at a disadvantage in confronting the so-called social "elite," who enjoyed status by virtue of money, power, or European heritage. I wasn't sure whom we would meet with, so I did not ask either of them to accompany us to the printer meetings.

Finally ensconced in my suite, Gabriel, Hector, Federico, Agustin Hurtado, Federico's partner, Rodrigo, and I sat down to discuss strategy for the meeting with the printing company management. Problem was, we had no strategy. None of us knew what to expect. I certainly had never been faced with this kind of a dilemma.

"I guess we'll just have to play it by ear," I said and then had to explain what that meant to Federico, Agustin, and Rodrigo. The only tactic I had was to simply say we could not, and would not, accept the 342% cost increase for the printing of our magazine. I did have a couple of wild cards I had discussed with our New York office and got their blessing if I needed to use them. I wasn't anxious to put them on the table. That option would surely create strong animosity by the plant management. We didn't need strong enemies in Chile.

The day after our arrival in Santiago was spent getting the lay of the land. We called our friends to get their view of Chile's present day economic situation. No good news at all. In fact, some of our Chilean friends alluded to the possibility of a coup by the military. We called the only other printer in Santiago for an appointment, but the president of the company, whom I knew well, would not take my call. He had surely been warned not to negotiate a contract with us.

The meeting was set for eight in the morning according to Federico, who had been in touch with the plant's general manager. However, Federico would not be allowed to join us. The exclusion of Federico was probably because they didn't want anyone present familiar with Chilean law. The morning of the meeting Hector and I took one of the hotel's taxis to the printing plant. No limo with driver this time.

DAY ONE.

We were ushered in to a very austere, small conference room. It was very different from the conference room we knew. The old one was stylishly comfortable, leather chairs, a long mahogany table that seated twelve, and beautiful oil paintings of Chilean wildlife adorning the walls. The new conference room had a wooden table and straight-back chairs. No amenities of any kind. We were not offered coffee or water or anything else. On three of the walls were poster-type paintings of Mao, Karl Marx, and Che Guevara. The link between the three was obviously Marxism. The whole scenario was set up to intimidate us. That was their first mistake. What they didn't know was that we were holding a wild card that even mentioning would rain on their parade. However, now was not the time. Whether they knew it or not, we were hardly in a position to be intimidated. After all, how are you going to intimidate an American eight-hundred-pound gorilla that was bound to have options? That's the trouble with these closed Marxist groups. They don't understand that power and money rule.

MAO, KARL MARX, AND CHE.

They introduced themselves, and we introduced ourselves. The three wore dark, nondescript Russian box-type suits. Their ties were the same yet different. All in all, they made an unremarkable impression. The one sitting under the Karl Marx poster was their spokesman and the official Unidad Popular Party Representative. A cadaver-looking individual sat under the "Che" poster. He was the new general manager. To my left was the third conspirator. The poster hanging behind him was Mao. He was the representative of the "Worker's Union."

Karl Marx spoke first and looked straight at me.

"We have a new set of rules for our customers," and for the next forty-five minutes he overturned twelve line items that had always been part of our standard operating procedure. All had to do with the production of the magazine. We could no longer do press checks. We could no longer check the paper quality. We could no longer recommend ink adjustments. We could no longer do a print order audit. He went reading his list in monotone, stopping after each item to explain what it meant, as if we didn't know. Finally, we would no longer be able to speak with the pressmen or any of the production department personnel, including bindery and warehousing. He wrapped up the presentation by saying the price increase would be 342% based on the exchange rate at the time of payment. When he had finished, he looked up at me with a slight sneer. He closed the file with the papers and sat back in his chair. The sneer changed to a satisfied smile that looked like the proverbial cat that ate the mouse. I had seen this approach done often enough before, usually with more polish and grace, but seldom with such dispatch.

I waited for several minutes before I said, "Your terms are totally unacceptable." It was like dumping a bucket of ice cold Gatorade on each of the red triumvirate. They glared at me wide-eyed but were unable to speak. It never occurred to them that we would turn down their proposal out-of-hand. At least they expected some sort of counterproposal. That led me to believe we had some negotiating wiggle room. I preferred to reach an agreement without playing our trump card. In fact, I really had two trump cards, so I said, "Let's adjourn for the day and come back tomorrow with our production costs to compare with yours."

That made them relax because I was sure they thought they were smarter than the two gringos sitting in front of them.

"De acuerdo, we agree," said Karl Marx. Hector and I stood and marched out of the conference room saying we would be back at eight the next day.

DAY TWO.

Again, a guard met us at the door and ushered us to the so-called conference room. To further increase the tension of our negotiations, I was carrying a two-liter thermos that I borrowed from the hotel. If they didn't offer coffee, we would bring our own. In my elegant Crouch & Fitzgerald briefcase, that was not all that brief, I also had two heavy kitchen-type cups and a couple of rolls and donuts. The coffee and pastries were strictly for us. None of the three over-rated commie front men uttered a word or made a move to object. They probably didn't want to give us the benefit of being offended or taken aback, so they just looked past the thermos and cups while we poured our premixed cream and sugar coffee. Karl Marx shoved a file over to me via Mao, and Hector shoved our file to Karl Marx via Che.

Still, I felt I should get a rise out of them if for no other reason than to put them on the defensive. Our goal, as agreed with our New York office, was to try to settle this situation by making them see the benefit of keeping the production costs at a reasonable increase. If they accepted our proposal, it would benefit them as well as us, but our strategy wasn't working. A newfound sense of power and authority made them think they couldn't lose.

BATMAN.

I took the file, but I didn't open it. Instead I stared at it for a couple of minutes. When I looked up, all three were staring at me.

Perhaps if I baffle them with unpredictable conduct, we will get a reaction, I thought. I began staring at the portraits of Mao, Karl Marx, and Che. First one and then another; back and forth, back and forth. I did this for several minutes until Karl Marx spoke up.

"You admire our portraits?" he said, "Painted by a Chilean artist."

"Not really," I said in my most critical manner, frowning. "I don't care for the subjects of the portraits who have been responsible for the slaughter of millions of innocent people or the amateurish work of the painter, which I find third-rate."

This shook up our inquisitors, who stared at us wide-eyed and seemed not able to say a word. Finally, Mao, who spoke very little during the negotiations, said, "You are insulting us, our country, and our leaders." It would appear I was finally getting to them.

Then Che chimed in.

"Do you have any pictures hanging in your office?" he said, almost spitting out the words.

"Yes, I do."

"Do you have a picture of the President of the United States?"

"No," I said. "I don't care much for politics."

Earlier in the year at a budget and management meeting in New York, I had bought my son Robby a poster of Batman. Printed at the bottom of the poster I had the words "Robby Really Is Batman."

"I have a poster of Batman hanging in my office," I said smiling, although the poster was hanging in Robby's bedroom. Now they were really frustrated and did not know how to respond.

"Who is this Batman?" asked Mao angrily.

I thought this over and decided to answer more or less the truth.

"Batman is a man who wears a mask with horns and a black cape and a suit to match. He fights crime and criminals all over the city, protecting truth, justice, and the American way."

"You are trying to humiliate and disrespect us," Mao said in a sharp tone of one who had been hoodwinked. These three either knew very well who Batman was and pleaded innocence, or the boobs really didn't know about Batman and our other crime-fighting heroes.

"You may not know this, Hector," I said in voice loud enough for our adversaries to hear, "earlier in the year Chile's Ministry of Education banned the reproduction, distribution and sale of all Walt Disney comics on the grounds that they were spewing capitalistic propaganda. They especially identified Donald Duck's rich uncle as one of the principle culprits. How can we negotiate with a mentality such as this?"

The verbal exchange had the effect I was looking for. It was hard for them to accept that the representative of a large publishing empire would stoop to comic book stunts.

Karl Marx finally found his voice and said, "Let's get back to the real reason of this meeting and proceed with the work at hand."

I opened the file, and Hector and I glanced at the figures. The difference between the two sets of numbers were apples and oranges. How in the world are you going to negotiate a printing and production agreement that is so far apart that there is absolutely no line item that has anything in common? I took our proposal and went down the line, item by item, explaining each cost and a corresponding increase. We were offering a bottom line increase of 19.5% that was most attractive by anyone's measure. Che, on the other hand, simply took the previous edition invoice and increased it by 342%. That was their scientific way of arriving at that figure.

Karl Marx decided he would give us an explanation about the 342% increase.

"The increase in production costs," he said, smiling and full of himself, "is to cover the expenses of producing free textbooks for our children from primary school through high school. Actually, your company is only paying half the cost of producing the textbooks. Our other American publisher has a similar increase, and that money will also be used for the free textbooks. That's the beauty of our society. The government serves the people, especially children. It's called Communism. You just don't understand."

Hector and I took out a donut and began eating it during Karl Marx's rhetoric. We watched their reaction with pleasure. They wanted to say something but preferred to act as if our demonstration of defiance meant nothing to them.

"We understand your desire to help children. We understand your desire to help anyone in need. What we don't understand are your attempts to blackmail third parties or governments to pay for programs that don't concern them. What we do understand is capitalism. In a capitalist society everyone produces and works in benefit of self and family. Capitalism is a successful society, but we're not here to give all of you lessons in capitalism versus communism. What we're going to do is come back in the morning and settle this mess."

Hector and I picked up our files, put them in our briefcases, took out the last two rolls apiece, and walked out chewing on the rolls.

DAY THREE.

This was it. I tried to be a nice capitalist so that we would have a mutual agreement to make our business relationship smooth and friendly, but they wouldn't budge. Of course, they thought they were holding all the cards and really didn't believe we had any options but to accept their terms in order to keep producing the magazine with the editions of three countries at stake. They were wrong, as they would soon discover. Hector and I had a hotel secretary put our proposal on paper with costs corresponding to each line item. Also included was a list of privileges we would have in the production of our magazine. We listed all of those Karl Marx had read to us as off limits and more. We signed the letter and would hand it to them for their signature. If they turned it down, as they probably would, we would drop the bomb.

THE BOMB.

Hector and I agreed if the letter of agreement was not signed when we arrived, we would give the printing company management team an ultimatum. I had to chuckle to myself. Here we were, in a business that should have been like any other business, and yet, we were about to negotiate an unconditional surrender as if it was the end of World War II, and our adversaries didn't even know it would soon be over for them. It didn't surprise me; we were dealing with Marxists.

Actually, I felt a bit like a bully. In spite of knowing we could not lose, I would have preferred a negotiation with an even playing field. So be it. Hector and I walked in their conference room carrying a throwaway cup of coffee and a file folder. The three representatives of the Neruda Printing Company were standing at the end of the table. They, too, were only armed with one file folder. Karl Marx, Mao, and Che had our proposal, and we had theirs. The three looked so smug standing there in their dark, box-cut suits and brown shoes that I almost laughed out loud.

Karl Marx spoke first.

"We do not accept your proposal, and what's more, we consider it an insult," he said, spitting out the word *insult*.

At that moment I stopped feeling sorry for the commie blackmailers, so I dropped the bomb.

I smiled and spoke softly and with self-assurance.

"Then we will print the Peruvian and Bolivian editions at our plant in Colombia, and the Chile edition we will print in Argentina. The only additional expense to us will be the airfreight from Buenos Aires to Santiago. Airfreight from Bogotá to Lima and La Paz is almost the same as Santiago to Lima and La Paz for the Peruvian and Bolivian editions."

The three were aghast. It took them several seconds to regain their composure. Finally, Karl Marx spoke up.

"Nobody," he said spacing his words, "nobody, especially an outsider, an American, gives us ultimatums." He took several deep breaths thinking over just what he was going to say next while staring at me coldly. "If the Chilean edition is flown here from Argentina or any other country, we'll meet the shipment at the airport and confiscate it. Then we'll take it out in the field and burn it. How's that for your ultimatum?"

"Well, now, the burning of our magazine will give us an international promotion that will produce worldwide press. Just think... We will notify all of the wire services, all of the leading newspapers, radio stations, and even TV networks in Europe and Asia, not to mention the rest of Latin America, of how Chile tried to blackmail us. I even see some of the headlines now: 'No Freedom of the Press in Chile,' 'Blackmail and Strong-Arm Tactics in Chile,' and article upon article about the magazine burning. You will do us a favor. We couldn't pay for all the free publicity we'll get from this strategy intended to intimidate us into accepting your proposal. What's more, advertising revenues for Chile are down to zero. No company wants to advertise in your country when consumers have no money to buy the products. Right now, it is costing us money to print the Chile edition, so go ahead, confiscate our magazine shipment and burn it."

The three were speechless. While they were digesting the effect of this bomb, I dropped a second one. This was the one-two punch of Hiroshima and Nagasaki

"You must know we pay in dollars for the production of the magazines. If you don't know, then your superiors aren't telling you the whole story or don't consider you important enough to bring you into their confidence. Until now, we have sent a collar check to the former owners, who live in Paris. Since they are no longer the owners, the plant and Chile would benefit from being paid in hard currency. In addition to losing our business, you will also be losing a guaranteed monthly dollar check, and in the face of Chile's economic situation and the dramatic drop in the value of your currency, that would be a hard blow to your interests."

It was easy to see they were not aware of how payments were made and in what currency.

"Allow me explain," I said softly and evenly, "a few months back, our office in New York had a visit from the Chilean Ambassador to the United States and explained there would be a change of ownership of the Printing Company in the near future. Our board agreed that with a change of ownership we would continue to pay for production in dollars direct to the plant or designated authority."

With this revelation, the negotiators across the table continued speechless. Before anyone of them could come out of their daze, I took advantage of their silence and spoke up.

"Mr. Treviño and I will fly to Buenos Aires tomorrow morning for the weekend. As you know, there isn't much happening in

Santiago these days." That was just one more dig aimed at their dignity. "We'll return to Santiago on Monday. If you decide to accept our proposal, sign the document and have it delivered to our office. If the document is not at our office by Monday afternoon, we will proceed with our plans to have the Chile, Peru, and Bolivia editions printed elsewhere."

I watched Karl Marx disintegrate. He slumped, caved in, really, and I wondered if he would ever get that ramrod-straight posture back. Che's hands began to shake, and he had to rest them on the back of a chair. Mao quivered visibly, and his face was no longer white but almost gray instead. If ever there was a defeated adversary, this was the group, and they knew they would be signing an unconditional surrender by Monday.

Hector and I put our throwaway coffee cups on the table, turned, and walked out. Future negotiations with anyone or all three individuals would be much easier the next time.

The Cabal

THE MARXIST REPRESENTATIVES OF THE EDITORA NACIONAL PRINTING PLANT

The conference room used for our negotiations for a new printing contract had been converted from a small reference library. It was small, dismal, and dark. Nevertheless, three of the walls were adorned by large poster- type paintings of Karl Marx, Mao Tse Tung, and Che Guevara. Hector Treviño and I never addressed any of the three by their real names, preferring to use the word "señor" or simply no prefix at all. Between us, we gave each of negotiating team the name of one of their Marxist heroes.

It was these three individuals that Hector Treviño and I negotiated an unconditional surrender for the printing of our magazine in Chile that included the Peru and Bolivia editions.

JOSÉ ANTONIO FERNANDEZ BARRIOS, known to us as Karl Marx.

Formerly a terrorist and a close friend of Fidel Castro, he was a senior leader of the Unidad Popular coalition political party. He had been appointed to the position of director of the printing plant based on his support of Allende's position on Marxism, Education Reform, and a strong critic of capitalism. He was little more than a thug with a limited education but considered a tough negotiator, using threats, intimidation, and bullying to win his cases.

JOAQUÍN MONTERO DAVILA, known to us as Mao Tse Tung, was a

member of the Carabineros National Police Force and later took a covert position with the Secret Police. His official position at the print plant was that of general manager. As such, he was a member of the Worker's Union. He was an able and conspiratorial organizer who used his affiliation with the Secret Police to undermine opposition. Without the Secret Police as backup, he was a coward, but nevertheless, he was feared.

ELÍAS SERRANO, known to us as Che Guevara, admirer of the Cuban

Revolution that brought Castro to power. He hero-worshipped Che Guevara. Prior to the election of Allende as President of Chile, he led guerrilla-type operations to harass the previous presidency of Eduardo Frei Montalva. He committed many atrocities and slaughtered dozens of Chileans. He was jailed and was to be executed but escaped and later came to the attention of the Editora Nacional Printing Plant. Forced to join the Worker's Union in order to work for the Allende regime, he was the printing plant's enforcer.

On the Town:
BUENOS AIRES, ARGENTINA

BUENOS AIRES, ARGENTINA. We flew Alitalia Airlines from Santiago to Buenos Aires. Next to Air France, Alitalia had the best first class service of the major airlines I was familiar with. Due to our heavy international travel, we were able to fly first class to all of our destinations. In fact, this policy included the States as well. Although we were looking forward to a long weekend in B.A. I was in a somber mood. Somehow, that rather hostile encounter with the plant management left a bad taste in my mouth. Although we won, I didn't like how the negotiations turned out. There wasn't much *negotiating*. Hector and I were holding all the cards. They didn't stand a chance, and they realized it too late. They were embarrassed and humiliated. I was wondering what kind of retaliation we could expect. They couldn't touch the magazine, but I had a strong feeling they would think of something. We would cross that bridge when we came to it.

I had contacted our printers in Buenos Aires and filled them in on our problem. Lorenzo Leone and his brothers owned and operated a medium-sized offset printing plant and were expanding. We were assured they could handle the additional printing of the Chile edition. After what took place with the plant management the day before, I was fairly certain we would continue printing there. On the other hand, if the senior plant management decided to act foolishly in defense of pride and national honor and elected to boot us out, we needed a fall-back position. We discussed this possibility with Lorenzo on the long ride from Ezeiza International Airport to Buenos Aires. The next printing schedule was still twelve days away, and we would have our answer one way or another by Monday. There was time to switch the Chile printing to Argentina if push came to shove.

They dropped us off at the Claridge Hotel and suggested we have dinner with them that night. *Why not?* I thought. *That will be a good beginning for the weekend.*

The Claridge Hotel is a small but very chic hotel located in the midst of business, banking, and entertainment districts on *Tucumán* Street. The hotel management knew us well and always gave us first-class service. I really didn't care for the hotel with its extra-small rooms and suites like something out of a miniature fairytale.

However, the option was the Alvear Palace Hotel, built in 1932, with a turn of the century baroque style building along European lines. It had a Beaux Arts façade and, according to the hype, each of the stones were shipped from Paris. To me it was one of those hotels where you could kill a person and the body wouldn't be found for three days.

Hector and I checked in and went up to our respective rooms. I took a shower and lay down on the bed. I wasn't tired, but I had much to think about. My thoughts went over the last four days of activities, and I finally came to the conclusion that I would not have done anything differently, so I put it out of my mind and finally dozed off. According to my nightstand clock, it was six-forty five when the phone rang. It was Hector. He was in the Claridge Bar and reminded me that the Leone brothers would pick us up at eight o'clock.

LA BOCA.

The Leone brothers had invited us to "La Boca," a working-class neighborhood in the port area of Buenos Aires where just about anything goes. It is the oldest, most original, and most traditional of all the "barrios" in the city. Italian immigrants that worked in the meat-packing plants and warehouses in the area settled "La Boca," meaning "the mouth." I'm not sure, but I believe the area was called "La Boca" because the "mouth" of the River Plate is nearby. One of the attractions of La Boca is Caminito, the principle street in La Boca, with more than enough restaurants and bars. The Leone brothers were well known in "La Boca" and were always greeted with hugs and kisses by the barmaids and very friendly handshakes by the owners. They were also among the few who would venture away from Caminito Street at night since surrounding streets were considered dangerous.

The Leone brothers, Lorenzo, Franco, and Dante, were a colorful trio, always laughing, drinking, or dancing. In fact, they were excellent tango dancers and proved it every time they took to the dance floor. They also dressed to the nines, which highlighted their extraordinary good looks. Lorenzo was in his early forties, and so was I. Franco was in his middle thirties, and Dante in his early thirties. Being from Italian ancestry, the Leone brothers took to "La Boca," and "La Boca" took to them. Among their unwritten rules was to avoid scenes and fights and help quell disturbances by the patrons. This was much appreciated by the bistro owners and the saloonkeepers.

Hector and I rode with Lorenzo Leone while Franco and Dante drove their cars. We arrived first and were ushered in to the dining area of one of Lorenzo's favorite restaurants. The owner, a good friend of the brothers, led us to a table set for ten people. The owner embraced Lorenzo, winked at him, and Lorenzo winked back.

"What's going on?" I asked Lorenzo.

Lorenzo smiled. "It's a surprise. Be patient. Have I ever let you down?"

Lorenzo kept smiling while he ordered three bottles of the house red wine. At a distance I saw Franco and Dante walk in with five outrageously beautiful women in the twenty-five to thirty age range. As they made their way to our table, I slowly got to my feet. Lorenzo and Hector were already standing.

Almost as if the matchmaking was preplanned, two of the women eased up to Hector and I. The four of us introduced ourselves, and thirty seconds later we were sitting down making small talk. Lorenzo passed one of the bottles of wine to Franco and the other to Dante. They poured the wine and began toasting. We toasted each other, we toasted our respective mothers, we toasted our health and our good fortune, and finally we toasted wine, women, and song.

When the band started playing a tango piece, the three brothers jumped up with their fair companions and walked out to the dance floor. All three were great dancers. Although we had socialized with Lorenzo and his brothers in the past, we had never received this kind of attention. It was a simple case of our business relationship evolving to one of friendship.

My *assigned* partner was petite with a dynamite figure that would stop traffic. She was a really beautiful woman with coal black hair and dark eyes. She was very friendly and accommodating with impeccable manners and a personality that made you feel as if you had known each other for years.

"*Bailamos?* shall we dance?" she asked with a smile.

"I don't know how to dance tango," I said, feeling a bit like a kid, "but I do dance."

More than feeling like a kid, I felt like an idiot. We were in Argentina, home of the tango, and in the kind of neighborhood where everything is traditional, including the music. Why would I think they danced to anything else besides the tango? That was as bad as thinking they would play anything else but a "somebody does somebody wrong" song from your favorite country hits in the Texas Ice House in San Antonio.

She kept looking at me and smiled again, coquettishly.

"*No importa,* it's not important."

Her name was *Beatriz*, but she was called Bette. All of us spent the evening drinking, eating, singing and, in general, having a grand time. One of La Boca's traditions, a custom I didn't particularly like, was to cut a newcomer's necktie in half. I wasn't sure we had ever been in that particular bistro before, so it appeared we were candidates for the tie-cutting ceremony. I had neglected to warn Hector, so he was wearing one of his new, flashy Pierre Cardin ties. I remembered about the tie cutting, so to be sure I wore one of my cheap ties. No sooner said than done, five waiters, wearing their tuxedo duty uniforms, and with their trusty scissors swept over us and proceeded to cut our ties in half. They kept the bottom half to nail up on the wall, along with dozens of others, and our names to identify the ties.

As they say, time goes by quickly when you're having fun. It was one in the morning when we left La Boca. Hector and I finally made it back to the hotel about four in the morning.

The next day we rolled out of bed around mid-morning and went down to the dining room for a late breakfast and a Bloody Mary or two to help us rejoin the human race.

"Let's do some shopping this afternoon," I said to Hector, taking a sip from my Bloody Mary. "Argentina has some of the finest leather creations in the world. They have shoes, belts, jackets, full-length coats, and more. I need to pick up some gifts for the home front."

Hector just nodded as he smoked a cigarette and worked on his second Bloody Mary. We finished our breakfast and went out to face the world. It was a bright, bright day, and the sun nearly overwhelmed us. We quickly made for the shade.

WELCOME, SHOPPERS.

Our first stop was Florida Avenue in *"El Centro,"* downtown B.A. It is the largest shopping street in the city and is permanently closed to traffic. The street is lined with every conceivable kind of shop offering a variety of goods, but you have to keep your eyes open for pickpockets. The pickpocket "industry" is practically an art form in Buenos Aires.

We skipped the Palermo neighborhood that offers chic clothing stores mostly for the twenties crowd. The weekend flea market in the San Telmo barrio is a good place for some leisure time and another Bloody Mary to continue the rejuvenation process. Finally, we made our way to Recoleta, B.A.'s most expensive and luxurious neighborhood in Buenos Aires offering only top-tier shopping. This is where Hector and I each dropped a bundle on some knicks and knacks for worthy people back home.

THE ENIGMA.

It is difficult to describe the character, personality, and overconfidence of the typical Argentine. On the one hand they are warm, generous, helpful, and generally easy going. On the other hand, when challenged, they become arrogant and aggressive and consider their countrymen to be the chosen people. They truly believe they are the center of the universe. This is especially true of the *Porteños*, the Buenos Aires residents. For example, they do not consider themselves as South Americans. They feel they are Europeans, who, through a twist of fate and a variety of circumstances, live in Argentina. When discussing fine goods and merchandise, they speak of it as European quality, not U.S. quality. In fact, they import European-made clothes and shoes. By comparison, they speak very little about the U.S. made design and quality goods. I do not believe they feel animosity towards the United States; I just think they consider themselves European who are above the capitalistic and materialistic North Americans. To them everyone else in Latin America are *Bolivianos*—Indians— because anyone that does not look European—Spanish, Italian, English—and has coarse, black, straight hair and a dark complexion is automatically stereotyped as hailing from Bolivia...a *Boliviano*, or Indian. At the end of the day, I don't much care what they think of themselves as long as they understand that I do not take kindly to anyone being severely critical of the United States. I take such comments as personal.

That night we had a repeat performance by the Leone brothers. They picked us up again at eight o'clock. Each was driving their own car and each had their date and one for us. By good fortune, it was the same arrangement as the night before, and Bette was my date. We said hello, embraced, and I gave her a kiss on the check as if I had known her for years. We sat in the backseat of Lorenzo's car and held hands. Strangely, we both began to open up about our personal lives. I say *strangely* more for me than for Bette. I have always been a fairly private person and never felt that past events in life were of any particular interest to anyone. Bette, on the other hand, loved to talk about her family. She had two brothers and a sister and was the youngest of the four. Her mom was a housewife, and her father and university professor. She loved them all dearly. We arrived at our destination before we could talk further. The place was lit up like a Christmas tree. There was a lot of action of people going in and coming out.

"This ought to be a fun place," I said to no one in particular as I stepped out of the car.

Mau-Mau Disco, modern music, and dancing hit Buenos Aires by storm. It attracted generations from the teens to the fifties. The two discos that led the pack were "Africa" and "Mau-Mau." I didn't get the connection, but I imagine the one named Africa is because the sound of the never-ending music. Mau-Mau, on the other hand, was an insurgency by Kenyan rebels against the British colonial administration that lasted from 1952 to 1960. Maybe the owners were just showing their dislike of the British in Argentina. Whatever the reason for the name, the place was always packed.

A MYSTERIOUS FRIEND.

Our choice for the evening was the Mau-Mau. Trouble is, with a rebel name, plus the loud, fast-paced music and the writhing bodies on the dance floor, it heats up the ambiance, produces a high level of excitement, and leads to some bad judgment calls by otherwise levelheaded individuals. To my surprise, as we walked in, the DJ was playing a calm, soft Sinatra tune, "Strangers in the Night," soothing music for the Mau-Mau disco.

Our table was round and in an excellent location: not too close to the dance floor and not too far. Sitting at tables around us were elegant, well-dressed males and fashionably dressed women. We ordered three bottles of chilled Dom Pérignon champagne in ice buckets to get our show underway. In looking over the room, I glanced at a large semi-circle booth with three couples. The women were classic Argentinean beauties with flashy diamond rings, pearl necklaces, and other expensive jewelry. The men were properly attired and gave the impression of people of importance and substance. I figured this was the boys' night out, and they had left their wives looking after the children. I didn't give it a second thought until I noticed that Lorenzo and the man sitting in the middle of the booth nodded to one another.

"Who is that?" I asked Lorenzo, and I guess I must have had a strange look on my face because Lorenzo replied in a very serious manner.

"A political friend," he replied quite seriously.

"It's none of my business, Lorenzo. I shouldn't have asked."

In the back of my mind I had the feeling that the Leone brothers had other enterprises beside the printing plant. I knew Lorenzo's relationship with "Mr. Mystery" would come up at another time.

118 / ROBERT AMPUDIA WHITT III

However, for the present, I was more interested in enjoying the rest of the evening.

Mau-Mau had either replaced their old DJ or the management had told him to slow it down. The music was now more for an older crowd than the young bunch, with such tunes as "I Can't Stop Loving You" and "Sentimental Me." It was probably a matter of economics. The young groups were not big spenders, although there were always a few of the wealthy kids that spent an inordinate amount of money in order to impress their dates. They would order Dom Pérignon champagne and single malt Scotch and not even know what they were ordering or drinking, only going by the price. Whatever. I was more than okay with the change. The DJ played some jazz, a few semi-fast tunes, and our traditional cheek-to-cheek slow stuff. It was my opportunity to show Bette I could dance.

The evening wore on with a lot of laughs, good camaraderie, and touchy-feely dancing. At one point, Hector whispered to me in a sort of slurry voice that he was in love and was going to get engaged. He wanted to know if I would be the Best Man at his wedding. Hector was a confirmed bachelor, but I didn't want to spoil his evening, so I went along with the champagne talk wondering how he would react the next morning when I would remind him of his marriage plans.

We didn't run out of bubbly. Courtesy of Lorenzo's friend, the Dom Pérignon kept flowing at our table. In the few hours that we were not dancing or eating or joking with the others, Bette and I chatted away and learned more about each other. She did most of the talking about herself, her aspirations, her family, and even some political thoughts. Discussing politics was classic for most of the locals, including women, and especially *Porteños*. My turn to talk didn't include much, but I did say I was born in San Antonio, Texas, and was a true-blue American citizen. That was a major surprise for her. After all, we spoke Spanish all night. By the end of the evening, I think we were more than just friends.

It was two in the morning when we finally asked for the check. The maitre d' came over with a box of Cuban cigars, and while he passed the box around, he said there was no charge for the evening. I looked at Lorenzo somewhat puzzled, but he just turned and looked at the maitre d' and nodded slightly.

We walked out of the Mau-Mau disco holding hands with our respective ladies. Bette was a very sweet young woman, and I thought I'd like to see her again, but she might prefer to let our encounter die on the vine. I would simply ask her on the way home and whatever her response, I was determined to follow-up or fall out. The Leone brothers left in their cars, and Hector and I each took a taxi. Bette and I continued our conversation well into the dawn. It was a "we'll see each other again" type of goodbye, and I was satisfied we would meet once more.

The weekend was winding down. Sunday we spent the day getting back our health and strength starting with a long, leisurely lunch and reading the local newspapers, having a cup of coffee, and smoking a cigarette. In *La Nación*, Buenos Aires' leading daily, I saw a picture of Lorenzo's friend from Mau-Mau. According to the story, it was rumored that this man might be a dark horse candidate for the presidency of Argentina. I'd have to ask Lorenzo about it and just what his connection was with the individual.

Argentina was renowned for outstanding championship polo players and polo ponies. I thought it would be an opportunity to see world-class polo. Hector, a horse lover, had never seen a polo match and jumped at the chance. Our concierge was able to locate a match that afternoon at the "La Martina Polo Ranch" about 50 kilometers from the city. We arranged for a hotel limo to take to us "La Martina" and bring us back. The match was hard fought and very close in points. Clearly, everything had to do with superior training of the ponies and riders, who knew what they were doing. It was worth visiting the polo school and the training of the ponies. We had a sumptuous lunch, but as we traveled back to the city, I felt I was a long way from my assignment on this trip.

CAFÉ TORTONI.

On my return to the hotel, I called Lorenzo and asked him to join me at the Café Tortoni at seven o'clock. I had a couple of things I wanted to discuss with Lorenzo, and it had been a long time since I had been in the Café Tortoni. It was the oldest and most traditional café in Buenos Aires. Some very colorful and talented individuals had put the Café Tortoni in Argentina's history books. It was identified with marquee names in politics, literature, and journalism. For a café, it was beautiful inside, with a memorable collection of antiques and artwork. The tables were set for two, three, or four places. Larger groups were situated in several back rooms. It was certainly a place to have a private conversation, do some business, or hold forth.

I was there a few minutes early to be able to select an out-of-the-way table. Lorenzo walked in and began moving about the restaurant until he saw me. I had signed in when I arrived, so he knew I was inside. He spotted me and walked over.

"Hola, Lorenzo," I said as he sat down.

"Hola," he replied.

He smiled and looked relaxed; he leaned back, pulled out an American cigarette package, and offered me one. I took the cigarette and put it to my mouth unlit.

"What's up, Bob?" he said, still smiling, lighting us both up with his gold lighter and taking a deep drag from his cigarette.

"Nothing we can't handle," I answered, flagging down a waiter and ordering a carafe of house red wine. "I want to talk to you about some things that I'm not clear on and ask you for a couple of favors"

"Fire away."

"First of all, are you hungry?"

"Not now. Maybe later when we finish our business... whatever it is.

"I saw a picture of your friend from the Mau-Mau disco in the papers today. Is he really a candidate for president of Argentina? And if he is, will there be any fall-out on you that may affect our magazine?"

Lorenzo stopped smiling.

"No problem, Bob," he said, speaking in a low voice and leaning forward on the table. "Your magazine will be better off, that is, if my friend becomes a candidate and then is voted in as president. You will have a confidential inside track, through me, to the Argentine government. I was going to tell you about these events at the right time, but you jumped the gun on me."

"I'm guessing, but I believe you and your brothers have other enterprises to look after. It's none of my business, of course, but is there anything I should know to cover my butt as well as the backside of my company?"

"Bob, my friend, everything is under control. If anything happens to me, and I mean anything, my two brothers will handle the business. If, God forbid, something happens to the three of us, the printing plant will be in good technical hands, and it is all arranged and in writing. What's more, the agreement states they will listen to you on prices and other technical matters in the knowledge that you will be fair and have both of our interests in your care."

"That is more than equitable on your part, my friend, and an unlimited amount of trust you put in my hands. We're a long way from anything happening to you and your brothers, but as you like to say, I won't let you down."

"Case closed," said Lorenzo. "What's next?"

"I may be stepping out of line," I said haltingly, "and this may be a premature and an unfair question, but what is your relationship with the 'dark horse' candidate?"

"It is not an unfair question, but it is premature. Rest assured that you will know about the relationship and many other details at the right time... that is, if the 'right time' comes into play. For the time being, you relax and just keep the subject filed in the back of your mind. I'll let you know the right time and, in fact, I may ask you for some help—nothing that will compromise you but will be of great help to me."

"Okay," I said, satisfied that Lorenzo was shooting straight with me. The three brothers were good friends, but the magazines came first considering that was what I was being paid for.

"I have a couple of personal things I'd like some help on. Bette is a very nice person. I like her very much, and I need a couple of favors from you. I'd like for you to look in on her once in awhile. If she needs anything, please help her get it. I'll cover the cost. Next," I said, pulling out a small box, gift wrapped with a ribbon, "please give this to her. This was supposed to be a gift for someone else, but I would like for her to have it."

"Done," he said very emphatically.

Our waiter brought our wine and a bottle of bottled sparkling water. Many Argentineans mix sparkling water with their wine, something I have never been able to understand. He also noticed the unlit cigarette in my hand and offered me a light, which I accepted, thanking him with a nod and a smile.

"One more thing," I said looking straight into Lorenzo's eyes. "Bette's father got mixed up in some sort of political problem that was not viewed kindly by the U.S. government. As a result, he and his whole family are considered non-grata in the United States. Bette tried to get a visa for herself, her mom, two brothers, and sister but was turned down. She asked to see the consul, and he pulled no punches in telling her it had to do with her father, but he was not specific. I have some friends in the U.S. Embassy in Mexico City and also in Washington, and maybe I can find something out and, perhaps, straighten out whatever it is. However, don't tell Bette. I don't want her to get hopes up and then not be able to deliver the goods."

The rest of the evening we spent discussing our party nights, the magazine, and other mundane subjects. We had a couple of ham sandwiches and drank our house wine. Back at the hotel we shook hands firmly and warmly and embraced.

"I'll be in touch, and we'll see each other again," I said.

Lorenzo nodded, got in his Cadillac convertible, and drove off. Hector was not in his room, so I left a note for him, saying we would leave the hotel for the airport at seven in the morning. Our flight was not until ten-thirty, but between the morning traffic, the charlatans at Ezeiza Airport who use uniforms to ask questions and review papers a half dozen times, and then the ticket counter, we really didn't have much time to spare. Nevertheless, we made our flight on time, boarded, and settled in for a relatively short flight to Santiago.

TOTAL CAPITULATION; SANTIAGO, CHILE.

On arrival we went through the usual drill with Customs and Immigration, and this time hailed a taxi, and drove straight to our office. There they were, standing tall, my first team in Chile: Rodrigo Valenzuela, production manager, who also doubled as our Chile manager, Federico de la Vega, our attorney in Chile, and Agustín Hurtado, law partner to Federico, who was holding an envelope in his hand.

The envelope was sealed, but it had the Pablo Neruda Printing

Plant return address in one corner. I took the envelope from Federico and slowly opened it. There it was, our agreement as it was written with no changes, duly signed by José Antonio Fernandez Barrios, alias Karl Marx, and his two cohorts, Mao and Che. We stood there while I passed the letter around and then began shaking hands, embracing, and laughing.

I placed a call to Roger in New York and got him on the line without any trouble now that the Latin American telephone system was operating with the satellite. Roger was very pleased, and I gave him the blow-by-blow details of our "mini war."

"My guess is that future negotiations will be much easier and smoother with this bunch. In fact, it wouldn't surprise me if they would just let us submit a proposed increase based on real costs and our good judgment."

"Good job, Bobby. Go back to Mexico City, tidy things up, and then come on up to New York."

I could sense he was smiling.

"Will do," I said and hung up.

I turned and was handed a glass with a "Pisco Sour." Federico de la Vega had picked up a couple of carafes of Pisco Sour at his club for the occasion. The Peruvians and the Chileans make claims as to the origin of this drink. It was of no matter to me. It is a fun drink made from Pisco grape brandy, sugar, lemon juice, and to make it a sour, an egg white and a drop or two of angostura bitters are added. That's the gist of it, but to mix a good Pisco Sour takes talent, and the ones we had in the office were excellent. We celebrated for a couple of hours, congratulating ourselves and laughing at our good fortune. Later, we went our separate ways, self-satisfied with the outcome of the challenge.

Two Social Extremes:
MEXICO CITY

I called Roger just to tell him I was back. He said he had taped my previous call on the blow-by-blow battle of capitalism over communism and played it to his senior staff executives. I was flattered, but I told him Hector was with me all the way for the Chile negotiations and certainly deserved credit as well. Still, it was going to cost Roger the next time the money train came by. The Peru tragic drama and the Chile humiliating disaster for the Red team was worth a substantial raise with which to keep score as Fielden himself had told me on several occasions. I wasn't going to let him forget it.

I told Roger I had my hands full in Mexico and would not be in New York for two or three weeks unless it was something urgent. He went along with my excuse and continued to congratulate me until we hung up. I planned to have R&R, celebrating, and picking up the pace as I went along. However, I had to take care of a couple business matters before the celebrating began. First, I had to go to the embassy for a debriefing. They were a bit upset that I did not check in with them on my return from Peru, but I didn't think I could add anything to the media reports on the coup. The press identified the military officers involved in the "mutiny," so all I could add were the details of the invitation and how the coup evolved. There wasn't anything my "handlers" could do but accept my explanation. Next came the blow-by-blow report on the Allende interviews. This session took much longer, and after two hours, I asked for a time-out.

"Let's continue this some other time. I have things to do."

"One more question," two of them said at the same time. "Does it seem to you that there will be a coup in Chile any time soon?"

"I don't know," I said, shrugging. "Things seem to be going well, although I did note a bit of anxiety among the locals. Maybe they're thinking it's too good to be true and are out there forcing fun and games while they last. You know what I mean, 'let the good times roll' and to the devil with the future."

"Thank you, Robert," said their new, peerless leader. His accent was obviously from Virginia or Georgia.

"It's nice being addressed as Robert," I said as I picked up my notes, stuffed them in my briefcase, and began walking out. "That's what I like about the South," I said over my shoulder.

THE FRIDAY LUNCHEON CLUB, FIRST SOCIAL EXTREME.

Several years back two friends and I would have lunch on Fridays when we could. It was just a friendly lunch. We didn't discuss business and took turns picking up the check. As time passed, we invited two or three others to join us. All agreed to picking up the bill in rotation. When we reached eight "members," we decided to have some rules. By coincidence the eight of us were all in the publishing business one way or another.

Rule number one: no new members would be considered unless they were involved or working in the publishing industry. Rule number two: the restaurant could not be one of the many Mexico City five-star establishments. There are dozens, maybe hundreds in the city all noted for fine dining. We insisted on a clean bistro, good food, and above all, a liquor license with a variety of first-class wines and spirits.

Mexico City, like New York City and other major cities in the world, did not abide by "no drinking" at lunch or dinner. In fact, not ordering a drink at lunch could sour and cancel a business lunch. Some felt that the person not drinking wanted an unfair advantage. In any event, having a drink or two was not a problem for The Friday Luncheon Club. Our last rule was that we would limit our "members" to thirteen. Once we were at full complement, anyone who would like to join our merry group would be on a waiting list until one of us would leave the city or simply go on to his "reward." I felt silly calling it a "membership," but I suppose that "membership" is better than gang, mob, hooligans, or even team.

The thirteen "members" represented five major international publications of U.S. origin, one represented an American encyclopedia company, another a Mexico branch of a major U.S. printing company that produced our magazine. Two represented a Mexico City-based direct mail company with corporate headquarters in Chicago. Another two represented a graphic arts company manufacturing printing inks and other products and finally two from a producer of paper coatings, the latter two with U.S. headquarters as well. The magazines, for the most part, used all the products of our "members."

Some of the lunches lasted two to three hours. Some "members" stayed on until the early evening. In spite of our "button-down" conservative position in the Anglo-American community in Mexico City and our image with the Mexican social elite, our get-togethers could become rowdy. Nevertheless, the bistros we selected were not the kind frequented by anyone in a position to comment negatively on our behavior.

This "unholy union," as we were labeled by some of the Mexican press, royally upset the management of Mexican publications. We were constantly spied on, so our enemies knew where we were at all times. We never came to bodily harm, but these were the days of the "Yankee Go Home" attacks. Although I never gave the groups or organizations behind it much thought, The Friday Luncheon Club provided ammunition for our strong critics.

SECOND SOCIAL EXTREME.

Having a cocktail at lunch was not important to me. I could take it or leave it. However, in some quarters it was a sort of ritual. I participated in an incident that will explain the tragic and, frankly, disgraceful consequences of what ego, pride, and lack of good manners can do to seriously harm a business relationship.

Two of my Mexican personal friends, Miguel and Jorge, successful industrialists, would soon be signing a joint-venture agreement with an American company. Teams representing each group had worked out all of the legal, financial, and operational details. The signing of the agreement was to get to know the principals firsthand and do a bit of celebrating. My friends had limited ability in speaking and understanding English, especially in business. As a personal favor, they asked me to join them at a luncheon meeting with their soon to be partners. They asked that I help them in saying the right and proper things and to help them understand what their opposites would be saying.

We reserved a room at the University Club for the signing event. The lunch was set for one o'clock. On the appointed day, I arrived about twelve thirty to see that everything was according to our instructions. Our American soon to be partners arrived at twelve forty-five, having spent the night in Mexico City.

The Americans included the CEO, a high powered and highly paid attorney, and the CFO. The CFO was a graduate of Harvard Business School and had been recruited by his current company from one of the top five international accounting firms. They were by no means professionally handicapped.

Miguel and Jorge finally arrived at one-thirty. Thirty minutes late is not unusual in Mexico City. With a population of more than twenty million, Mexico City has the dubious honor of being the largest city in the world, and lateness for an appointment is always forgiven.

"We're sorry we're late," said one of my friends. "Traffic was unusually heavy today."

The CEO looked straight at my two friends and said with a trace of sarcasm, "I always give myself enough time to make an *important* appointment."

Miguel and Jorge stared back at the CEO and didn't flinch. They also didn't respond. Making that statement was the CEO's first mistake, and from there on it was downhill all the way.

The silence was broken by one of the barmen pushing the portable bar into our room, although the two parties continued to stare at one another.

"*Que desean, caballeros?*" asked the barman.

"What is your pleasure?" I said to our guests.

"We'll have Pellegrino bottled water, and please have the waiter bring the bottle unopened," said the attorney smugly.

What in the heck is it with these guys? I thought. *Do they think they're holding a winning hand, or do they even care how the meeting goes?*

"*Una botella grande de agua Pellegrino para estos farsantes y no la abran. Estos creen que los vamos a envenenar,* Pelegrino water for these clowns and don't open the bottle. They think we're going to poison them."

I wondered if they thought we didn't have imported bottled water in Mexico. In fact, we not only had Pellegrino water from Italy, we also had imported water from France and several other countries, including the United States.

"What did you say to the waiter?" asked the smug lawyer.

"I told him to bring a large bottle of Pellegrino water and not to open the bottle. Please take note that this man is not a waiter but an accomplished barman. Now that we've cleared up the water situation, what cocktails would you gentlemen like?"

"None," answered the CEO. "We'll stick with our water."

Wow, I thought, *mistake number two.*

"*No quieren alcohol los señores.*"

Miguel and Jorge ordered an eighteen-year-old MacAllan double malt Scotch each, and I ordered a Kir, which is nothing more than white wine with some drops of Cassis syrup. I needed to keep a clear head for what looked like trouble coming up with the visitors.

I initiated a conversation of sorts, discussing our families, children, their names, and trouble they got into. The atmosphere lightened up, and we all began to relax. We followed up with golf over tennis as businessmen's leisure activities. In the interim, our barman came and, without asking but seeing a slight nod from one of my friends, proceeded to serve us a second round. Our guests raised eyebrows and just shook their heads and rolled their eyes. I now knew what my friends were planning. If the joint venture went up in smoke, so be it. This is our country, and we do what we please.

Another welcomed interruption came in the form of the maitre d' with menus and the usual routine of explaining the specials of the day. We asked our guests to order first. The three ordered chicken and rice soup and a club sandwich. They pointed to a bottle of Pellegrino water on the portable bar and asked for a second bottle. It was clear what message our guests were sending in ordering plain-Jane food and not asking for our recommendations or the specials of the day offered by the maitre d.' I knew Miguel and Jorge would do the opposite, so I took the lead.

"*Que tal esta el escargot?* How is the escargot?" I asked the maitre d.'

"*Magnifico!*"

I ordered escargot as my appetizer. For my entrée, I selected brick-frilled baby squid with tamarind-mint dressing. Miguel and Jorge ordered grilled marinated London broil with a side of caramelized onion. By the look on the faces of our guests, it appeared they were wondering what in the world we had ordered or how anyone could eat snails and squid or candied onions. Miguel smiled at the maitre d' and asked for two bottles of Marqués de Cáceres wine, one red and one white.

"Please have the white wine chilled and open the red to allow it to breathe," said Miguel, still smiling.

Our meal appetizers were served, as well as our wine. I had the white, and Miguel and Jorge enjoyed the red. The terrible trio had their soup and ate the club sandwiches, examining each portion, and removing the lettuce and tomatoes. Our second course had arrived, and I made comments about how delicious it was, hoping they would ask me about the snails and squid, but they didn't bite

Just to further annoy our guests and to keep some semblance of the conversation going, Miguel began to explain the origin of the wines.

"They are from the Province of Rioja, Spain. Some say it resembles the Bordeaux region in climate and soil and—"

The CEO interrupted Miguel. It was obvious he had given considerable thought to whether or not the business was worth taking all this verbal abuse and mental anguish. He had to think of his shareholders and investors, but enough was enough. He needed to move on to business.

Then came mistake number three.

"Do you people drink like that on a business day and go back to work?" asked the CEO. The "you people" was an Archie Bunker one-liner.

Jorge didn't hesitate for a second.

"We go back to work if we feel like it. If not, we go to our Country Club and take a steam bath or simply go home. We have trusted and capable management employees who look after our business when we are not available and have for years. Doesn't everyone?" asked Jorge with a smile and a twinkle in his eye.

"Are you okay to make serious decisions?"

"Yes we are."

"Then let's get down to business." The CEO put on a face that he must have used to deal with some of his juniors. "We need to read over the contracts, sign all twenty-two pages, and discuss anything that is not covered in the contract."

"Excellent," said Miguel, "we'll just have some coffee and a bit of dessert. Then we'll have some cognac or brandy and smoke one of those delicious Cuban cigars. I think the club has several excellent brands: Monte Cristo, Romeo & Juliet, and even Sublimes. Cuban cigars are not allowed in the Unites States, you know."

Whereupon, the CEO pushed away from the table, as did the attorney and the CFO. In the interest of privacy and because the club did not permit its members to conduct business in the principle dining rooms, we reserved the private room. Our guests had their briefcases with them, so they picked them up, turned on their heels, and walked out without uttering a word. Miguel rang for a waiter and sent him to tell his driver to take the three gentlemen to their hotel, the airport, or anywhere they would like to go and to tell him that if they refused to accept the offer, just turn and walk away.

We sat in silence for a few minutes and then began chuckling and finally laughing. Miguel and Jorge were self-made multi-millionaires. In addition, each was an heir to a small fortune. Nevertheless, they worked hard at their respective industrial businesses. Today's fiasco took place because the CEO walked in with an attitude of "I'm doing you a favor." Nothing could have been farther from the truth. The fact that the business did not reach fruition was not important to Miguel and Jorge in terms of money. They were taught that idleness and complacency produces stagnation and finally loss and failure.

They were sorry for the teams that worked hard and dedicated so much time to the project only to have it go up in smoke.

"I'll make it up to my team," said Miguel.

"And I will also take care of my group," repeated Jorge.

So who was at fault for the debacle? On the one hand, the pompous CEO not only was giving the impression of doing the Mexicans a favor but also insulting them by criticizing their lifestyle and mores. Miguel and Jorge, on the other hand, while not giving up on their customary drink before lunch, noting their guests had only asked for water, should have ordered a simple glass of wine and gone on to discuss business. Pride and ego got in the way of both sides, and what could have been a successful enterprise died a shameful death.

Somebody, somewhere said, "What we have here is a failure to communicate."

Marching Orders:
NEW YORK CITY AND BEYOND

NEW ASSIGNMENT. Everything had been going so well for us in the Mexico City office, with little or no interference from New York, urgent assignments, or verbal thrashings. It was about to end. Roger only called me on my "private" line to beat me about the head and body or to perform some task no one else would do.

"Bob, I need for you to come to New York as soon as you can. We have some legal business with our so-called partners in Brazil, and we need somebody from our company with authority to sign off on the papers."

"First off, Roger, I'm not that proficient in Portuguese, let alone on a legal matter, and secondly, I don't know beans about legal business in Brazil."

"You don't have to know anything about legal business in Brazil. We've been in touch with our lawyer in São Paulo, and he will be with you at the meeting. I'm going to give you power of attorney so you can sign for our company. What I want you to do is have the lawyer translate their proposal and call us if it makes sense to you. If it doesn't, we'll make a counterproposal, and if they don't agree, leave and say I'll get back to them later."

Here I go again. I feel like a traveling salesman only instead of a car over bumpy roads, I'm on an airplane flying over bumpy skies.

"When do you need for me to be in New York?"

"As soon as you can make it. How about Monday? Come up on Friday, and we'll have theatre tickets for you and some friends to the best shows in town on Saturday night and Sunday matinee. Let me know how many tickets you need. Sunday you can enjoy lunch at The Tavern on the Green. By the way, we want you to fly to São Paulo from here, so be prepared. Altogether you'll be gone about a week. Okay?"

Why ask if it's okay? He knows I won't say no. I also noticed he said "we." This must be a decision of the board of directors, or at the very least, the executive committee.

"I'll be there," I said. "Please have someone make hotel reservations at the St. Regis."

A LONG, SHORT FLIGHT.

The best airline reservation I was able to make on short notice was AeroMexico non-stop to New York City. I tied up a few loose ends I had pending and met with our staff clearing up an advertising misunderstanding with one of our larger advertisers and left the office in Hector's good hands.

AeroMexico was not a bad airline. In fact, it had the best accident record worldwide. They served good food and had excellent wines and spirits. However, like many things in Latin America, rules were "bent" to fit the situation.

We were served champagne before takeoff and had an on-time departure. The movie was so-so, so I sipped a couple more flutes of champagne and dozed off. About three hours out I woke feeling as if we were losing altitude. I always take an aisle seat, so I asked the window seat gentleman to tell me if it looked as if we were preparing to land. We certainly were landing, and it didn't look like Idlewild International Airport in New York. It tuned out to be Dulles International airport in Washington, D.C.

At first, I thought we had mechanical problems, so I called The Purser, whom I knew from previous flights, and asked what the problem was. The Purser smiled at me and put his hand on my shoulder squeezing lightly.

"No problem. There are twelve Mexican congressmen and their

wives on board, and they have to be in Washington tomorrow morning. They asked us as a special favor if we could land here, seeing it's on the way to New York."

I couldn't believe what he was saying.

"You mean to tell me I bought a non-stop ticket to New York and we are landing in Washington just to let some people off? For all I know, they didn't even pay for the airfare."

He withdrew his hand from my shoulder.

"In the first place, it is always good policy to be kind, friendly, and *giving* when dealing with political friends. For your information, they did not pay the airfare. What's more, you forget, or you do not know, AeroMexico is owned by the Mexican government. Would you like another champagne?" he asked in a snotty manner.

Astonished, I nodded, and he walked away. Immigration and Customs were not at all pleased. In fact, they were downright pissed off. Here was an unscheduled flight landing not because of mechanical problems, but because some passengers wanted to get off, which posed several problems for them relayed to us by a friendly flight attendant. They did not have the personnel to handle a hundred and fifty international passengers at this time. The dilemma was, do they wait for the next shift several hours from now, or do they allow the twenty-four passengers to deplane and have them go through Immigration and Customs? The American senior officer on duty, considering the possible political fallout, decided to allow the congressmen and their wives to deplane but not until their baggage was located. The Mexican baggage handlers were alerted at the Mexico City airport to keep the VIP luggage separate and near the door so it could be offloaded quickly. Nevertheless, the operation took more than an hour.

Finally, we were ready to continue our trip. It was not to be. We sat on the tarmac for another two hours. According to the Washington airport tower, we were not cleared to land at Idlewild due to heavy traffic. My guess was that the senior officer in Washington called Idlewild[1] and asked them to hold up permission to land for a couple of hours just to punish us.

You have to ask yourself, *How can a government official be so disrespectful of rules and regulations of another country? Easy, when they don't respect their own country's policies, they feel they can bend or even break another country's set of laws.*

AeroMexico knew in advance that they would not be able to get landing permission at the time and day they wanted on such short notice with just a smile and a gift. The gifts in this case was going to be free air tickets to Acapulco and a week of complementary hotel accommodations for their trouble. These "gifts," bribes might be a better word, would be distributed to the four or five senior officers.

The free gift for me from The Purser was the smile and a flute of champagne and an unopened bottle of the bubbly to take with me. The gift didn't appease me, but I had no choice but to take it and shut up. The Customs officers probably accepted the gifts and a little bit of Latin American *modus operandi* took place.

NEW YORK CITY.

The city that never sleeps. I love the place, but then I'm a big city boy. We were four hours late so instead of landing at two-thirty in the afternoon, we arrived at six-thirty in the evening. It would take me an hour to get through U.S. Customs and Immigration and another hour or more to go from Idlewild to mid-town Manhattan and the St. Regis hotel on 55th street.

What the heck, I thought. *I'll just go to the Carnegie Deli around the corner from the hotel. on 7ᵗʰ Avenue between 54ᵗʰ and 55ᵗʰ streets. I'll order a huge, hot pastrami sandwich, a couple of bottles cold beer, take it up to my room, and I'll turn in early.*

The weekend went well with two good Broadway shows and some very fine dining. For company on Saturday night I invited a married couple that were native Texans but now lived in The Village. Both of them were old high school friends. They were articulate, well educated, and very colorful. You could hire him as a speaker with experience as a ship's captain of unlimited tonnage, an emerald treasure seeker, a pearl diver, and a stalwart individual who would fit the classic mold of a soldier of fortune.

She was a highly paid model who had been on the cover of *Life Magazine*. She could speak on some very juicy subjects of what goes on behind the scenes in the top tier-modeling world. She explained there are no free lunches for models. When she graduated from high school, she set her sights on the glamour of modeling, and she fought hard to reach the op of the industry.

Sunday I took an old friend from our New York office to lunch at Tavern On The Green and a Broadway matinee. She and I had a very platonic relationship, and she was a barrel of laughs. All in all, it was not a bad weekend for me in spite of having to face Roger and his merry band of second-guessers on Monday.

NEW YORK HEADQUARTERS.

One of my favorite streets in New York City is Madison Avenue. If you're looking for a hard to find item, you'll find it in one of the terrific shops on this street. It is also a prestigious address and a "must" for advertising agencies, public relations firms, executive search consultants, and other similar enterprises that are peddling goods and services and above all, themselves. Even if I wasn't sure, I knew Roger had insisted on a Madison Avenue address for the company. It was all part of the trappings he put on for the world to see.

I walked in our offices at eight-thirty in the morning, although the meeting with Roger was scheduled for nine o'clock. I wanted to say hello to old friends with whom my only contact was the telex or telephone, and in some cases, not at all. Even though I flew to New York at least once a month, I went straight to the meetings and only came out after they were over on my way for drinks or to my hotel, so I missed socializing with most of my friends. Our company was a melting pot of nationalities and a madcap world of egomaniacs, braggarts, eccentrics, hangers on, a few who lived in a bottle most of the time, and even a couple of Slick Willies. Nevertheless, they, or I should say *we*, put out a superior magazine.

Promptly at nine o'clock I walked into the boardroom. The table was set up with tablets, pens, two carafes of coffee, and water. One of our board members was already there. He was what I called a "Whiffle Bird." When I was asked to explain what I meant by "Whiffle Bird," my response was always: "It's a bird that flies backwards. It doesn't see where it's going; it only see where it's been." "Whiffle Bird" was a term I applied to second-guessers, nitpickers, and who otherwise would not lead, follow, or get out of way. What "Whiffle Birds" did was to comment at length about something they knew nothing about, nitpick it to death, and then walk away leaving some chump holding the bag. He never got to me, but he tried awfully hard. I said hello and quickly sat down, opening my briefcase to avoid talking to him.

The boardroom was the second most elegant space on the executive floor after Roger's office. The conference table was Brazilian rosewood trimmed with leather and chairs to match. The walls were adorned with signed LeRoy Neiman lithographs of *Club Saint-Germain, Alpine Skiing, Casino, Defending Victory*, and a monoprint of *Satchmo at Chez Paris*. There were other Neiman serigraphs scattered around the office, but those in the boardroom were Roger's favorites.

Roger walked right behind me along with his entourage. The key people for this meeting were all there—the company CFO, the company comptroller, our high-priced lawyer and his partner, and our Portuguese language expert from our own staff. The six of them could have been right out of Central Casting. Roger and Josh, the CFO, as usual, wore their Wasp dress uniforms. The others were attired in a variety of costumes. The Comptroller was in an ill-fitting brown suit with a horrible tie that looked like a Christmas gift from a thrift store. The two lawyers were very professional in their three-button suits and very Jewish. Finally, there was our Portuguese language expert, who looked like a fugitive from Greenwich Village.

Once again, I asked him why the matter couldn't be handled in Brazil. Once again, he said he and his senior people, including the lawyers, would not agree to the proposal until it was examined and reviewed by a senior executive of our own.

"Then, Roger, you better explain just what the situation is because at this stage I'm confused. I don't know what editorial arrangement you have made with them, and I certainly have never been privy to what financial deals have been made with the Brazilians."

"It's time to renew the agreement with our so-called partners in São Paulo. Usually, we just change the date on the agreement, both parties sign it, and that is the end of it for the next two years. This time our Brazilian *friends* made some changes in the agreement, as they pertain to the editorial content of our Spanish language publication. Now then, our attorney and his associates understand the legal aspect of the agreement, but they don't know anything about publishing and who does what to whom. So your charge, dear Bob, is to read over the translation and the Portuguese version of the agreement and let us know if it makes sense to you."

"First of all, I do not read Portuguese well, and secondly, if I'm going to read the translation to English, why don't you do it here?"

"We have, and we're not quite sure of the implications of the changes. Your job, Bob, is to read it very carefully and tell us if those guys are trying to get away with something. I have never trusted Al. He's just too smooth and too slick. He acts as if he attended charm school."

Al, as he liked to be called by Americans, was really only part of his name. His complete forename was Al ʿAbbas. It had something to do with being a lion and akin to a prophet or seer. I didn't like Al, and I didn't like his Arab henchmen, so this was not going to be a fun trip. Even more, I thought Roger was putting too much stock in my evaluation of what I would discover. As usual, I had no choice. I was proud of taking on this responsibility, but I felt I was in a no-win situation for me.

"If you have the translation in your hands, why don't you let me work on it here?"

"Good question. Your work has always been in the field. You may have a different view of the agreement, and we want to know if your conclusions jive with ours. It'll be a walk in the park for you, Bobby."

"No it won't," I said. I think that was part of the schmoozing Roger had laid on me. First, the Broadway shows tickets, then calling me a "senior executive," and how he has confidence in my opinion and all that jazz.

"Call me as soon as you have analyzed it, ripped it apart, and have reached a conclusion. There's no hurry but try to make it quick," said Roger smiling.

Nobody else had spoken a word, so then why were they there? Maybe they wanted to impress me about the importance of the matter. I think he was, in fact, trying to impress me but also to keep his "team" in the loop and be able to lay off some blame, or all of it, on the others if it went sour. That's the way big-time corporate business works. On the one hand, he had me, a good soldier, in the field and on the front lines. On the other, he had the people who attended the meeting, including the all-knowing, all-seeing member of the board of directors. He was covered on all sides of his butt. Actually, I didn't think badly of Roger. It was just that he had a very special way of manipulating people to do his bidding, making them think each had made up their own mind. In my case it was a bit different because I didn't see or speak with Roger everyday. I was left pretty much to my own devices as long it was for the good of the company and I didn't interfere with policy.

I booked a Pan Am non-stop flight to São Paulo, Brazil's largest city. It was a traffic nightmare but not much different from Mexico City or, for that matter, many other major cities around the world. I didn't care for São Paulo, but it could be that I didn't know my way around and I didn't speak Portuguese. During the times I visited the operation there, I had never made an effort to make friends, and since I didn't like the management, my trips to São Paulo were "in and out," consisting purely of business and my hotel. No dinners, no invitations, no shows, no nothing. I preferred it that way.

Often times the meetings would be held in Rio de Janeiro, a place I should have enjoyed, but again, it was Brazil, and I didn't get much of a kick out of it. My mother constantly chastised me for not sightseeing on my travels. This was especially true of Rio.

"Have you visited the Christ the Redeemer statue atop Corvacavdo Mountain? What about the Sugarloaf? Have you seen the Carnival?"

I had to say no to each question, but I did say I had walked on the Burle Marx designed sidewalks.

"Of course you did. They're right in front of your hotel."

She was right. I always tried to stay at the Copacabana Palace Hotel right across the street from the beach. It was a grand hotel built in the twenties along European style and tradition and had the Burle Marx sidewalks right in front.

"You're a know-nothing country bumpkin with a chip on your shoulder, but I love you," she said and then she hugged me and kissed me. "Someday you'll wish you had taken advantage of all your trips, the opportunities you missed in not seeing history and the wonders of the world that most people only dream about."

She was right, and I would change my ways on my next trip anywhere and see and visit places and landmarks besides offices, restaurants, saloons, and hotels.

THE FREE WORLD.

My window seat partner was a gorgeous blue-eyed blonde in her middle twenties. She looked quite serious and was reading. I decided not to interrupt her, but the stewardess did it for me.

"Would you like something to drink before takeoff?" she asked the young lady and then me.

"I'll have a glass of champagne," she said in a sweet and low voice.

"I'll join her. What brand are you serving?"

"Tattinger."

"Comtes de Champagne?"

"Yes."

"1955?"

"Yes"

"Terrific," I said turning and smiling at my seatmate. She had closed her book, and I noticed the cover was a compilation of John O'Hara's short stories. She appeared to be a true American reading a true American author's works. I was to be surprised.

We had our champagne without speaking and finished just as the stewardess came by to pick up the glasses preparing for takeoff. She went back to her book, and I started reading the current issue of *Time Magazine*. We were in for an eight-hour flight, so we would have two meals and a movie and arrive about 8:00 p.m. With all the time we had on our hands, I tried to break the ice with my seatmate with a bit of general, unimportant topics, but she didn't bite. In spite of her glamour, she was not all friendly or talkative. So be it. She was deep in her O'Hara book, and I went back to my *Time Magazine*.

After takeoff, I had a Jack Black. Gorgeous didn't have another drink. An hour later the movie came on. It was *Fiddler On The Roof*, a rather innocuous film suitable for adults and children. Lunch was served during the movie with all the trimmings, including some fine white and red wine. After lunch was over, I asked the Stewardess for a Rémy Martin VSOP cognac.

"When ordering a martini, James Bond says, 'Stirred but not shaken,' or vise versa, I don't remember which. For cognac, I always say in a flute or shot glass and not an inappropriate snifter."

She smiled, nodded, and walked to the galley.

When I had my cogñac in hand, I reclined my seat and began sipping my delicious Rémy Martin.

Suddenly, the gorgeous blonde turned to me and said, "Mr. O'Hara writes about a lot of tragedy, don't you think?"

I was taken aback and was speechless for a few moments. When I finally regained my senses, I said, "I suppose there is just a lot of tragedy and sorrow in the world. However, what do you think of him as a writer?" I pushed my recliner button and put the seat back in a sitting position.

"He certainly is descriptive and his stories, even if you don't like them, make sense. By making sense, I mean he makes a point you may not like, but you agree with the outcome."

She had a slight accent that I couldn't place. Not Latin American, not Portuguese, not European, although it could be Eastern Europe. She was very well mannered and her accent only added to her attraction.

"Well, you know, O'Hara is one of America's most acclaimed authors, and he is highly praised by the Free World," I said proudly.

"Only an American would use the word *America* to identify the United States. Are there not a Central America and a South America? Americans could say *North America* when discussing the United States, but Americans believe the word *America* belongs to them, and no other country is worthy of using it in any way, shape, or form."

Whoops, I thought. *What did I get in to?* That sweet-looking face had suddenly changed composure to a more serious and somewhat defiant look.

"My name is Robert, but my friends call me Bob. If we are going to continue this discussion, let's at least get on a first-name basis."

"My name is Soñia, and I prefer to call you Robert. I don't like American nicknames."

I didn't like the way the conversation was going, and I was sure we would never reach an understanding on the use of the word *America* or anything else.

"Everyone in the world, the Europeans, the Asians, use the word America when referring to the United States. I rarely use the word and speak of my country as the United States. I don't know why I used it when we spoke earlier. However, even the term 'the United States' when speaking with Europeans or Asians or many other nationalities doesn't mean much or explain that I am speaking of The United States of America. I don't see where we're to blame for the name game."

"You're making light of it!"

"No, I'm not," I replied vehemently. "I just think it's silly arguing over something that we can't do anything about. Probably the only phrase that could be used is "U.S.A.," such as the way the fans shout at the Olympic Games." I raised my voice slightly and chanted, "U.S.A., U.S.A., U.S.A."

My explanation and my suggestion of using U.S.A. seemed to infuriate her.

"All of it is the fault of the United States," she said heatedly. "What about the use of the term the 'Free World'? What is the Free World?" she continued just as defiantly.

What am I doing as a forty-something businessman arguing geopolitics with a twenty-something woman?

"The last time I looked, the Free World is the United States and her allies in Europe, Asia, Latin America, and whatever country is not ruled by a totalitarian or dictatorial government."

"We are the Free World," she said, balling up her small fist, "and we are offended by those in the West who claim the words 'Free World' as their own."

"First of all, what do you mean by 'we'?"

"The Soviet Union," she replied with something of a sneer, ruining those beautiful red lips. "My father is the Soviet Ambassador to Brazil."

Double whoops. I was dumbfounded and speechless. That explained the accent. Talk about being faked out of my mind. I was Bozo the Clown sitting there and might as well have been sucking my thumb. Until then I thought I was a *people expert*. The trouble with my people expertise was that I actually lived in a cocoon. Most of the people I knew, or met, fit a certain set of specifications that I had personally devised. For all my world travels, I was not as worldly as I painted myself. It was clear the problem with my formula was that it was about as effective as creating Frankenstein.

She had me.

"Soñia," I said coming out of my stupor, "I think people on international flights, if they choose to speak to one another, should introduce themselves with a brief verbal background description."

"First, you initiate the conversation by claiming the United States has usurped the word 'America' and followed it up with the 'Free World' assault on me. I should have said, 'Nice to have met you,' and taken a nap."

Without waiting for a response from beautiful Soñia, I turned, leaned back on my reclined seat, and closed my eyes. With luck I would sleep until dinnertime.

A Serious Warning:
SÃO PAULO, BRAZIL

We arrived about 8:00 p.m. It took less that an hour to get through Immigration and Customs. I saw Sonia being picked out of the passenger crowd and quickly ushered through the paperwork. Customs didn't check her luggage, and she was gone. Sonia taught me a lesson, and in the future I would be more careful about whom I spoke to on an international flight and try to get some background information before we began getting chummy.

THE PROPOSAL.

Guarulhos International Airport is located about twenty miles from the city of São Paulo. To my knowledge, São Paulo didn't have an El Rutas terrorizing the countryside. However, for possible reasons of safety, taxis were not available in the early morning or at night. Pan Am made available a Greyhound-type bus to shuttle passengers from the airport to the city.

At the Pan Am terminal I took a taxi to the Grand Hotel Ca d'Oro on Rua Augusta just a couple of blocks from the office. I was drained from the eight-hour trip and the verbal fencing with Sonia. If we had really been fencing, she would have easily won. A pity; knowing Sonia better would have been nice. I called the reception desk and asked for a 6:00 a.m. wake-up call to read and study the Brazilian proposal with a fresh mind and a rested body. I took a hot shower and got in bed, falling asleep as soon as my head hit the pillow.

In the morning over breakfast I went over the proposal again. There were two clauses that were very one-sided in favor of the Brazilians. On another clause, in a very roundabout way, it gave them certain control over our magazine's editorial content and, even more, gave them the right to reprint and rewrite our opinion articles. There was no way we would accept the proposal as it was written, and there was no way it could be salvaged in its current presentation. The bottom line was a meeting would be pointless. What the proposal wanted was clear as a bell: control over our editorial content. Why did Roger insist that I come to São Paulo if he knew in advance I was going to reject the proposal?

Clearly, Roger wanted me, his boy in the field, to turn down the proposal. This way he could lay the blame on me. Roger was buying time. With this feint he would open up the negotiations again, go back and forth with the Brazilians until it was time to renew the old contract in order to keep publishing the Portuguese edition. After that, he would have two years to negotiate a new contract or find a way to dump the current partners. That was at the very least. At best, I would put the Brazilians in their place, and they would no longer be a problem.

So much for Al 'Abbas' power play. My hat was off to Roger and his devious ways. As always, it was a simple case of who does the work and who gets the credit. Unfortunately, most companies are not fair and do not play by any set of rules except their own. If you accepted this premise, no matter the company, you would do well in a corporation and then take advantage of your own opportunities when they came to your door letting the blood and bodies fall where they may.

CARIOCA TIME.

I walked in the Brazilian offices purposely smoking a cigarette to show my disdain for the required etiquette in visiting someone's office. I continued to smoke as I was ushered in to Al's ostentatious workplace complete with oriental rugs, an oil painting of a golden Mosque, and several desert scenes. There was even a trace of incense in the air. I hate incense. Al was sitting behind a reproduction of an Egyptian and French combination desk. It was ugly and a horrible piece of furniture. Behind him, on a credenza, was a picture of his wife and children. They were ugly as well.

Al didn't get up when I walked in, so I sat down on a small sofa facing his desk about fifteen feet away with a couple of chairs and a coffee table surrounding the sofa. We were either going to half shout at one another or he would have to get up and join me. Reluctantly, he got up slowly and made his way to one of the chairs opposite the sofa.

"Hello, Al," I said smiling, "how's it hanging?" I knew he didn't know what "How's it hanging?" meant, but he would ask someone after I left. I didn't have to be nice to this clown, full of himself, about to be taken down a peg or two. I crushed my cigarette in an ashtray and looked him straight in the eye.

It was obvious he was put out, angry. "What are you doing here, Robert?" He was being hostile and belligerent. I almost laughed out loud.

That will change shortly, I said to myself.

"I'm here representing the president of our company with authority to act on his behalf and the corporation as well."

"So go ahead, Robert, act on his behalf," he was still speaking arrogantly.

I threw my copy of their proposal on the coffee table.

"We reject your proposal, Al. Clearly, you are trying to take control of the editorial content of our magazine."

"You can't do that," he said and smiled as though he held the winning hand. Leaning forward, his elbows on his knees, he was wondering if I was bluffing. Al thought I couldn't get away with rejecting the proposal.

"Robert," he added, "you don't have the power to make any changes in the proposal or to turn it down out-of-hand. You don't have the authority."

I looked at him for a time and then smiled.

"I can, and I just did. Why don't you try reading the power of attorney?"

The smile on Al's face disappeared and was replaced by a sour look. He picked up the power of attorney but didn't read it. His demeanor had changed and he took a deep breath before he spoke.

Stunned, he said, "What do we do now?"

That was too easy. Why didn't he challenge the power of attorney, or me, or try to stall, buy time, call his lawyer, or do something to keep the ball in play? When I spoke to Roger about Al folding so quickly, I learned Al was up to his neck in debt and was going to need our company's co-signature to secure a loan. The co-signature would have the entire Brazilian operation as the guarantor for the loan. Al would have to meet the obligation or forfeit his company to us.

"If I were you, I'd pick up the phone, call Roger, and apologize profusely for the stunt you tried to pull. I would also apologize for thinking American executives are martini-guzzling egomaniacs and numskulls. Then I would tell him the next phase of negotiations would be in good faith. Finally, I would beg him not dump you and your collection of hangers-on."

"Thank you," he said and walked out of the office.

This was just another victory for the eight-hundred-pound gorilla from the States. I went back to the hotel to call Roger, my office in Mexico City, and book a flight back home.

Roger sounded pleased, but I think he was pretty certain what the outcome of the negotiation with Al 'Abbas would be.

My call to Mexico City presented another problem. Our distributor in La Paz, Bolivia, was threatening to cancel our distribution agreement. As in most cases in small countries, there is only one to choose from of whatever connection you are looking for. Generally, there would be only one dental products manufacturer or distributor and so on for practically any product or service with very few exceptions. We had no choice but to clear up whatever problem the distributor was having with our company. I wasn't about to give up the circulation in Bolivia

There was one other incident of a more personal basis. I had unconsciously granted corporate credit cards to several of our key executives to be used for company business matters only. Our newsstand circulation manager had married while I was away on a trip. For his honeymoon he used the card to pay for everything: hotel, meals airfare, entertainment, incidentals, and everything else where he could use a credit card. He ran up a substantial bill, but was unrepentant when Hector called him on the carpet. He brazenly said that if he were fired, the company would not ever recover the amount he spent using the credit card. On the other hand, if he continued to work, the company could deduct a fair amount monthly from his pay.

"What do you think, Bob?" asked Hector, obviously upset with the situation.

"Let's just wait until I get back. I've just been through one gunfight at OK Corral, and I'm about to head for Tombstone for another. I may as well do this Bolivia thing as long as I'm in the area. I'll be in touch."

What a pretentious thing to say: "As long as I'm in the area," as if you're in Dallas and you're talking about a nearby town such as Denton or McKinney, only a few miles away. But to say, "As long as I'm in the area," when you're talking about thousands of miles over the Amazon jungle from São Paulo, Brazil, to La Paz, Bolivia, is simply an overstatement of self-importance to the nth degree. I had to watch myself before making these kinds of statements, or I would lose my friends, who had no patience with snobs and the like. Remember, you're just a guy.

I booked a flight with Varig, a Brazilian airline, non-stop São Paulo to La Paz, Bolivia, for the next day. I spent the rest of the day following my mother's instructions and did some sightseeing.

With limited time, I had only selected two sites. The first was *Patio do Colegio* that marks the place where the city of São Paulo was founded. It was originally a Jesuit school and now a center for cultural activity in São Paulo. I was told it had a high rating among locals and tourists. It was okay, but I've seen some more impressive landmarks in Brazil.

In the short time I had left, I was curious about the *Leberade*, an oriental-influenced neighborhood home to Japanese immigrants. There is a considerable population of Japanese immigrants in Brazil that began in the forties. I had been told it was worth visiting. It was, and worth the time and effort, and I told myself I would visit the neighborhood again.

The management of both sites had done a good job of making

available a wide variety of brochures. I armed myself with several of the most interesting ones and even bought a couple of soft cover, magazine type, four-color booklets. I was now a real, live tourist. In addition, I had purchased an inexpensive camera in Mexico City for this trip and used it to take snapshots, using a couple of rolls of film. I thought my mother would be satisfied this time. I never meant to look down on tourism, it was just that I was always so concentrated on what I went to do and then leave that I just didn't pay attention to sightseeing opportunities. Of course, it was my loss, as I have come to realize.

Mending Fences:
LA PAZ, BOLIVIA

PRESIDENT GENERAL HUGO BANZER SUAREZ, 1971–1978

President Banzer came to power as a result of a rightist *coup d'état* that deposed the military president, General Alfredo Ovando. He was overthrown almost immediately by a countercoup by General Juan José Torres Gonzalez, a leftist official. Banzer then masterminded a "revolutionary" uprising and was given full powers in 1971 and ruled Bolivia as a dictator.

All of these coups and countercoups have been going in Bolivia since its independence. They obviously had an effect on the mindset of the local citizens. It's the same all over Latin America, and it shouldn't surprise us that "bending" the rules, which can lead to corruption, is a mainstay of this part of the world.

LA PAZ, BOLIVIA.

They say La Paz is the city that touches the sky. It has some dramatic differences in altitude depending on what part of the city you are in. For example, the elevations vary from about 3,000 meters to 4,100 meters. In feet, it means you may be standing in one part of the city of from 9,000 feet to another part at 13,000 feet. If you have trouble acclimatizing to these altitudes, you had better think twice about visiting La Paz.

I had a night flight that was delayed leaving São Paulo by four hours. I was unable to sleep on the plane and pretty worn out by the time we landed. Add to this the meeting in New York, the meeting in São Paulo, the flights, the drinking, and just being away from home gave me every reason to self-destruct from fatigue. You would think I'd be used to it by now, but I wasn't and probably never would be. It reminded me how people asked me if I got used to jumping out of airplanes with sixty-five jumps under my belt. No, I never got used to it, and I was scared every time.

Bolivia is a very poor country. There has always been instability since its independence in 1825. Some say it has had sixteen constitutions and 250 governments. Others say it has only been 190 and still others claim 150 is the correct amount. Whatever the figure, it is easy to see Bolivia has lived an unstable period since 1825, especially since most of those changes were due to military coups.

Wars with neighboring countries have proven disastrous. Bolivia lost a war with Chile, losing their seacoast as a result and therefore becoming landlocked. Another loss with Brazil gave way to the cession to Brazil of the Acre region, rich in natural rubber. Finally, in 1932, Bolivia warred with Paraguay and lost the lowland area believed to be rich in oil. Often you would meet locals that would have a chip on their shoulder over the losses, and it was decidedly difficult dealing with them.

Such was the case of our distributor. I constantly had to stroke and schmooze him, after which he would settle down and we would reach an agreement on whatever was troubling him. This time his complaint was with the Chilean printers in Santiago. Chileans didn't think much of Bolivians, and they treated them as second-class people. When the magazine shipment was late, the printers ignored his calls and did nothing to locate or expedite the shipment. With the feeling of inferiority to start with and being ignored, he just didn't want to have to deal with the Chileans any more.

"Calm down, Eusebio," I said, "I know the Marxist owners of the Chilean printing plant, and you can rest assured that relations with them in the future will be cordial and friendly. You may not like Chileans, and they may not like you, but they will play by civilized rules of conduct. You can take my word on that. I will call them on my return to Mexico City specifically about business relations between Chile and Bolivia. It will be taken care of."

"Thank you, Roberto. I knew you could handle the Chileans."

"It's a two way street, Eusebio. You have to do your part and be just as cordial and polite."

"We won't let you down. By the way, you look worn out."

"I arrived at four in the morning and was not in bed until five. You picked me up at eight-thirty, so in combination with several tough days between New York, São Paulo, and here, I seem to be fading."

Fiddling with my pen, I tried to concentrate and focus on the business at hand while trying to keep from falling asleep.

THE MINISTER OF EDUCATION.

"Taking advantage of your visit, I set up a lunch with a high government official and our Customs brokers that I think will be good for the magazine and for you as well."

Eusebio didn't add that the meetings with the high-ranking government individual and the Customs brokers would also be of benefit to him. After all, he had one of the top executives of our magazine as his guest. An opportunity to have a verbal exchange on global issues in a personal setting didn't happen with any frequency in Eusebio's life. However, he had overestimated my importance and my connections with world leaders. I was pretty much of a front-line soldier with the credentials to open doors otherwise closed to everyday grunts. I wouldn't disappoint him. Still, I would play the part and make a good account of myself.

It was about eleven in the morning when we took a break. Eusebio asked his secretary to have tea bought to us.

"I think the tea will help you get some of your energy back and relieve you of some fatigue," he said smiling with a twinkle in his eye.

While I was drinking two cups of tea before we left for lunch, Eusebio excused himself to take a private telephone call. He came back to the conference room with a somber look on his face. I asked him if the call was anything serious, but he said it was nothing important. The tea helped my fatigue and state of mind. I was in much better shape when we met with the Minister of Education of Bolivia. It was easy to tell the minister belonged at the top Bolivia's rigid caste system. The minister was an intellectual and a former university professor. In spite of his high social level, his conversation was vaguely socialist/nationalist. He was quick to remind me that Bolivia expropriated Standard Oil of New Jersey's proprieties in 1937. He didn't need to remind me; I didn't know about it in the first place.

As a ploy to get in the conversation, I offered to send him a selection of books we had published on agriculture, farming, construction, and other very useful topics by well-known authors. I didn't tell him USIA funded them. I also told him I would send one hundred copies of each title so they could be used in class if acceptable to the University.

He was more than pleased. He thanked me profusely and asked that I return to Bolivia for a vacation.

Wonderful, I thought, *we are finally ending our exciting and educational lunch meeting.*

"One more thing," he said. "When you return, I would like to have you as my guest at my country home."

It was my turn to thank him as we stood up, shook hands, and he turned and walked away.

Eusebio and I drove back to his office chatting about the minister's vast estate in the country. He said it was a Bolivian showpiece, a true marvel carved out of the Bolivian jungle and worth a return trip to La Paz. All told, he considered our lunch with the minister a productive meeting. I didn't, but then I couldn't see anything productive about it except that it had given Eusebio a small chip with the minister that he might collect in the future.

Once back at his office, I thought I would take a nap until we left to meet with the Custom brokers at five in the afternoon. No such luck. After a couple of more cups of Bolivian tea, I felt wide eyed and alert, so we spent the rest of the afternoon talking about the magazine and various distribution problems in La Paz and some of the other major cities in Bolivia. I was particularly interested in Cochabamba, a city that I always considered to be the dark side of the moon, where we paid the post office management and postmen "on the side" to ensure the magazine was promptly delivered. In fact, as in other cities, we paid to have our magazine actually reach its subscriber destination. Our record keeping in Mexico City always received a lower level of complaints from Cochabamba than any other city in Latin America. For all intents and purposes, our money "sweetener" to the post office personnel worked fairly well. Even if the system was less than perfect, it was the only game in town. Eusebio assured me Cochabamba was under his personal supervision, whatever that meant, in terms of efficiency. This was "protection" money in reverse.

Another "backward" custom was for a client to visit his business or service supplier bearing gifts. As is the case of the sweetener for the post office personnel, it was a great help in getting better service from the supplier. Latin Americans are very gracious in giving or receiving gifts, and in all honesty, I like any act of generous and courteous cordiality.

According to Eusebio the brokers were hardcore Johnny Walker "aficionados," but in reality they would drink any brand as long as it was Scotch. I borrowed Eusebio's office boy to have him buy three bottles of Johnny Walker Black Label. Imported quality whisky is especially expensive in Latin America, even when you deal with your friendly bootlegger. So a bottle of Johnny Black made a nice gift even if the recipient was wealthy.

THE BROKERS.

Their office was located in the warehouse area of the city. They needed the space since brokers were sometimes required to warehouse goods while completing the necessary paperwork and having the shipment clear Customs. The business office itself tried vainly to be elegantly dignified. The result was chrome, glass, a mirrored wall, and the rest of the walls had centerfolds from *Playboy Magazine* pinned to the cork texture. In the middle of all the glass, chrome, and centerfolds was an antique Bolivian desk and chairs. The combination was a horrible concoction of "low-rent" décor and high-priced accessories.

The owners turned out to be two cousins and a son-in-law. You could tell they were not used to wearing suits and ties fidgeting and standing on one foot or another while shaking my hand and personally embracing Eusebio. In Latin America embracing among men is reserved for relatives, friends, and close associates. Score one for

Eusebio. Being a personal friend of someone vital to your own enterprise is a smart move anywhere in the world. Greasing the rails to release our magazine within hours of its arrival in La Paz was very important for the distribution phase in order for copies to reach newsstands and subscribers as soon as soon as possible. As a fortnightly, our flagship magazine ran stories and articles that were already news, but we did an in-depth report that went behind the scenes for details. Mostly, our information complemented the blazing headlines of a newspaper or the exaggerations of the radio and TV. Nevertheless, it was important the magazine be available on a timely basis.

The two cousins and the son-in-law were no different from many of the "good ole boys" I had met through the years in the South and Southwest of the United States. About the only difference between these "good ole boys" was that the son-in-law was bald and the cousins were not. They reminded me of several I did business with in San Antonio, Texas, except these were Bolivians instead of Americans and spoke Spanish instead of English. I was sure both groups had the same principles: patriotism, God fearing, and their own moral code that allowed for certain infringements on local law. However, the Bolivians had better opportunities to breach rules and regulations considering nuisances in the face of worthless local and federal red tape and bureaucracy that stifled their business.

Eusebio introduced us, and I shook hands with each one, but since we had just met, we did not embrace. Johnny Walker Black Label gifts came next. They were all smiles. They nodded their appreciation and thanked me in anticipation of our *hora feliz,* happy hour, that was soon to come. The son-in-law, who acted as the leader, began opening one of the bottles. One cousin ushered us in a room that appeared to have several uses: a conference room, a discussion room, an entertainment room with a TV and audio equipment for music or taping conversations, and even a single bed in one corner for anyone who was tired or had other plans.

The other cousin went to a built-in bar and brought out an ice bucket. The two cousins, Eusebio, and I sat down while the son-in-law poured the drinks. His drink was in a straight shot glass. I guess he felt like mainlining. The rest of us asked for Scotch on the rocks. We began our happy hour by first toasting ourselves, and then we toasted the rest of the toast list. What toasts were on the list depended on the country we found ourselves in. When the toasts were over, we had half of our drinks left except for the son-in-law, who had killed his neat drink.

The room was decorated with more beautifully framed *Playboy* playmate centerfold posters. Three numbers were written on the poster before framing. The numbers were from one to ten and each was a vote from the son-in-law and the two cousins. The numbers, in turn, represented a grading system on where the centerfolds rated with each of the owners. I could see these three were really hung up on *Playboy* playmate centerfold posters.

After the usual complaints about the government, taxes, bureaucracy, and red tape, the son- in-law directed the conversation to the *Playboy* clubs and the *Playboy* mansion. They wanted to know if I had ever been in any of the clubs or in the mansion in Chicago. They were thrilled when I told them I had been in three of the clubs: New York, Dallas, and San Francisco. They refilled their drinks; I begged off and began smoking. Pretty soon the room looked as if it was a set for a black and white gangster movie. Consider five men, drinking, smoking, wooden furniture, and even a roll top desk against one wall with posters of semi-nude women plastered on the walls and you get the picture. Maybe plastered wasn't the word. Actually, the posters were well framed, and there I was, describing the clubs I had been in and what the girls looked like.

"The Bunny girls were beautiful beyond reason," I said, shaking my head and rolling my eyes as if it was too hard to believe.

One of the cousins leaned across the coffee table and asked me in a low, almost whispering tone, "Do you think if we showed one of them enough money, she would go out with us?"

"I don't know. You can always try, and if you're nice and offer the Bunny enough money, she might go with you."

I couldn't believe I was talking about this with a grown man, albeit one with money. That just goes to show you, money doesn't always mean brains.

That seemed to satisfy the three of them. The next question came from the bald-one.

"What about the *Playboy* mansion? Is it everything we see in the magazine? You know, the girls, the pools, the games?"

"I've never been in either of the *Playboy* mansions."

"You mean there are two mansions?"

"Yes. The original is located in Chicago, and that is probably the one you have read about. The other is called *Playboy* Mansion West and is in a suburb of Los Angeles. I have a friend who has been to both mansions. He spent several hours at both of the mansions, and he hasn't been the same since. In fact, he is on the verge of divorce."

My friend had actually been to both mansions but he was not on the verge of divorce. I added the divorce bit to make it a salty story.

"Wow," said one cousin, "does a visit to the mansion really affect you that way?"

"As I said, I've never visited either mansion, but my friend has never been the same since."

"Did your friend tell you about the mansions and what goes on inside?"

"Sort of. Apparently, the mansions have some sort of 'Code of Silence' that forbids a visitor to speak in detail about what goes on inside with the exception of discussing the mansion's amenities."

"I love that secrecy stuff," said the bald one. "At least tell us what he *did* tell you."

"Well, the original mansion was a seventy room residence. I don't know how many bedrooms it had, but you can bet that at least half of the rooms were sleeping quarters. The one in Chicago is now closed. The one in Los Angeles includes twenty-two bedrooms. It has its own wine cellar with some really dynamite wines from the entire world. It also has a game room, but my friend wouldn't tell me what kind of games they played there. Part of the 'Code of Silence,' I'm sure. The have tennis courts, an Olympic swimming pool, and, of course, the famous grotto with a sauna and bathhouse. My friend was fortunate enough to be allowed to stay overnight. He said he didn't sleep all night. He didn't, or couldn't, go in to detail, but he said he can die happy now."

The three just sat there dumbfounded. They took a long pull from their drinks and a deep drag from their cigarettes.

After a few minutes of thinking it over, he asked, "What would it take to be invited to the mansion?"

"That's a good question." I shook my head and made a vague kind of helpless gesture. The three brokers were in their cups by now, and I guess I could have said anything to make them happy. Instead I decided to try to give them a possible "entry card."

"The three of you and your father-in-law," pointing to the bald one, "probably have clout with the Bolivian Ambassador to Washington and other politicos. I would get the ambassador to write a letter of introduction to the owner of the *Playboy* Mansion West to ask for the opportunity of visiting the mansion on your next trip to Los Angeles."

If this didn't get at least one of them in, nothing would.

They kept drinking, making small talk, and I reminded them I had to be at the airport about 7:00 p.m. for an 8:00 p.m. flight. I stopped drinking after my first drink knowing I was in for a long night from La Paz to Lima and from Lima to Miami and finally, from Miami to Mexico City. The Lima to Miami flight was the best I could do. If I didn't get that flight, I would be stuck in Lima or La Paz for three days. I didn't need that.

Eusebio, who had been silent most of the evening, finally spoke up.

"It's 6:15. Let's get going."

I thanked the brokers and was awarded with an embrace to seal our friendship. Whatever the rest of the night held for the brokers, our discussion about the *Playboy* playmates had turned up the volume, but the Scotch would dampen their plans.

We arrived at the airport and parked the car. Eusebio suggested we go straight to the gate since I had no luggage to check. I had my nifty Crouch and Fitzgerald briefcase and a Hartman tweed garment bag that I could fold and make into a carry-on. I never checked luggage in Latin America when I had to make a connection to another airline; even to the same airline was a gamble where your luggage might end up. If lost luggage was a problem in the United States, in Latin America you were playing luggage roulette where around and around it goes, and where it stops, nobody knows.

There was standing room only at the gate. There had to be at least fifty people bunched up against the door. After standing there amid the smoke, body odor, and bad breath for an hour, it was announced that our flight was two hours late. This was an Eastern flight that flew Lima to La Paz and back to Lima. It might also be the same plane I was to connect with in Lima for the flight to Miami.

I suggested to Eusebio that we go to the bar and get a drink, but the bar was as crowded as the gate.

"Why don't we just go and sit in the car?"

"Good idea, Bob. I'll see I can find a couple of bottles of beer or drinks and bring them to the car. I'll meet you at the car, here're the keys."

Eusebio walked off heading for the bar. I kept walking outside out of the terminal to the car. When Eusebio got back, he had a pint of some local *Singani* liquor concoction. *Singani* is the liquor of Bolivia and tastes like Manchurian dragon stew. We sat and drank and talked about the brokers and their fetish about *Playboy* Playmates. We talked about Butch Cassidy and the Sundance Kid, who were killed in Bolivia. Eusebio gave me a thumbnail sketch of the official Bolivian account of Butch Cassidy and the Sundance Kid while in Bolivia. The pair's demise came in a shootout in San Vicente, a small miner's settlement near the town of Tupiza. The two Gringo gunfighters, or *Pistoleros*, as they're known in Bolivia, also lived in Argentina as honest cattle ranchers and in Chile before making Bolivia their final resting place. Eusebio said someone had set up tours to Tupiza, where Butch and Sundance lived, and to San Vicente, the place of the shootout. You can even see their gravesites.

"That might be worth seeing," I said. "I have a friend in San Antonio who would just love to make that tour. Butch and Sundance are his heroes. Maybe we'll give you a call and ask you to set it up for us."

"Be happy to do it."

"It's been nearly two hours, Eusebio. I think I better make my way back to the terminal and battle that mob. I don't think there is any reason for you to stand with me; there isn't more you can do. You've been a great host, and I hope I'll have the opportunity to reciprocate in Mexico City some time soon."

"I'll stay, Bob."

"No, don't get out of your car. I'll make it the rest of the way alone. Think, Eusebio, I'm in and out of airports in Latin America as a way of life. I've handled these situations before, even though my mother doesn't think so. Take care, my friend," I said, opening the door and stepping out.

Eusebio wouldn't leave it just like that. He got out of the car and came around to shake my hand and gave me an *abrazo*, an embrace.

"You take care as well, Bob."

A Tough Ride:

MEXICO CITY

THE LONG ROAD HOME. I turned and walked back to the terminal. Nothing had changed, same mob, same odor and breath and smoke and kids crying. I stood there smoking like the rest for another hour and half when an agent finally came to the door, opened it, and called out *"Primera clase, unicamente,* first class only."

I took out my ticket and held it over my head and began pushing my way through the crowd shouting, *"Primera clase, primera clase."* The throng parted just enough to let me and a few other passengers through. Then down the hall to Immigration and Customs, which went quickly for a change, and boarding without any further delay. I guess the flight was trying to make up time.

There were only four of us in first class. I laid the garment bag and my briefcase on the seat next to me. I leaned back and closed my eyes for a few minutes. Between the drinks at lunch, the drinks with the brokers, the *Singani*, not to mention the Bolivian tea, I was ready to cash it in, and I still had to make a connection in Lima, if my flight was still there. If the flight wasn't there, then what would I do next? I didn't want to think about it.

We took off at 10:00 p.m. I didn't accept a drink offer and sort of dozed, but my adrenaline kept me anxious, thinking about the Lima connection, keeping me from a real deep sleep. Less than two hours later we were landing at Lima's Jorge Chavez International Airport.

I looked out of the window and saw an Eastern Airlines plane on the tarmac.

Good grief, I thought. *That is my flight.* You could see lights on in the cabin and the boarding stair was still in place at the door in the front of the plane. We taxied and came to a stop about fifty feet from the other plane. Our own door opened and an Eastern agent rushed on board.

"Are you making a connection to Miami?

"Yes, I am."

"Hurry, we have an Immigration officer at the foot of the flight waiting to check your passport. I assume you have your luggage with you."

"Yes, I do."

The stewardess helped me with my coat. I grabbed my garment bag and briefcase and followed the Eastern agent off the plane. I guess my adrenaline was still pumping, because I managed to keep up with the agent as we ran to the plane. The Immigration officer took the passport that I had in my hand, gave it cursory glance, stamped it using a small inkpad, and returned the passport. I was up the stairs in record time. Again, there were few people in first class, so I had the next seat for my garment bag and briefcase. I was breathless and near close to collapsing from the few hours sleep and all the drinking. Without asking, the stewardess brought me a glass of champagne that I did accept.

"You were lucky," she said, smiling. "We knew you were on the other flight and that you would have to wait until day after tomorrow for another flight to Miami, so our captain decided to wait for you."

"How long did you wait?"

"About half an hour. Our flight was also delayed. Nothing new. It happens pretty regularly in these parts"

"I know. I've been kicking around Latin America since I had to fly prop planes."

She rolled her eyes and couldn't imagine anyone "old" enough to have flown prop planes. I guessed she was in her early twenties. There was a time spread of about twenty years between us. I guess I was "old" to her.

I didn't have the heart to tell her that my final destination was not Miami but Mexico City. I had only booked this flight to avoid spending the night in Lima and having to go into the city for a hotel and all the trouble that entails. I had really wanted to fly Canadian Pacific Lima to Mexico City, but the first flight out was booked solid and the next available one was two days away. Anyway, here I was on my way to Miami and a few hours later reversing my direction and flying to Mexico City. Sounds ridiculous, but this is Latin America under the best of circumstances. You rolled with the punches or you got out.

The champagne put the finishing touches on my exhaustion. Fifteen minutes after takeoff I was in dreamland, and for the next five hours, I didn't wake up. The stewardess woke me about an hour from Miami and offered me breakfast. It was a good first-class breakfast, and I devoured it. I had not eaten since the day before at lunch with Eusebio and the Minister of Education. The other passengers in first class had already finished their breakfast, so I thanked the stewardess for not waking me until the last minute.

We made a good landing and slowly taxied to the gate. At the time, I didn't know Eusebio had slipped a small paper bag inside of a manila envelope with fifty coca tea bags inside my briefcase. My briefcase was fairly large to allow for the many papers and even a book I was reading, so he put the envelope under some files and a couple of magazines. If Customs had caught me with this cache of coke, I'd be doing twenty-five to life at some less than fun penal complex. When I finally did open it at home, I realized Eusebio was just giving me a Bon Voyage gift with the best of intentions. In his note with the tea bags he said that was the tea I had been drinking to keep me alert and sharp during my stay in La Paz. With a friend like that, who needs enemies? Of course, living a rather cloistered life high up in the mountains of a developing country, he had no idea of the consequences of being caught smuggling drugs. I could have never been able to talk my way out of the facts of the scenario.

Since I was unaware I was smuggling coca tea in my briefcase, I went through Immigration and Customs nonchalantly. The Customs officer only opened my garment bag, unzipped it, and felt around the clothing. He told me to close the bag and went on to my briefcase. I opened it for him and turned it around for him to see. He only gave it a glance and was about to wave me through when he stopped and picked up a scarf I had neatly folded on top of my papers.

"This is a torn gore (panel) from a parachute," he said, smiling.

"Yes, it is," I said smiling back. Not many would recognize the identity of the scarf. It has a camouflaged design, silky to the touch, and very light. He was obviously a former paratrooper. "I had a blown gore in one of my jumps and managed to cut away a piece with my knife to have the scarf made."

"What was your unit?" he asked.

"The 11th Airborne Division," I said. "I was a Rigger and an Aerial Delivery Heavy Drop specialist. What about you?"

"The 82nd and proud of it. I only caught the tail end of the Korean war, but I have to thank you Riggers and the heavy drop boys.

"Thanks."

"You guys fly so low to drop supplies and then get shot at by the bad guys."

I just nodded.

"Airborne all the way," he said giving me a thumbs up. "I'd like to talk to you some more, but I have to keep this line moving. Good-looking scarf. Good luck and Happy Landings."

We shook hands and I moved on.

I headed straight for the Eastern VIP room and checked in asking the receptionist to send somebody to wake me in a couple of hours, knowing I was going to crash in one of the soft and inviting leather sofa chairs. She took down my flight number and time of departure that would be three and a half hours later and waved me into the room. I was drained and exhausted, ready to send up the white flag. I wanted to shout, "I quit!"

DRUG SMUGGLER.

After an uneventful flight, we landed at Mexico City's International Airport on time for a change. Although I was the first passenger off the plane, there were two flights of tourists and locals in front of me. Each of the five Immigration agents was fully occupied clearing all passengers.

My personal policy was to be extra nice and kind to the Customs and Immigration officers. Like anyone else in the world, if you treated them well, they would reciprocate. This was especially true of the Latin American officers. I never gave them money, but I tried to bring back inexpensive souvenirs from whatever country or countries I had been in. This time I had half dozen hand-carved Brazilian good luck charms. They represented a balled-up fist with a thumb stuck through the forefinger and middle finger and two-thirds of the forearm. They looked like they were made of ivory, but my guess was it was it was just an excellent imitation. A keychain was attached to the forearm of the hand.

There were three queues, and my queue had about forty people in front of me. I was just slowly shuffling along, needing a shave, and looking very haggard when one of the officers I had made friends with spotted me. He walked over and stood next to me flashing his badge so that other people in the queue could watch. Then, without saying a word, he took me by the arm and walked me over to a small office next to the Immigration check booths. Once inside the office, he shook my hand and we embraced.

"Did you have a good trip?" he asked, giving me a "you look terrible" look.

Jokingly, I said, "It was a bit rough. I traveled to four countries, spoke Spanish, English, struggled with Portuguese, and had enemies attacking from all sides. It was the New York three-button suit militia, a Russian female spy with a license to kill, a Portuguese scam artist, and Bolivians and Chileans about to face-off with six-guns in the street. All I needed was for a terrorist gang to show up for a plane hijacking. I thought I was at the Alamo on the American side."

The officer began laughing uproariously. While he was laughing, I unlocked and reached in the a side pocket of my garment bag and pulled out one of the Brazilian good luck charms and handed it to him. He finally stopped laughing, and I explained the story of the balled fist as it was told to me. Actually, the charm looked expensive due to the imitation ivory, so my officer friend was pleased.

We chatted while he walked to the Customs area and delivered me to another officer I knew well. The Immigration officer said, "Tell him about your latest trip." I repeated the story and they both began laughing. I had another charm in my hand and handed it to the Customs Officer. He came around from behind his work area and shook my hand and embraced me.

I walked away smiling at them and saying *"Nos vemos en la proxima,* I'll see you the next time."

Thankfully, my driver was waiting for me outside the international area.

"Hola, Benito," I said. *"Como estas?"*

"Bien gracias," he replied.

Benito was a man of few words. He would respond to any question you may have, but his conversation was limited to saying hello and goodbye.

Benito took my briefcase and my garment bag and put them in the trunk. I just fell into the backseat and asked him to drive me home. My thoughts were on the trip on the way home. I lay back on the seat of the car, studied the passing cars and business scenery, and tried to decide how I felt about the culmination of my efforts. I was pleased with the results and let it go at that and dozed off. It was about a forty-five to fifty minute drive home. Benito woke me as we pulled up to the house, honking the horn with our special signal, and the maids were quick to open the gates. I got out and mumbled a hello and walked in the house. I went straight to my bedroom, undressed, and fell into bed asleep as if I had been drugged.

The next day, I awoke about nine and decided to unpack before I went down for breakfast. My garment bag was first so I could sort out what clothes needed to be laundered and what needed dry cleaning. Everything needed cleaning of some sort, so I just separated the laundry from the dry cleaning and put them on the bed for the maids to take care of what needed to be done.

My briefcase was next. I took out the papers and files to put them in order by country and by event, and that's when I saw the large manila envelope that had been somewhat hidden. I opened it and a sort of sweet fragrance filled my nose. There was a note inside. It read, *To Roberto from Eusebio. Take this tea when you need to have your mind alert and quick. This is the tea you were drinking the day you visited me in La Paz. Enjoy. Your good friend, Eusebio.*

I pulled out the small bag and found fifty bags of tea. The label on each bag read *Te de Coca* (Coca Tea). Good grief. I had been carrying coke around in my briefcase through the Customs of two countries. I almost passed out. Eusebio had no idea what possession of drugs, especially coke, could mean. At the very least, jail time. Customs officers and no one else would believe I was innocently carrying *Te de Coca* as a gift from a good ole boy.

Thank you, Lord, I said to myself, *for the kindly Customs officers in Miami and my Customs friends in Mexico.* I just sat there on the bed my hands shaking slightly and tried not to think of what would have been the consequences had the tea been found.

When I recovered, I brushed my teeth, took a shower, and put on my robe. Still shaky, I went downstairs to get some breakfast. Rosita was in the kitchen. I asked her for a hot cup of coffee and a glass of orange juice and some *huevos rancheros*, ranch style scrambled eggs with tortillas. The newspaper was lying at my place in the breakfast room, so I sat down to read while the coffee, juice, eggs, and tortillas were brought in.

The Legal Aliens:

MEXICO CITY

MEXICO-PRESIDENT JOSÉ LOPEZ PORTILLO 1976-1982
YANKEE GO HOME. All of the Mexican newspapers generally ran a political banner. The stories on the front page were mostly political as well, but there was one that caught my attention. "Yankee Go Home" was the title of an article that only had a couple of paragraphs but continued later in the newspaper. The reporter had cruised Mexico City and photographed all the "Yankee Go Home" graffiti he could find. The graffiti appeared on main thoroughfares, avenues, boulevards, on outdoor signs, on bus stop benches, the bullring, the Olympic stadium, the National University of Mexico and its own football stadium, and practically everything else that had a good amount of rolling traffic and foot traffic. There are exactly forty-three photographs of "Yankee Go Home" graffiti.

I had lived with anti-Americanism since I moved to Latin America, but this was going a bit far. What the heck is going on? I called one of my Friday Luncheon Club friends in the news business and asked him if anything important had happened to provoke all the "Yankee Go Home" graffiti.

"Where have you been, Bob? Were you on a 'round the world cruise, on a yacht, on the high seas with no manner of communication?"

"C'mon, old friend," I said somewhat impatiently. "I've had an extremely hectic and draining ten days, but I won't bore you with the details. Just tell me what is going on?"

"Sorry, Bob, I thought you knew. President Allende has been assassinated, and they're blaming the CIA and ITT. The official party line is that he committed suicide, but people in Mexico are not buying it. You know that the Chilean and Mexican governments have become fast friends. Echeverria and Allende were tight. However, the Mexican Government is not discouraging the local communists, Marxists, leftist groups, and radicals from claiming thugs from the CIA and ITT murdered Allende. Hence, 'Yankee Go Home,' and it's for real."

"When did this happen?"

"On September 11."

"Are we, the Gringos, under siege? I didn't notice anything different when I came in from the airport yesterday afternoon. Has anyone attacked the University Club or the American School or the American British Cowdray Hospital?"

"The competition hasn't gone that far, but the game just started. You take care, Bob. With the business we're in, I would hire a couple of eyes, ears, and knuckles to help Benito keep a look out for you and even for your backup in case you need it."

"Thanks a bunch. You take care yourself."

Now I knew what that private call to Eusebio in La Paz was about. He just didn't want to tell me so I wouldn't get distracted from my visit with him or that I might cancel everything and try to get out of La Paz earlier, that would have been a miracle anyway. I wasn't surprised I didn't learn of the assassination during the trip. I was exhausted and not paying attention to anything but getting myself home.

I called Roger, but he wasn't in. I told his secretary to tell him I was on the Chile matter and would get back to him. Next, I called our office in Santiago, Chile. I spoke with Gabriel Vidal, office manager, and Rodrigo Valenzuela, production manager.

"*Que pasa?* What's happening? *Diganmelo todo* (Tell me everything)."

Rodrigo was first.

"The ones you call Mao, Karl Marx, and Che have fled along with other higher and lesser-ranking Communist officials at the plant. Nevertheless, the pressroom and bindery are in good operating condition. The only thing the plant people are concerned about is how they will be paid and when."

"How about it, Gabriel? Can we cover them for a few weeks, maybe a month?"

"I think so. We may need a support check from New York, but it will be worth the investment. I call it investment because if we come to their aid, they'll never forget it, and we need friends at that plant. Besides, I think we can deduct the cash outlay we make by deducting it from a production invoice"

"I agree. Gabriel, write up a cash flow and telex it to me by day after tomorrow. Rodrigo, you get to the plant and tell them we are not going to let them down. They should keep the magazine in production, and we will pay their wages if the plant does not come through right away."

My next call was to Federico de la Vega, our attorney in Chile.

"*Hola*, Federico. Do you have your hands full?"

"I do, but I'm thankful it's finally over. More than year ago, the rumor was there would be a coup of some kind. So now we have it, and we're all very pleased."

"Hold on a minute, Federico. Do you or any of your friends know anything about this new man?"

"His name is General Augusto José Ramón Pinochet. He is a just and fair man, but he is also brutal with his enemies."

"Federico, those are just platitudes. Do you or any of your friends know his character, his ambitions, what he wants for Chile? After all, you and your friends didn't put him in charge or make him president. No Chilean did. He appointed himself believing that he is the solution for Chile's problems. Is he?"

"You're right, Bob. We don't know who or what he is other than a highly decorated soldier who has always shown that the country of Chile is his first priority."

"I hope you're right. Now tell me. Will this change in government affect our company in any way?"

"Not at all. Your company is a legally constituted organization in Chile. It has no tax liens or credit problems and has the financial support of an American corporation in high standing globally."

"Then we can go about our business without obstacles or trouble?"

"Bob, I would worry more about the reaction to the fall of Allende will have in Mexico. Remember, Mexico and Chile have long been close friends and there was a special bond between President Allende and President Echeverria. So take care, my friend. I'll be looking to hear from you. Thank the Lord for our satellite telephone system. I can hear you as if you were next door."

"Please let me know if anything comes up that we should know about concerning the magazine. Thank you, Federico. I'll be in touch."

I called Roger again, but he still wasn't in. It was time to have a staff meeting to catch up and learn the good and the bad that happened during my time away from the office.

THE NEWSSTAND WAR.

The newsstand circulation manager reported that the "Yankee Go Home" crazies were already mobilizing, on the march, and painting over our logo on our magazine kiosks. We paid for the kiosks although the man who operated the kiosk was really the proprietor. A small shop in the warehouse area in Mexico City manufactured the kiosks according to our specifications. They had four sides, and the crown also had four sides with a metal flag stuck on the very top. The kiosks were ten feet tall not counting the crown, which was seven inches in height and had panels on each of the four sides. The kiosk door opened to the sidewalk. It was a half door so that the proprietor could stand behind the door inside of the kiosk and use it as a counter. Magazines and newspapers of all kinds adorned the kiosk from top to bottom around each side except the side that faced the street.

Our logo was painted on that side in red, identical to our magazine logo. The crown panels were also painted with our logo much like the kiosks you've seen in Paris with "Cinzano" or some other brand of liquor on their panels. The flag also carried our logo on both sides. Not too shabby. We had forty-three kiosks scattered around the city in the downtown district, the financial district, museum area, the largest bullring in the world, the Olympic stadium area, and the middle-class and affluent residential areas.

The kiosks had three missions: one, they drove our competition crazy; two, newsstand sales were important for our ABC circulation audit. Many of our readers were newsstand consumers. Finally, we made friends with the kiosk proprietors not only by giving them the kiosk free-of-charge, but during the year we would award them at special times such as Holy Week, Christmas, and other festive days with gifts. In return, the proprietors would give our magazine priority displays. It was a win-win situation for the proprietor and us.

"How many of our kiosks have been damaged or defaced?" I asked Pepe Colmenares. Pepe was our Newsstand Circulation Manger. He was hardworking and industrious, tough and a good negotiator. Unfortunately, he was also the culprit who had used the company credit card to pay for his honeymoon. I had no choice in choosing him for the job. He had the experience we would need and the contacts that would be needed as well. I also did not have a choice in giving orders for an assignment that would include the use of force. Still, we were in their stadium, it was their ball and mostly their rules. So be it.

"We've identified three kiosks, but they're just gearing up. I think they'll soon have enough teams to cover the city. They are striking at night when the kiosks are closed. Those Rojos Reds are well organized, and they have plenty of manpower."

That set my blood boiling. The kiosks are private property. They have been bought and paid for by my company. We have to face up to the enemy, or they will just keep coming. The answer is just to fight fire with fire. Slap them around; tell them we are not going to take their intimating methods and keep doing it until they calm down. I should say *hope* they will calm down.

"Pepe, get a half dozen of your headbuster friends. They'll get their usual fee. Then cruise the city tonight and stop at those with the *Rojos* doing the dirty work. Without warning them, I want your boys to give them a beating they won't easily forget. I don't want any dead bodies, or permanent bodily harm, just a good, sound beating. They can have a broken nose or black eyes and bumps and bruises but nothing serious. While they're lying there, tell them if they don't stop, the next time the beating will be more intense and then leave."

"Dicho y hecho, spoken and done," said Pepe and walked out of the room.

I didn't like using Pepe's headbuster friends but, unfortunately, the situation needed to make a strong statement in order to be understood. In many ways, it was no different than making a bully back down. Intimidators are generally cowards, and with a show of strength they fold their tent and disappear. These Reds were not university students on an ideological crusade. These were trained Communist agitators sponsored and paid for by the Russian Embassy. Whatever training they had, they were not used to having a gang of headbusters who were a bit crazy themselves, beat them to a bloody pulp. We were not offering them détente.

STRIKEBUSTERS.

Our next order of business came from Juan Rodriguez, production manager in Mexico. Our printing plant was a joint venture between our company and our printing contracts, a large U.S. national printing conglomerate, and an American financial services group. The plant site was selected next to the small town of Tecoloapan, State of Mexico. We wanted to be out of the city limits and the high tax and high-crime area. Rather than hiring skilled personnel from Mexico City, our cadre of U.S. and Mexican professionals decided to take on the task of training locals for positions normally in the hands of seasoned and experienced technicians. The result was miraculous. These small town Indians and *meztizos* were fast learners, and although some of them couldn't read, they mastered machines in six months. Several of them were wearing shoes for the first time in their lives. Of course, they were well paid and increased their standard of living tenfold.

According to Rodriguez, they were threatening to strike. However, the strike was not limited to the printing company; they would strike against our company and the magazines. They figured they had us in a chokehold. We couldn't afford not to have the magazines printed and sent for distribution according to our schedule.

"What do they want?" I asked Rodriguez.

"More of everything," he said looking angry, "more food coupons, more gasoline allowances, more school allowances, more and better schools, more time off, and just more and more."

"What did you say?"

"I said they never had it so good. I said they were being ungrateful after all the training the company had given them, after how their families had benefited from their jobs at the plant. It didn't faze them. To me it appears they think they are holding all the cards, and what's more, they are acting very arrogant and aggressive."

"Set up a meeting at the plant for all employees at ten tomorrow morning. Attendance will be strictly enforced. Those absent from the meeting will be docked three days' pay. No excuses will be allowed, and no superior will authorize an absence under penalty of losing his job. Have Paco in the warehouse make signs announcing the meeting, and take them to the plant before lunch today. Make sure that all of those who can't read are aware of the meeting and have their immediate supervisors sign an attendance card guaranteeing the workers' attendance. Call me from the plant this afternoon. I want to know what reaction there is from the plant personnel and from the plant management. If it's late, call me at home. This is vitally important."

The rest of the agenda dealt with housekeeping matters. There was nothing of real importance to deal with. Hector took care of recovering all the company credit cards. He explained why to the group of executives and began the old one bad apple story and so on and so on.

About six in the evening I received a call from Rodriguez.

"What's the bad news, and is there any good news?"

"The strike is for real, and it's imminent. There are three *liders*, union organizers, who have infiltrated the plant. They have the press room, bindery, warehouse, and shipping departments ready to follow them out of the door on this foolish and illegal strike."

"It is foolish, yes, illegal, no. They have every right to strike any time they feel they are being abused by the company. That isn't the case, so something else smells rotten here. There is no good news. They are confident they can get what they're asking for."

"Okay, Juan. Thanks for the information. Good job. I'll see you in the morning."

I began thinking the why and wherefores of the strike. Obviously, it was sponsored by the three *liders*. A *lider* in Mexico is a union organizer or a front for the union or a senior management person in the union. They are tough and tough to deal with. Our printing plant was a non-union company. We had already done better for the employees than the union would have had they been in charge. The best thing to do with a union organizational plot is to nip it in the bud. Develop a sort of strike in reverse. First of all, you have to show the personnel that you are in charge and not the liders. If possible, you have to humiliate the *liders*. Make the *liders* look silly, impotent, toothless tigers. If you let them get away with this first-test case, you will always have them with their hand out asking for more and more under the threat of a strike. In addition, the *liders* are corrupt. They demand and get payoffs, bribes, and other "favors" from the management of a company. All in all, they are bad news. I had no option but to strike first and strike hard.

Later that night I got a call from Roger at home. I gave him an hour's worth of details about Brazil and Bolivia. I also touched on the Chile situation and that we were in good hands. Reluctantly, I told him we might have a strike in the Mexico printing plant, but I would have to wait until I had more information tomorrow morning before I could report on what exactly we were facing.

"Come to New York when you get the Mexico mess under control. I want you to give a full report to the board of directors.

"I will, Roger, but it will take several days before I can get away."

"Just make it as soon as you can." He hung up.

Hector and I left our office in Mexico City about nine o'clock in the morning. It was a good hour drive to the plant. Hector did the driving while I smoked a cigarette and decided on my strategy. I would not speak to them about all the good things we had done for them, how their families and children had benefited from our generosity. They knew that. No, I was going in there to show them what an eight-hundred-pound gorilla can do.

Showdown. As Rodriguez had said, they all looked full of themselves and were laughing and joking. Most of them were seated on folding chairs, and those that couldn't find a chair stood in the rear. In front of the seated group were three instigators behind a small table with tablets and pencils. They were obviously the *liders* and were thinking we would capitulate and be forced to negotiate their demands.

Hector was standing so close to me I could smell his after-shave lotion. I looked the group over with a serious face, threw down my cigarette, and stamped it out on the cement floor. I unbuttoned my coat and put my hands on my hips. Here we go.

"I'm going to introduce you to an eight-hundred-pound gorilla," I said loudly. "I am that eight-hundred-pound gorilla. When I'm finished speaking here, if you do not follow my instructions, I will do the following: you will all be fired. I will take the magazine to another printer that can handle both publications and stay with them until we get this plant up and running with another crew that will be trained on the premises. If necessary, I will take the magazines to Texas where they were produced for many years. In either case the magazines will be produced, distributed, and in circulation as scheduled. Not one of you will ever work at this plant again. I am also ordering a special police unit that will guard the plant twenty-four hours a day and anyone jumping over the fence will be shot. Either all of you go back to work or none of you go back to work. I will not tolerate having part of the group leaving and part staying. One more point, there are several of you that will be fired no matter if you all decide to stay. I give you one hour to decide. I'll be back here at eleven-thirty this morning for your answer."

With that Hector and I walked out and headed for the administrative offices. The general manager and the plant manager greeted us at the door. Both men were trusted, bilingual, U.S. factory trained individuals.

"We were standing behind some boxes, but we heard your whole speech," said David Flores, the general manager. "That's quite a bluff you're running, Bob."

"It's not a bluff, David. I've dealt with these commie bullies all over Latin America. The best way to deal with them is to call their threats, tell them whatever they're proposing is unacceptable, then throw the eight-hundred-pound gorilla at them, and beat them down. In the first place they're cowards and will back down. In the second place just make sure that the eight-hundred-pound gorilla will come through for you. In this case, if they don't back down, we'll just close the plant, as I said we would."

"Won't that be a costly strategy?" asked David

"Yes and no. If we give in to these Red blackmailers, over the long term it will cost us much, much more. This way, we cut off the head of the snake before it can strike."

I smelled coffee.

"Can I have a cup of your java?" I said, sitting down and accepting a cigarette from David Flores. "What I want to know now is who the bad guys are really and who of the supervisor level are on our side?"

"I'm the plant manager, my name is Jesse Brant," said the young man serving me a cup of coffee. "The only bad guys are the three *liders*. They've got everybody worked up thinking they are overworked and underpaid. Until these *tipos,* guys, sneaked in, everybody was happy and satisfied. The good guys are the seven supervisors. There are two in the pressroom, two in the bindery, two in the warehouse, and one in shipping. They are honest, hardworking men who have been trying to convince everyone the rabble-rousers will only bring us trouble."

"Okay, call in the seven supervisors. If this plant is to have a future, assuming the workers stay, the supervisors will be key in seeing that each department runs smoothly and legitimate complaints are looked after and solved as soon as possible within company policy."

Jesse picked up the loud speaker and asked the supervisors to come to the administrative offices. They filed in one by one and all had a wide grin on their faces.

"What's going on?" Jesse asked.

"Everyone has gone back to work," one of them said.

"What about the *liders*?" I asked.

"They went back to work as well but saying that they were all making a mistake. They were sure you were bluffing and that they would have had what they asked for, but nobody paid any attention to them."

"They are going to continue to give us trouble," I said to Jesse and David. "Fire them and fire them now."

"We'll have to give them the complete severance package," said David.

"I don't care; do it now," I insisted.

Jesse stared at me for a few moments thinking over what he was about to say.

"That's more than fine with me, but the union isn't going to like it. They'll give us trouble. I may need outside help in defense of the plant and the workers."

"No problem, Jesse. I've just the cure for that. I call them our headbusters. If the union wants to play rough with us, we'll play rougher. When and if it happens, let Hector or I know, and we'll bring in the cavalry. You're probably going to find the worker themselves will put up a heck of a fight. They like what they have, and they don't want to lose any of it. Okay?"

"Thanks for the help," said David, shaking my hand. "It was worth watching a pro at work."

"You bet," said Jesse, shaking my hand as well. "It was a good lesson for everyone."

"Thank you for your kudos. I'm not a pro; I just hate bullies and I hate anything that smells of communism. Speaking of smells, your coffee is terrific and smells like coffee my grandma used to make. Have it brewing for my next visit."

Hector and I shook hands with the supervisors and walked out. Many of the workers were out of the plant and waved to us as we drove away. By the look on their faces, they were happy and pleased. They didn't get anything extra, but in many cases for what had just taken place, they would have been punished and some of their benefits could have been cut back. As Indians and Meztizos, they knew that on *haciendas,* farms or ranches, the *patrones,* owners, would punish their workers for insubordination and a variety of other "crimes" by cutting back on their meager privileges. I think they saw me as a kind and fair *patron* (owner), or I would have never been able to dictate terms to union representatives. What's more, there was no punishment for even listening to the union spokesmen.

We got back to the office just before lunch. Pepe Colmenares was waiting for me and came over to my office when he saw me walk in.

"How did it go last night, Pepe?"

"We caught four teams just getting started or in the act, sir," he said proudly and smiling. "The Reds got a good beating they won't soon forget. They were no match for our headbusters. Each team had one or two that had to be carried away. We didn't leave any dead bodies. No broken arms or legs. Then our guys slapped paint on the team's guys, including their hair. You should have seen them. They looked like clowns at a kid's birthday party. I think they'll seriously consider not going on paint duty again, perhaps even getting into a different line of work."

"Good work, Pepe," I said in a not too happy voice. I didn't want him to think that his success with the kiosk attacks would forgive the credit card abuse.

Within days the rest of the paid vandals were cutting and running. It had been hard for Pepe Colmenares to keep the headbusters in check, so some of the Reds were hurt badly enough to require medical help. It didn't matter to me. I was defending private property and our investment in the kiosks. People in the states were used to anti-anything graffiti, burning the flag, and other acts of so-called civil disobedience, but where I live and work, you must fight fire with fire.

A Frontal Attack:

MEXICO CITY

PICTURE PERFECT. The next day was our weekly Friday Luncheon Club meeting of friends. I was ready for some fun. The last ten days was nothing but grief.

I called one of my closest friends in the group.

"How's it going, Matt? I'm ready for some friendly faces, some good food, and a lot of laughs."

"You've been out of town, my friend. You don't know the latest, do you?" asked Matt.

"After the past ten days, I can't imagine what could be worse news except an eight point five earthquake or a revolution."

"Besides the 'Yankee Go Home' fuss, *El Futuro,* The Future Magazine, has thrown down the gauntlet for foreign publications to pick up and defend."

"What do you mean, Matt?"

"Well, you know they've always been trashing us about anything they perceive to be anti-Mexico? Now they've turned up the heat."

El Futuro is a Mexican fortnightly tabloid-size magazine. The magazine's editorial policy is one hundred percent passionately nationalistic. "Viva Mexico" is their cry. It was not communist but would lean with the commies when it served their editorial purposes. Their beef with the foreign publications was that we had all the advertising and circulation but that was a result of our superior editorial package and marketing technique. *El Futuro* was taking advantage of the "Yankee Go Home" hysteria with their brand of yellow journalism.

"So what did they do this time?" I asked.

"They found an ancient toilet in an old home in the Colonia Éscandon, The Escandon, neighborhood. You know the kind. It has the water tank attached to the wall about ten feet high and a pipe that is screwed on to the water tank that leads down to the toilet. Then comes the chain that must be pulled to make it work. Bob, you know what I'm talking about."

"So what came next?"

"Obviously, the toilet was no longer in working order. They took our magazines and stuffed them in the bowl so you could see the logos and part of the magazine's body. *El Futuro's* logo also appears in the center of the page as if it's a cover story."

"Then what?"

"They took a full tabloid-size picture and published it in their last edition. It's created quite a commotion among our friends and the business community in general. In fact, some creative gangs have reproduced the page on cardboard and are displaying the cards all over the city."

"Has anyone done anything about it?"

"No."

"Good"

"We're supposed to talk about what we should do tomorrow at our Friday Luncheon Club."

"What was the tagline on the reproduction?"

"*Para lo unico que sirven,* the only thing they're good for."

"Up 'til now, nothing *El Futuro* has done sounds too serious to me," I said and chuckled. "We can counter these so-called journalists easy enough. It might be time to unleash my eight-hundred-pound gorilla again.

"What in the world is an eight-hundred-pound gorilla?"

"I'll tell you tomorrow at lunch. Hang in there. Bye."

Tommy, our host for the lunch, picked a small restaurant in the *Colonia Condesa,* the Condesa neighborhood. According to our requirements, the restaurant had a liquor license but not much of a selection of brands or liquor categories. No matter. Tequila, rum, vodka, gin, or beer would be would be acceptable, and we'd have our rip-roaring fun as usual.

According to our Friday Luncheon Club requirements, the restaurant had to be able to sell spirits. A good wine or the like served to enhance the camaraderie we felt for one another.

As expected, the conversation was about *El Futuro* and what to do, if anything, about the one-page reproduction in the magazine and the reproductions that were appearing all over the city. The argument against action was that we were guests in a foreign country. Could we take the law in our hands without serious repercussions? The argument for action was if we let them get away with this attack, there would be no end to it.

I agreed with those who felt we should do something that would have an important effect and discourage *El Futuro* and others from taking this road again. So what could that be?

"I have a pet eight-hundred-pound gorilla that I use in special situations where a diplomatic solution is impossible and a show of action is the only option."

I described what we did in the case of the newsstand kiosks and the threatened strike at the plant.

"That's what I call an eight-hundred-pound gorilla," I said, leaning back in my chair. I savored the aroma of my *Hornitos Reposado*, one of my favorite tequila brands. The restaurant was filled with cigarette smoke and probably looked like a den of iniquity to a passerby, but was one of many Mexico City *cantinas*, saloons, for men only to enjoy the company of their close friends and to discuss anything away from the sensitive ears of their families. As I savored the *chicharrones*, pigskins, that had been served as hors d'oeuvres, I explained how we would pay back the president and publisher of *El Futuro* for making the mistake of attacking us.

There was silence all around. They all began discussing direct action as an option. The main argument was how physical should it get? What if someone from our side or their side gets seriously injured? What are our legal liabilities? Can they sue us as individuals or as companies? On and on went the discussion until about an hour later they turned to me and asked details of the plan.

I began by saying, "We can start by getting our headbusters on the job. However, we're going to need an additional contingent of headbusters for the job I have in mind. Don't worry; our boys have an army of relatives they will press into service. The first group will go around and discourage the competition from distributing any more toilet cards. They will also tear down the ones that are up already. The second group will search the city for graffiti that is painted on walls, buildings, billboards, and anywhere else it is seen prominently. This group will have paintbrushes and paint and will paint under each graffiti the words 'but take me with you.' So each graffiti will now read 'Yankee Go Home but take me with you.' This will drive the *El Futuro* people berserk, and it will be a barrel of fun."

They all looked a bit hesitant and cautious. One of them said, "Bob, you think we can get away with this without getting sued by *El Futuro* or having the federal government step in with an astronomical fine, or worse, start a street war?"

"I'm surprised at you guys. All of you have been expats for ten or more years. You know how things work in Mexico and in Latin America. What we're doing here is defending our name, our reputation, and fighting back. If we do nothing, it will be more of the same, and pretty soon we'll be walking around afraid of the shadows, possible physical assault, and the laughingstock in Mexico. *El Futuro* can't sue us. What they're doing is just as illegal as what we will do. The Mexican government won't go up against us because they'll be going up against the eight-hundred-pound gorilla. Stop and think about it. Together we represent the entire free press of the world. Our gorilla is the major publications of the U.S., Europe, and Asia, and our own magazine that wields a very big stick in Latin America."

One of them said, "Maybe we should just let this brouhaha blow over."

"I prefer not to wait," I said. "If we let this go on, they'll only think we've backed down and have bent over for a few more assaults. I have something else in store for the *El Futuro* boss. We've all heard and read how he proclaims himself as 'A Man of the People.' He is using that tagline to run for mayor of Mexico City. We all know he is a very flamboyant individual, so I am having our interns dig up all available photography of our erstwhile publisher and owner of *El Futuro* in action. We'll have shots of him in his Cadillac with driver, playing golf, going in a nightclub with a babe on each arm, entering his mansion in Lomas, having lunch with Mexican movie stars, even a shot of him walking away from two beggar women and their babies outside of a major hotel. The frosting on the cake is a shot of him entering the U.S. Embassy with one of the main U.S. diplomats laughing as the guards' salute them. There is probably more, and we'll pick out the best. Then I'm going to have a collage of the pictures with the tagline: 'Is This a Man of the People?" printed on poster board. Stacks of the posters will be distributed to our newsstand proprietor friends and have them sell for three pesos apiece, and they get to keep the entire income amount since we won't charge them for the posters."

They brightened up at this possibility, a couple even laughed.

"The *El Futuro* bunch will send out their own troops to pick up the remaining posters, but it will be too late by then. We're printing five thousand posters, so about half should be sold by the time they get to the kiosks. We've got photographers standing by at all the large and centrally located kiosks to stop the bad guys as they try to take the posters without paying. The kiosk owners have been told to say they paid for the posters, and hence they are private property, if anyone takes them without paying, it will be considered theft. So while they're getting authorization to pay for the posters, more time will elapse and more will be sold. Pretty foolproof scheme, I'd say."

The Friday Luncheon Club boys came through agreeing the complete plan was the way to go. They were still concerned about exposure of their companies and publications, so I explained the plan that made it palatable for the group.

"This will be a cash operation," I said. "The headbusters will be paid through a third party. The printer is a small shop hidden away in Ixtapalapa, where none of you have ever treaded. I will have Hector at my shop make up a required amount of needed cash and divide it evenly between the thirteen of us. I will need to have the money in my hands by next Tuesday. Now let's see what this program will do for the *El Futuro* president and owner in his mayoral campaign."

They all seemed to be smiling and happy and ready for a bit of knuckle drill on the green, wishing they could be active participants. Yes, there was a risk, but it needed to be taken. Our headbusters were a bit more than simply mercenaries. The money was important to them, but that wasn't what it was all about. Many of them had suffered under the *patron* style of management. It went back to the days of the haciendas when the owner family of the big ranches owned everything on the land as far as the eye could see. "The owner gave, and the owner took away," depending on his interpretation of the "grievous" circumstances that were presented concerning the *peon,* ranch hand. The punishments varied from cutting privileges at the company store to not getting paid at all. The scenario was something out of the good old plantation days in Southern United States.

We finally got back to our drinking and eating. Terry, who was always good for some new jokes, didn't fail us. We laughed boisterously, maybe too loudly, some feeling a bit nervous about our upcoming campaign against *El Futuro.* Nevertheless, it all ended on a good note about four o'clock, and we left the restaurant with different destinations.

Two weeks later at our Friday Luncheon we were toasting and celebrating our success with *El Futuro.* Our headbusters started attacking the day I received the money from my colleagues. They went after the *El Futuro* bunch with gusto, first tearing down the photograph reproductions of the toilet scene and then painting the slogan "but take me with you" on all "Yankee Go Home" graffiti where it fit and painting over "Yankee Go Home" when it didn't fit. When the "man of the people" posters were finished being printed, they immediately distributed them to the major kiosks. The third week they spent "mopping" up. It cost more than we had estimated, but by all accounts it was an inexpensive way to show the *El Futuro* organization, and any others that may be entertaining such thoughts, that they couldn't fight the eight-hundred-pound gorilla.

About a week after the newsstand turmoil had come to an end, I received a call from the president and publisher of *El Futuro.*

"What I don't understand," he said, "is why you, an Ampudia, whose great-grandfather, General Ampudia, fought Zachary Taylor to a standstill in Monterrey, would side with the Imperialist invaders. We call those people like you the worst kind of traitors because they sell themselves and their brute force for money or power or both. They have been known since Attila the Hun as mercenaries—"

"And you, sir," I replied, cutting him off before he could continue with derogatory remarks, "have allowed your own political gangsters, thugs, thieves of every stripe, and even so-called Mexican captains of industry to sack this noble country. With your help by standing by and saying nothing, you have abetted the Mexican version of Attila the Hun. You, sir, deserve worse, and you will get it."

"*Vete al Diablo*, go to the devil," he said furiously and hung up.

I finally called Roger and gave him a blow-by-blow report on all of the action from the beginning. He told me that in the future he didn't want to know the details of the headbusters and whatever action they were taking but to go ahead and do what I thought was best for our company and our magazines. I also told him how much money we had spent on the newsstand wars and gave him an estimate of what it was going to take for the "man of the people" initiative. He okayed it, but again, he said to spend what I needed to spend in defense of our property. He reminded me to come to New York as soon as I could schedule it.

"I want you to report everything about your trip, Brazil, Bolivia and the current Chile situation. Also be prepared to report on all of the details of the newsstand wars, the *El Futuro* attack, and how you solved each of the evils."

"Of course," I replied. "I'll let you know my schedule as soon as I can make it."

Roger used the word "evil," and that surprised and amused me. He was obviously dressing up my presentation, but I wasn't sure why.

The man on the front line was really Pepe Colmenares, our newsstand circulation guru. He had done an exceptional job of spearheading the newsstand war and the *El Futuro* attack and of controlling the headbusters. We had to get the credit card wrongdoing resolved. He was a valuable player in our company and with the magazine, and I didn't want to lose him.

Hector and I huddled up and worked out a plan that would punish him but would benefit us as well. First, we would deduct twenty percent from his salary on a monthly basis. That would take him about two years to pay off the debt, including interest. This deduction would surely have a negative effect on his and his new wife's lifestyle and may prompt him to look for another job. I didn't want that, so we came up with a plan that would not only make up for the salary deduction, but he could earn additional income. The plan consisted of having him increase newsstand circulation by setting up new points of distribution in the city and the environs that had been neglected in the past. The increases were based on percentage points controlled by our accounting department. Pepe went for the plan. Hector and I were pleased the problem was resolved. That called for a celebration at one of our favorite restaurants down the street from the office with Pepe Colmenares as our special guest.

THE DEBRIEFING.

The U.S. Embassy was three long blocks from my office, but it was a nice day, and the walk gave me time to think about my upcoming New York trip. It was as good of a time as any to begin pleading my case. I wanted more than just money. Heck, I was the lord and master for our company in Latin America, so in my early forties I was doing well. There had been talk about launching a magazine in Europe. Maybe I could deal my way into that project, but I didn't just want more money, although I would ask for it on general principle. I needed to have some stock in the company, and I should be close to getting elected to the board. I'd have to sort things out and prepare a presentation to sell the board.

This time, in addition to the director for Latin America of USIA and my two "handlers," there was a new face hailing from Washington, D.C. He identified himself as no one important and was just going to sit in and listen to my report. Whose chain was he trying to pull? He had CIA written all over him. The one thing that really annoyed me about Washington types was their omnipotent attitude to the rest of the world. In other words, they felt they were head and shoulders above the rest of humanity and could even jump tall buildings in a single bound. Of course, many times they had their heads handed to them on a silver platter by the competition.

Meeting the new man from Washington was to be a very pleasant surprise. He was called "Hank" by the three embassy individuals and sat quietly through the debriefing. At their request, I went over the Peru so-called "bloodless coup," but this time they had me do a step-by-step report on this episode. The names of the senior officers leading the coup were a matter of record, so I only described the cloak and dagger scenario. I said I was met at the airport and did not go through Customs or Immigration. At the hotel I didn't have to register, so for all practical and impractical purposes, I was not in Peru.

I brushed over the incident with the Russian Ambassador's daughter on the flight to São Paulo and was about to move on when Hank spoke for the first time. He wanted to know every detail of the conversation I could recall. Now I knew this debriefing was more for Hank's benefit than for his USIA pals. By the look on his face and the notes he was taking, plus the tape recorder, it was obvious he was dead serious about this debriefing.

"Was she wearing excessive clothes and jewelry? Was she intelligent? Did she speak good English? Was she beautiful? Was she looking for a war of words, thoughts, and political views?"

"Affirmative to each question," I replied.

"Thank you, Bob. Let's move on. What is your opinion of Brazil?"

"Brazil has never been one of my favorite countries, and this leg of the trip was somewhat distasteful to me. In the first instance I was meeting with an individual whom I considered less than honest and caught him in a company power play to takeover part or all of our Brazilian operation. Secondly, Brazil was far and away a country I did not look forward to visiting. In fact, I never had a good time in Brazil, including the city of Rio de Janeiro with the glitz and glamour of the *Ipanema* and *Copacabana* beaches. I was disappointed when I saw that one block away from those two world-renowned landmarks were office and apartment buildings and shops of all kinds as if you were in mid-town Manhattan. Then there was the language. I never did well with the Portuguese language, so Brazil was not on my list of favorite swinging playgrounds. I took a lot of ribbing from my friends, who insisted Mardi Gras in Rio and the hot-looking babes on those equally hot beaches was something out of a dream. I preferred Acapulco many times over Rio. Acapulco was exactly what it was supposed to be; a fun-filled city with little or no business to distract you.

"The only thing I found strange was when the hotel manager said he would give me a twenty percent discount if I would pay in cash. Since Brazil has been under a dictatorial regime, there might have been a change on the horizon. I accepted his offer and paid him in cash. Apparently, there has not been a change... at least so far.

"The brief stopover in La Paz, Bolivia, was successful insofar as business was concerned. I managed to settle a racial dispute between two longtime enemies: Bolivia and Chile. It had to do with the distribution of our magazines that are printed in Santiago, Chile, and air freighted to La Paz. The Chileans, and for that matter, the Argentineans, treat Bolivia as second-rate citizens of South America. Bolivia has a huge population of Indians. Chile and Argentina do not. I don't know what these two countries initially did with their Indian population. Both countries lean heavily on their European heritage, and that may give the non-Indian folks an attitude of superiority over anyone else. Maybe they put the Indians on reservations much like we did. Anyway, the problem was solved for us.

"Our distributor set up a lunch with the Minister of Education. The conversation was very boring and may have been a total loss had it not been for the excellent Bolivian dishes we ordered.

"I told him about our book-publishing operation, which interested him, so I offered to send him one hundred copies of each title. This generous gesture on my part was not so generous. Properly handled, it could be free promotion for our book operation and good public relations for our company. It turned out he was a member of Bolivia's ruling class and a millionaire. In fact, he was very pro U.S.A. and very pro capitalism, so our lunch meeting wasn't a total loss after all.

"Before going to the airport, we met with our magazine distributors and custom brokers and had drinks and discussed *Playboy* centerfolds, the *Playboy* mansion, and anything to do with *Playboy* in general. Stop me if all this is irrelevant.

"However, the whole Bolivian one-day trip could have been a twenty-five to life nightmare. Without telling me, my friend Eusebio slipped an envelope of coca tea in my briefcase in appreciation of my help. I was a drug smuggler and was not aware of it."

Hank spoke for the second time. "Hold it!" he exclaimed suddenly. "Do you mean you went through two Immigration and Customs checkpoints carrying an envelope full of coca tea bags? How many tea bags?"

"Fifty."

"Good grief," he said in a lower tone. He stood and paced the room, recovering his self-control. Hank was tall, over six feet. I guessed his weight about one-eighty to one-ninety. He was attractive, age somewhere in the mid-thirties, with an Ivy League look and properly attired in a Brooks Brothers three-button suit and prep school tie. He was properly packaged for the Washington, D.C. scene but not so for Latin America.

"How long have you lived in Latin America, Hank?" I asked.

"I've never lived in Latin America."

"Do you speak Spanish?"

"No."

"Why do you think you were selected for this particular assignment?"

"I guess I fit the job description."

"Did the job description include having lived and worked in at least one country in Latin America? Did it include command of the Spanish language? Not fluency, just a working knowledge of Spanish?"

"No."

"Hank, I need to spell a few things out for you. I know you were alarmed that a run of the mill Bolivian, or any Bolivian, gives coke so little importance. He gave it to me as a gift, not thinking for a moment that in the eyes of Americans I would be smuggling drugs with unimaginable penalties. You see, Hank, you filled the job description perfectly except for the emotional, psychological, philosophical, and sentimental side of the Latin culture and the individual. In other words, the job description did not include how you reach the heart and mind of a Latin American. You can be a very successful management executive in the States and fall right on your can in Latin America. Many have.

"Let me tell you how little knowledge those characters in the States have, and I don't just mean D.C. The private sector is just as guilty among some very senior management gurus. An 'efficiency expert' was sent to a company's Mexico branch to study and analyze why that branch was so productive and successful in hopes that their system could transfer to other plants located in Latin America. While there he noticed that each production room had a picture or statue of the Virgin of *Guadalupe* located on a wall high enough that it could not be touched. Around the Virgin were lights, candles, or both and other decorations. He noticed that many of the workers would bless themselves when they passed the picture or stature. Although he was not in Mexico to offer any suggestions, he took it upon himself to have all the religious items put in a vacant room. The plant manager, also an American with only three months on the job, agreed with the 'efficiency expert,' and the icons were moved. Then the 'expert' went merrily on his way.

"Production began to drop after the first week and kept dropping until it reached a crisis level. The American plant manager had no idea what was happening, but the Mexican supervisors did. Lo and behold, the icons were put back, and just as quickly the production levels began rising and continued to rise until they reached their former levels. There was nothing wrong with the technical qualifications of the American plant manager or the 'expert from afar.' Nothing wrong at all except they didn't know the sensibilities of the Mexicans."

Hank began to squirm in his chair. Two of the three USIA functionaries sat upright in their chairs and stared blankly at Hank. The third one seemed bored by the view through the window.

"I don't know what to say. I don't know how to proceed, but I have a job to do, and however I may stumble I have to complete the assignment and report to my superiors in D.C."

"Admitting what you just did is a very good start. I'll be in town for a few days before my next trip. If you like, I'll give you a hand with your report, and I promise it will be our secret," I said, smiling. "And I'll give you some tips on some social and business nuances of operating in hostile territory."

Decisions:

WASHINGTON, D.C.
NEW YORK CITY

The only difference with my last trip to New York City was that I would make a *planned* stopover in Washington, D.C. Hank had said that Jimmy Warren, the former head of the USIA book production program in Mexico, had sent his regards. Great. I called Jimmy and asked him for some time on his schedule and explained that I wanted to investigate the case of Bette's father, don Vicente, and why he had been categorized as "persona non-grata" in the United States.

I had met the man and had a long, pleasant, and educational conversation with him and could not imagine don Vicente as a terrorist or any other kind of troublemaker, but I really did not know him. At least through Jimmy Warren I had the resources to find out for myself what kind of danger the United States and our citizens would face by allowing this man to enter the country.

THE WAR ON TERROR IN ARGENTINA.

In March 1976, a military junta under
General Jorge Rafael Videla took power in Argentina. They disbanded the government and broke the back of the trade unions. Their first priority was to search and destroy the *Montoneros*, a guerilla group that favored Peron. The Anti-Communist Alliance, an

extreme right-wing group, became known as the Death Squads and flourished under the junta.

According to the Socialists, the phrase "War on Terror" did not mean war on external terror. It meant war on terror on its own citizens by the government and the military. Democracies around the world labeled it Argentina's "Dirty War" and were revolted by the junta's atrocities. It was brutal repression and subjugation in its highest degree. During the years of the junta, between fifteen thousand and thirty thousand *desaparecidos,* disappeared, without a trace. Mass murder, mostly of students and workers, was the order of the day. The military junta was now being compared to the ideology of Nazism. These were bad people.

Even the *Madres de Plaza de Mayo,* Mothers of Plaza de Mayo, became a political group of mothers whose children had disappeared. They organized a series of continuing demonstrations in front of the Presidential Palace on the *Plaza de Mayo.* They demanded that the fate of the victims be made known. The mothers created a formidable national network gaining support of international organizations, but on the home front little was gained.

The problem for our side—the U.S.A.—was that to keep Argentina from going socialist or communist, or worse, Marxist, we had to support the junta. It appeared that several very senior Washington State Department officials, including Secretary of State Henry Kissinger, were backing the brutal military regime. They had no choice. It was clear the United States was involved and was exposed by the many documents, telegrams, telexes, and memos that passed between the U.S. Embassy in Buenos Aires and the State Department in Washington. There was very heavy pressure from every conceivable left-wing group around the world, including some heads of state, for the U.S. to end support of the junta. In an effort to clean up its own act, the CIA prepared a secret memorandum outlining steps to be taken.

"As I see it, Jimmy, the fear of subversion was the background that sucked don Vicente into the vortex of brutal reaction by the government forces. Among the documents sent to the White House and the State Department were names of individuals considered "enemies of the state." There were also lists of the organizations considered subversive and names of its members. This is where don Vicente ran afoul of the American and Argentine bureaucracies."

"What was don Vicente's profession?" asked Jimmy

"He was a university political science professor at the University of Buenos Aires. The university was a hotbed for radical groups of one kind or another. Somehow his name appeared on one of the lists of members of the group known as *Montoneros*. It is a strange set of circumstances that got don Vicente on the list to begin with. First of all, the *Montoneros* group was formed as an armed guerilla movement. These were advocates of the former dictator General Juan Perón. It was obvious don Vicente was too old to be a guerilla fighter, and he never cared for Perón".

"It appears your friend is a victim of mistaken identity," said Jimmy in a serious voice while thumbing through a telephone directory.

I nodded and said, "By the time don Vicente's name appeared on the rolls of the *Montoneros* group, they were including students as young as high school level. By virtue of being a professor of political science at the University of Buenos Aires and through confusion with a notorious terrorist with a similar name, the professor was now labeled a senior-level terrorist. At that point he went into hiding. He said he felt like a Jew being chased by Nazi storm troopers. For months it was a nightmarish existence. What saved don Vicente were the testimony and character witnesses who spoke up on his behalf. Although they cleared and deleted his name from police archives, somehow his name continued to appear on the member list of the *Montoneros*. The family tried to clear up the identification mess, but they failed. They had no contacts at the U.S. Embassy, any contacts of importance in the local or federal government, and simply no one to intercede for him, so they gave up."

Jimmy made a face and began writing on a note pad. "Sounds like the making of a real tragedy. How did you get involved in this state of confusion?"

"I came to know about their trouble thorough a mutual friend. The family didn't realize the father was "persona non grata" in the United States until they tried to get a tourist visa for him so they could all visit Disney World in Orlando, Florida. He was turned down for the visa, and the family wouldn't go without him, and that's where I came in. The daughter had nothing to do with my initiative to bring this matter forward. In fact, she was not aware of my "connection" with the movers and shakers in Washington."

Leaning back in his chair, Jimmy shook his head a bit and said, "I'll be honest with you, Bobby, this is one of those cases where it can easily be fixed, or not at all. If it's turned down, there will be no appeal by don Vicente or any member of his family."

"Okay, Jimmy, I understand, but even if don Vicente is turned down, he will be no worse off than he is now. As a sidebar, you should know that the Argentine friend who brought the don Vicente case to my attention is an individual who will be a strong player in an upcoming government administration. You should know him, and if you like, I will make the introductions sometime soon in Buenos Aires."

He and I sat there for another hour drinking strong, aromatic Argentine-style coffee and smoking a cigarette. Jimmy had what seemed like a myriad of questions, and I understood that getting the "persona non grata" label off the professor's name was serious. In the end, I told Jimmy I would vouch for don Vicente and his entire family and would accept responsibility for any of their actions outside the law.

Jimmy wanted to know if I was in love with the girl or anything else that was making me go this far out on a limb.

"Not at all," I said in calm, low voice. "We are not close physically or emotionally. I have met the family, and I consider what has happened to them an injustice of the terrible times taking place in Argentina even as we speak. I want to fix it."

I offered to get whatever documents he might need to move this matter along, including references of unimpeachable people of stature from Argentina. That did it. We let it go at that, and I left his office with a promise that he would very diligently look into the matter and fix it if he could. Either way, he would get in touch with me and took my New York phone numbers and address as well as the name of my hotel. We said our goodbyes, and he thanked me for the work I was doing for our country, especially now that USIA was asking more and more of me.

ON TO BIG TOWN, U.S.A.

I took an Eastern Airlines shuttle to New York City late in the afternoon and finally arrived in my hotel room at eight o'clock. I was too tired to go out for dinner, and it was late as well. I ordered a couple of hot pastrami sandwiches and potato salad and a couple of bottles of beer. About ten o'clock I got a call from Roger to tell me our meeting was set for ten the next morning. *Was I prepared? Did I have all my information confirmed? Did I this, did I that?* I felt like he was prepping me for a long and arduous trial. I answered yes to all of his questions, and he hung up. That was Roger. He never said hello or goodbye; he said what he needed to say or received answers to what he needed to know and that was the end as far as he was concerned. I had the feeling he played the "hang-up" game so as not to give the caller time to ask for something. He had a nutty approach and some would call him an even nuttier guy.

THE SABER TOOTH TIGER AND HIS MERRY BAND OF CO-CONSPIRATORS.

The board members were all seated and waiting for me.

Roger and his three closest collaborators were seated at one end of the conference table. I was seated at the other end. He insisted everyone at the table introduce himself. Each person gave his name, title, and responsibilities and stopped there. I had been around long enough to know their true capabilities, so they didn't need to give any more information. Leo went first. He was second in command of our publishing empire and executive vice president and publisher of all our magazines. He was also in charge of the European project. In my mind Leo was responsible for taking our magazines to their current high level of recognition and credibility on a worldwide basis. Leo and I were close friends, and I give him much credit for my own progress in the company.

The third in command was Jacques, our CFO. He was a dour individual but an expert at financial games and ploys, especially with the IRS.

Next was good-time Charlie, perfect in his position was Vice President of Marketing and Advertising. He could drink without getting drunk. He had a library of clean and off-color jokes and was handsome, blue-eyed, blond, about six feet two inches tall, and weighed two hundred pounds. He was probably thirty-five or thirty-six. His usual poise reminded me of his football playing days—as a quarterback, I later learned—whose ego would never let him be off the playing field.

The three served on the board along with six other board members. Counting the three extremely qualified and talented senior level secretaries, Roger, and me, we were thirteen in the boardroom for my report on the state of the countries I visited as they related to our publications. Roger wanted my report to include all highlights of each country starting with the Tlatelolco Massacre. Reporting everything was going to take the two full days Roger had scheduled for the meetings. Roger wanted the board to know how deeply involved our magazine was in local matters and the prestige we had earned through our fearless editorial content. I was sure he was thinking of El Rutas and the "Bloodless Coup" among other actions.

I emphasized what I felt the board should know and what could or would affect our company now or in the near or distant future. As far as trying to use a crystal ball to anticipate if there would be a coup or a legitimate change in government or a devaluation of the country's currency was near impossible to prognosticate.

When I described some of the precarious situations I found myself in, they shook their heads, took deep breaths, whistled, and applauded enthusiastically. They laughed their heads off when I told them all about the coca tea. They got a kick out of how I used the "eight-hundred-pound gorilla" in Mexico and Chile. What I had not realized at the outset of my two-day report on my activities in Mexico and South America was how beneficial it would be for my presentation. I had planned to plead my "case" to the board, but here I was with the entire board of directors listening to how I was Batman, Dick Tracy, James Bond 007, and many, many others. They concentrated on what I said. Later their questions were intelligent, targeted, well thought out, and made sense. They asked nothing off the wall. They didn't to try to embarrass or trick me. All in all it was a tremendous opportunity to set the stage for what I had in store for them.

MY TURN.

I had hurried my presentation so that I would have the afternoon of the second day for my presentation. Fortunately, we had lunch in the conference room without alcohol. Drinks always muddied the water one way or another. I didn't need whiffle birds for this part of the meeting.

I stood up and looked at each person at the conference table.

"You have all heard my part in carrying the flag for our company and our magazines in Latin America. That is part of my job, and while it is exciting and gives me much satisfaction, it is not without risk. The risk is not only bodily harm but the possibility that I could end up in one of their jails for an indeterminate time.

"In addition to the actions in which I played a key role and which I have described earlier today and yesterday, I am on the road about fifty to sixty percent of the time. Finally, I am still responsible for running the business side of our operations, including production, circulation, financial, and advertising, among other line items.

"My reason for this presentation is threefold: one, I will need a substantial salary increase, two, I want to participate in a stock ownership plan, and three, I want a seat on the board of directors. Although Latin America is the market, we sell our advertisers in the States, in Europe, and in Asia, we are poorly represented in the hierarchy of our company. In fact, we are not represented at all. We are being treated as second-class employees by virtue of living and working in Latin America. There is no one else in this company that can handle my job, not anyone."

I stood for a few more seconds and stared at each of the board members, including Roger. He looked surprised. I'm sure he didn't expect my presentation to be as explicit and forceful and to the point, leaving nothing to doubt.

The board members just sat there. They didn't know whether to clap or sing "Dixie." They looked at each other until one of them suggested we adjourn for thirty minutes. With that, everyone began standing and walking out of the conference room. Leo winked at me and nodded slightly. Whatever was going to happen in those thirty minutes, he would back me up. I thought Roger would also go along with my "case," but I couldn't be sure. I had no idea about the others. The six outside board members were a strange lot to be on the board of a Latin American operation. Three of them were mainline New Yorkers. The other three were mainline Philadelphians. I could not imagine that anyone of the six had even visited Latin America. Mexico was a possibility, but only because it had tourist destinations such as Acapulco. What I described to them about my activities in Latin America were movie fantasy to them even through they were true. I don't know if they could even truly understand that kind of bizarre activity went on in modern twentieth century countries.

Whatever they would come back with, if it wasn't favorable, I would let loose my pet eight-hundred-pound gorilla. They wouldn't be ready for it, and I didn't think they would have an alternative plan. Few times in my life did I think I was in the driver's seat like this one, and I planned to take advantage of it.

As everyone left the conference room, one of the secretaries, who was also Leo's right hand, gave me a smile and a thumbs up. I smiled back and returned the thumbs up. I just sat there drinking coffee from a fresh pot someone had brought in while smoking a cigarette. I didn't want to lose my focus and reminded myself that I had faced tougher adversaries than this bunch of wimps.

Forty minutes later the board members started filing in. One by one they sat down but avoided looking at me. They served themselves coffee, some lit cigarettes. Finally, my number one nemesis on the board spoke up.

"We would like to ask you a few questions."

"Fire away."

"Do you live comfortably on the money you are paid? Is it enough?"

This was the time for them to know what I was really after. He had just opened the door for me to present what a compensation package means to me.

"I live fine on the money I'm paid. In fact, I could be paid half of what I'm currently earning and still live comfortably. The truth is, I could still make it on half of the half and survive financially, but that isn't the point, is it? Our peerless leader sitting there at the end of this conference table has told me the acquisition of wealth is not an end in itself; it is just the means to keep score. In my particular case, how valuable am I to our company? I am not here on my knees asking for a dole. I am here to have you acknowledge my importance to this company and our magazines."

"That is very straightforward and of you, Robert. It also rings of a threat or an ultimatum. Before we get into your personal and professional position with our company, we have one more question. We would like to know the details of one of our magazine shipments that was confiscated and burned in Montevideo, Uruguay. As far as we know, nothing was said or done about that incident."

"Much was said and much was done over that episode. The Uruguayan government had warned us that the word *Tupamaro*, the name of the terrorist group operation in Uruguay, had been officially banned from use in all media including TV and radio. In 1972, a state of internal war was declared, and Uruguay was placed under martial law to help the police and military marshal the resources of the country against the guerillas. In the middle of all of this, our editorial department decided to run an article on the *Tupamaros*. The Uruguayan government blew up. We had been forewarned. We knew exactly what was going on with the *Tupamaros*, yet we opted to go ahead with our editorial story. The *Tupamaros* were engaged in terrorist activities. They killed, maimed, and tortured Uruguayans and foreigners. They kidnapped prominent people to fund their terrorist activities. These were sadistic, extremely cruel, and brutal monsters. They were one of the worst of the many terrorist organizations that exist in Latin America. You might have read about some of their atrocities.

"The government decided to teach us a lesson and confiscated that particular edition. As a first step, I decided that instead of flying to Montevideo, I would visit with the Uruguayan Ambassador to Mexico. We had a cordial visit, and I offered our apologies for running the story and assured him it would not happen again. I couldn't threaten him with the same eight-hundred-pound gorilla I used in Chile. I don't know if any of you are aware that Uruguay is a small country of less than three million population. I felt that this matter had to be handled diplomatically. It wasn't hard to convince him that we were on his side and would profile the president, Juan Maria

Bordaberry, and his cabinet and explain what a fine job they were doing with the economy and growth of the country. Further, I told the ambassador he could take credit for setting up meeting and the upcoming story. He loved it.

"Of course, I had already spoken with our Editor in Chief about this matter, and he agreed with me. Besides, he felt that Uruguay was an excellent reader interest story of a small country that has always brought itself up by its bootstraps. Frankly, I didn't think it was worth mentioning it at this time. Thank you for correcting me on this oversight. Is there anything else you would like to know?"

Major League:
NEW YORK CITY

CAN YOU AFFORD IT, AND WHY? The board members sat there speechless. There appeared to be no more questions. Then it was Roger who spoke up.

"You have certainly enlightened us by explaining the various events that have taken place in Latin America with our company, our magazine, and yourself. I think now you had better tell us why you think you are worth an increase in your compensation package, stock in the company, and a seat on the board of directors. Remember, Bob, no matter how much value there is in what you have to offer, a company is not much of a company, nor does it have proper leadership if it responds to internal or external threats."

"I couldn't agree with you more," I said, rising from my chair. "What I'm about to tell you is not a threat at all; it is simply a way for all to evaluate my position, my capabilities, and my future with this company.

"First, this is a very brief list my credentials: I have native fluency in English and Spanish. I fully understand the social and business nuances of doing business in Latin America and, of course, the States. I have a decent university education. I work tirelessly for the benefit of the company and am willing to spend fifty to sixty percent or more time of my life in countries other than my home base. I am a personal risk taker, also to the benefit of the company. I know the publishing business, and I'm good at it, especially in this Rube Goldberg world of producing a magazine in four countries simultaneously for formal distribution in eighteen countries on a fortnightly basis."

I took a swallow from my fresh cup of coffee and a drag on my cigarette and went on.

"This is only a partial list of my work. I won't call it my duty and responsibility because you would never be able to attract a candidate for this job with the requirements I have just listed. I won't bore you with more, but if you recall some of the events I described yesterday and this morning, you will bet get a fairly complete picture of what it will take to replace me. Understand this is not a threat. It is a statement of the facts, not really known or considered, by anyone except two in this room."

The board members just stared at me, hardly moving, and surely wondering how I was able to speak so bluntly to the "mainliner" shareholders of the company.

"At one of our previous meetings, one of you asked me if it was true that I paid our key people above the average according to a study by the American Chamber of Commerce of Mexico that included all of Latin America. I said it was true, and I explained that in Latin America executive talent is at a premium. There is constant stealing from one company to another.

"Searching for replacements for key positions is not an easy task. To avoid losing key personnel, I made sure their compensation was above average and added other benefits, such as longer vacation periods. This policy kept me from having to spend valuable time and money searching for a capable staff member to replace one that had been lured away."

Our chief financial officer finally spoke up, "It appears our executive staff was loyal to money more than to you or our company."

"Yes, I pay them as much as thirty percent more than I have to, but it has its rewards. Even more, if one asks for three weeks' vacation instead of two because he is traveling from Bogotá, Colombia, to the States and needed the time to make it worthwhile for his wife and children, I gave it to him. What is one week in the face of what it means to a family? There were other bennies I gave them. You can say I bought their loyalty, but in the eyes of Latin Americans, I was taking care of our own inasmuch as I had the power to do so. Take a look at the names of our staff in the different countries. There is very little movement or none at all.

"So what I am asking for is not just for me but for the recognition of our most valuable asset, our marketplace, the reason for the existence of our magazines. It is four-thirty in the afternoon, and I have spoken for several hours. You have been a good audience. You listened to me and asked questions that needed to be answered. I know this has never come up before, so I appreciate your time. I hope it has been enlightening and clarifies what our Latin American operation is all about on a day-to-day basis. Thank you, ladies and gentlemen. I will be in New York until day after tomorrow staying at the St. Regis Hotel. Obviously, I want to hear from you and am prepared to answer any other questions you may have."

I gathered my papers, although I didn't use or need them, and stuffed them in my Jim-Dandy-almost-brand-spanking-new Crouch & Fitzgerald briefcase and walked out of the conference room. Leo's secretary handed me a note saying he would like for me to join him for drinks and dinner about six-thirty in the evening at the 21 Restaurant.

AN EVENING WITH LEO.

I enjoyed going out with Leo. He was full of life used to only the best in everything in which he participated: his clothes, his cars, his office personally decorated, the restaurants he frequented, the best seats in the house at the theatre, and he was a barrel of fun and laughs. I was looking forward to tonight, and it didn't matter whether or not we talked about the meeting. Going for breakfast, lunch, dinner, the theatre, or any other form of leisure activity with Leo was an adventure in entertainment.

We met at 21 at the pointed time. Leo was able to get his favorite table in the Bar Room, which I believe was also Humphrey Bogart's favorite table, for laid-back drinking and dining. The Bar Room is my favorite of all the available areas for food and drink in this glorious establishment. This has been, and still is, the watering hole of celebrities, from movie stars to politicians, sports heroes to world leaders and dignitaries. It's available to anyone who has the price of a premium drink and is wearing a coat and tie. It doesn't matter who you are; if you are not wearing a coat and tie, you will not gain entrance. The Bar Room is simply legendary and well known around the world. 21 was once a "speakeasy" in the days of prohibition; today it is one of the most celebrated restaurants in New York City. It is not a tourist trap or a tourist attraction in the sense of seeing a tour group taking in the sights at 21. Those people do not feel comfortable at 21 and generally avoid it or simply do not know about it. It is very much a New York bar and restaurant mostly for New Yorkers or other movers and shakers that know New York City from sleaze to glitz.

A waiter who knew Leo well approached us.

"Which one of your 'usual' drinks will you have this evening?" he said, smiling at Leo. The waiter was a huge man with a red face, dirty blond hair combed straight back, and could compete with Leo in size for clothes. Both had Russian accents. Actually, Leo was a Lithuanian but a genuine white Russian prince. The waiter was simply a waiter but a very good one.

Leo had a habit of ordering for his guests without consulting them on choice of brand, type of beverage, and so forth. He was pretty much of a "take-charge guy." It was okay with me if what he ordered was what I wanted, but if it wasn't, I would just jump in and change the order. Leo would never say a word about the change in his order, but most people would go along with whatever Leo ordered for them.

For our drinks, Leo ordered vodka martinis, an ounce and a half for each drink straight up, four drops of Noilly Pratt white vermouth each, and five olives on the side for each of us. Leo had set up everything in advance. The cocktails, the whole menu, the wine that he had called ahead to have it opened and "breathing," and finally the desert.

Leo had left the after-dinner drink choice up to me.

"Thank you, oh gracious one, for leaving one choice up to me. What a guy," I added. I started laughing, and he joined me. We had good drinks, a great dinner, and over cognac we got serious.

"Tomorrow afternoon," said Leo, "your election to the board of directors of our company will be announced and an interoffice memorandum will be distributed to all department heads. There will be a press release packet with your bio and some of your accomplishments, as well as other public information for the media. Happy so far?"

"You bet."

"It gets better. This is the private side of it. Your compensation will basically be doubled. You really impressed the board with your daring-do activities as a sort of real-life model of Butch Cassidy and the Sundance Kid. They were overwhelmed. In fact, so was I. They discussed that these episodes for more than an hour and wondered where in the world they could find somebody that would take your place. While the iron was hot, I brought up the subject of your stock participation plan. They all agreed to have Jacques design a program just for you based on the stable growth of our enterprise in Latin America. You are now joining the special 'in' group of our company. Believe me, it isn't that easy to get in, but to get out it only takes one fatal mistake against any one of the 'mainliners,' and it's all over. No defense. No recourse. No way out of your gaffe or affront or disrespect if it was intentional or not. If, on the other hand, you just goofed and can prove it, admit to the crime and all is forgiven. You are going to find that as a private company, we set our own rules after we meet all federal, state, and local rules and regulations. This is a very close-knit group. Over time we all get to know one another in a very personal way, a sort of camaraderie that you might find in a special and precarious way in an Airborne, Ranger, Special Forces, or Seal unit. However, the rewards are far better. Roger and I will explain more of our infrastructure tomorrow before the board meeting. So for now, let's just enjoy the rest of the evening."

I was pretty tired both physically and mentally after a very late night that ended at the Oak Room Bar in the Plaza Hotel, but I couldn't sleep. Instead, I just lay there and thought about what Leo had put on the table for me to digest. I felt like I was being initiated into my fraternity back in college. What appeared to be a cut and dried, run-of-mill, one-size fits all was turning out to be some kind of a "secret society" in league with the United States of America, whose mission was to battle communism, Marxism, and any other radical extremist group that infringed on the vital interests of our country. In other words, our company, our magazines, were the MLR—the main line of resistance. Wow! I just said a mouthful. This mission was okay with me. I couldn't be happier. But what were the rules of engagement? What was our backup, if any? Did anyone of our principle players have a way out? The more I thought about it, the more it seemed like a script for a movie.

Roger called at mid-morning and suggested we have lunch. Leo would join us. He wanted to know if I could clear my agenda from lunch on. Suddenly, Roger was a different person. Gone was his "boss-to-employee" tone and attitude. He was now addressing one of the "boys." The "boys" that kept the ball in play and kept us in the game through either money, political clout, intelligence, hardball effort, the most senior worldwide connections, or any other available leverage.

We met at his club and went directly to a small, private dining room. Leo walked in right behind us. Roger and Leo ordered sandwiches and salads. So did I. The food was not the object of today's lunch. We were there to talk. That is, we were there for Roger and Leo to talk. I was there to listen.

Roger went straight to the point.

"The original mission of the magazine was purely a commercial initiative. It was to develop a Spanish language business and news magazine for all of Latin America. Until now, readers had to rely on several English-language publications for their Latin American and worldwide information. If I were a native of any country in Latin America and spoke and read only Spanish, I would consider it an affront to my language and culture to be offered a publication in a foreign language as my primary source of information.

"We were pretty much of an instant success, but to publish this magazine on a fortnightly basis for audited circulation in eighteen countries, you need money. We were doing okay financially with advertising revenues coming in from stateside, Europe, and a bit from Asia. Still we needed for Latin America to play a role in generating advertising and circulation income. That's where the USIA came into the picture. They had been following our progress and soon realized we were successful but cash poor. We were invited to Washington and were offered the opportunity of a lifetime.

"In exchange for our support in battling communism and Marxism in Latin America through our magazine editorial, they would put all of their far-reaching resources at our disposal. You can imagine, Bob, what that meant for our editorial department. It was a treasure chest of top-tier information at our fingertips. Of course, this led to our excellent editorial reputation, and we were able to hire the absolute best writers and editors available. They were not only good at their craft; they were widely recognized as the best at their particular area of expertise.

"It is obvious that our straightforward reporting has put us at the forefront of credibility with our readers and a strong influence in Latin America. By this I mean we have created respect in our editorial product in every country south of the Rio Grande. How do you think you received the invitation to the 'Bloodless Coup" and the Allende interview and so on and so on?

"By the way, the affair with your friend's father, don Vicente, has been fixed. You may be surprised we are involved. We knew about it from the moment you contacted Warren. The name of don Vicente no longer appears as a former or current member of the *Montoneros*. There is nothing on paper to tie him to this group, and as far as we were able to determine, there isn't anyone that would claim don Vicente to have been a card-carrying member of this or any other terrorist band.

"Also, he will be sent a letter through our embassy in Argentina naming him as a special envoy with all the rights and privileges of a diplomat for himself and family during their visit to the United States. Once in the States, he will be addressed as Ambassador, and the U.S. Government will cover all expenses for him and his family for a period of one month. We hope that in a small way this gesture will compensate for the inconveniences caused by our government as a result of the confusion with his name and that of a known terrorist."

I just sat there quietly awed. I didn't know what to say, so I said nothing.

"You will not be doing anything differently than what you have been doing," said Leo, "only now you know we intend to continue to fight communism and Marxism any time, anywhere it pokes its ugly head in our battleground. But let me caution you: we cannot abuse of our strength. If we do, we may come up short. Truth is important, Bob. Our agreement with the USIA is a two-way street. Our country's intelligence service needs all the information it can get its hands on. We did not approach USIA. They approached us as a result of our work in Latin America. We are hard working and fair-minded Americans. We are the leaders and defenders of the 'free world' in spite of what your little Russian girlfriend said. Defending our friends and ourselves is not just a matter of guns—firepower—it is also a matter of being quicker and faster than our enemies at determining where and when they will strike next. For this, our leaders need information. They need all kinds of information.

"Bob, you are in the unique position of being able to enter through locked doors, seeing through blacked-out windows. You can identify the royal pimps from the true pretenders, the two-bit con artists from the million-dollar swindler. You and I have become close personal friends, and I know your head is screwed on right insofar as our country is concerned. To use one of your own very descriptive terms, you're ready to do a bit of 'knuckle drill on the green,' as you call a few rounds fighting, and you do not hesitate to parade your pet eight-hundred-pound gorilla when necessary.

"We are going to have to spend some time in laying out the 'terms of engagement'; how far you can go and when you need to put on the brakes. We will do all that and more, and you will find us to be excellent and faithful partners.

"This meeting and everything connected with it will remain confidential. If the competition gets hold of any connection we may have with the U.S. Government outside of our book distribution agreement, they will pounce on it like a dog on a bone, and our credibility will suffer. In fact, as of this moment and as far as anyone outside our board and the three of us is concerned, our Mexico office works with the Mexico operation of the USIA in the distribution of their books period. This is logical inasmuch as we have a book and magazine publishing distribution network in Latin America. So it is a simple 'capitalistic' venture. The USIA provides a product and needs us to get their product to market. We get paid for this service and this part of what you have been doing with USIA remains the same. According to their Latin American operations officers, they are very happy with your work. Just keep it up."

"I don't want to be a spook," I said. "I'll do my job for the company, and I'll report about my conversations and meetings with people that may interest them. Outside of that, I'm not going to be slipping around dark corners in a trench coat."

"Not to worry," said Roger. "Nothing in your 'job description' is going to change. Still, as a soon-to-be board member, you need to know everything the company is involved in. Of course, you can always back out."

I didn't back out. I told them both how much I appreciated their trust and confidence and agreed to move forward as always. We finished our lunch and walked over to the office. A few minutes later we had the board meeting. I was officially named Vice President and Chief Executive Officer for Latin American operations. I was elected to the board and was presented with a letter signed by Roger as chairman of the board that within a period of not more than ninety days I would have a stock participation plan in my hands. Everyone clapped, gathered around me, and shook my hand and toasted my new status from a couple of bottles of Dom Pérignon champagne that had been brought in ice buckets prior to the meeting. There were several invitations to celebrate later that evening. I declined as gracefully as possible, saying I had plans but really wanted to get back to my hotel and digest everything that had taken place in the last couple of days.

I always enjoyed having something to eat and drink in my hotel room. When in New York, it was my way of ducking out of invitations with people I didn't want to be with or if I simply wanted to be alone to read, watch television, or relax, and do a replay of whatever took place that day. This evening was no different as I sat back in a leather easy chair with my feet up on an ottoman and began to think about the day's activities. Everything had changed and nothing had changed. I got what I wanted. Really, more than I wanted or could have asked for, so why didn't I feel like I had just opened my own treasure chest?

My thoughts were interrupted by the ringing of the telephone. It was Jimmy Warren calling from Washington. He knew everything had been taken care of and wanted to know if I was satisfied with the result.

"More than satisfied," I said. "Your friends did a super job with the whole matter. I'm sure Bette, her father, and the whole family will be overjoyed with the outcome. Thank you. You're a good friend, Jimmy. I owe you one."

It was a littlie late to call Bette in Buenos Aires, but I was sure the hour would be of little concern when I told her the good news. When I got her on the phone, I could tell by the sound of her voice that she was given over to her emotions as she listened to the details of the good fortune that had been bestowed on her father and the whole family. Equally as important, she was delighted that her father's good name had been vindicated and restored to its proper place in Argentine society. When might I be traveling to Buenos Aires again, she wanted to know? She and her family would want to thank me properly on my next trip. Unfortunately, I had no idea when I would be in Argentina again in the near future. That was going to change in short order, but for the moment, my immediate agenda was to Mexico City in a couple of days.

Thanks to turning down the drinks and dinner invitations the night before, I awoke bright eyed and bushy-tailed. Even though an interoffice memo had not made the rounds as of yet, the word of my promotion and election to the board of directors had made it to our key staff. Congratulations, handshakes, pats on the back, and kudos began as I walked in and continued until I closed Leo's office door behind me. Leo was sitting behind his desk drinking a cup of coffee and smoking a cigarette.

"Did you get all you wanted?" he asked with a big Cheshire cat grin on his face.

"Yes, I did," I said, smiling back. "More than I expected. What do you think, Leo? Too much, too little, just right?"

Leo looked back at me and continued to smile. He offered me a cigarette and a light and had one himself.

"Don't think about it. Just enjoy what you have achieved and call it an achievement, because that's what it is. You didn't steal your accolades and everything that has now gone with it. You earned them. Don't think about it anymore; just go on with your life and do your job exactly as you've been doing. You have now joined the company's big leagues. Act like it, and have a ball doing it."

That bit of advice from Leo has been ingrained in my mind ever since. Who was I to question my good fortune? In the final analysis, I was who I was, and whatever trappings I was wrapped in were just part of the package.

Leo and I talked over some business, and around mid-day I excused myself, went back to the hotel to pick up my bags and head to the airport for a five o'clock flight. If the flight was on time, I would be back in Mexico City about ten, with plenty of time to get some much needed sleep and rest.

Pornography:

MEXICO CITY

CRITIQUE. It was good to be back in my office and among familiar surroundings. Unless Hector or someone else asked what I had been doing in New York, nobody asked or cared. As long as the status quo was in place and their own jobs or areas of authority were not in jeopardy, they knew that whatever took place in the city of Oz was of little concern to them.

I asked Hector and Pepe Colmenares, our newsstand circulation manager, to come in for a meeting to give me an update on the newsstand circulation wars. The enemy had backed off, and our kiosks were being left alone. Our headbusters had to exert some extra muscle in a few instances to make them understand the game was over for good. As a result, a few of the opposing players were sufficiently hurt and had to be taken to the hospital. However, their injuries were not life threatening. The injuries included a few broken legs or arms and noses, maybe some ribs, but more importantly, Colmenares said, total defeat for the opposition. I asked Pepe if we had gotten any negative publicity for our "strong-arm" tactics from the local or federal government, the police, the Mexican media, or anyone of importance. From Pepe's description of the aftermath of our "blitz" on the attackers of our kiosks, they weren't the only ones that were surprised. The authorities, as well as senior management, of the perpetrators were left speechless as witnessed by their silence and the lack of fortitude in developing a counterattack. At the end of the day, the enemy "attack squadron" collected their fees and went home, never to return. Pepe said our boys confronted a few that were on their way back but turned and ran as soon as they spied our head-busters. That was the somewhat brutal end to the newsstand circulation wars. We now knew how to head off the next flare-up. I thanked Pepe, and again I was in a quandary as to how to proceed with the credit card mess hanging over his head.

Next I asked Juan Rodriguez to join us for a call to the plant in San Mateo Tecoloapan. We put in a call for David Flores, general manager of the printing plant. I wanted to know if everything had calmed downed since the union strike fiasco. When he came on the telephone, I asked him to get Jesse Brant to join us using the plant's speakerphone as well as ours. Speakerphones were a big luxury in those days, but we had one installed in our office and the plant to avoid, whenever possible, the need to keep repeating the conversation to others involved in the discussion.

While we were waiting for Jesse, I thought about the last few days in New York. Was being part of the company big leagues something I wanted? Of course it was. It was a matter of keeping score, as Roger had emphatically put it. Still, I left New York without getting as much as a ballpark figure as to what my compensation package would be. Leo had made the remark that it had been doubled, but just what did that mean? I also did not have the letter about my participation in a stock plan. Then there was my election to the board of directors. So far, it was only words. So what did I have there? It was all a bit confusing. Nevertheless, I enjoyed my work to the nth degree, and any frosting on that cake would only make it sweeter. I was sure Roger and the board would clear up the whole matter soon enough. New York couldn't afford to play word games with me or, for that matter, anyone else key to the organization.

David and Jesse came on the line and gave me a big hearty welcome back. After some small talk, as usual, I asked about the aftermath of the strike.

"Very calm and quiet. Everyone was back at their schedules and routines and moved on as if nothing had taken place. The union men were ostracized, and eventually they left the plant of their own accord. I don't believe we'll have union organizers back with us for some time to come."

"You know Juan Rodriguez, our production manager?" I asked David and Jesse. Keep him up-to-date on anything of importance that may affect our company and our magazine, and Juan will report it to me. David, you and Jesse are doing a fine job out there in the wilds of Mexico. Keep it up, and let us know if there is anything you need from us. We're here to give you a helping hand anytime you need it.

ABSURD CENSORSHIP.

For some strange reason that I was never able to understand, I was elected to the Board of Directors of the Mexican Chamber of the Publishing Industry. Maybe it was because I spoke perfect Spanish, although they knew I was an American. Maybe it was that our magazine was a headliner in Latin America with considerable influence and power, or maybe one or more members of the board had a secret agenda. Whatever the reason, I never knew. What I did know was that it was a mistake to elect me to the board, and it was a mistake for me to accept.

I tried to be present at as many of the monthly meetings as I could and even some of the special meetings that popped up once in a while. I don't think anything I said at the meetings had any impact on the subject being discussed. I never saw my name on any document of importance except those that were signed by the entire board. It was becoming clear to me that having my name and that of my company and magazine on the list of members of the board was another reason why I was elected to this august group.

One of the main duties and responsibilities of the publishing industry board was to give their blessing and authorization to any new print media about to be published. Without this authorization, publishing a magazine, newspaper, or whatever would be against the law and punishable by a substantial fine and prison time. No one ever wanted to take that risk. This was especially true of what would be considered pornographic material. However, there was nothing in the bylaws or any sort of document describing exactly what consisted of "pornographic material." As a result, most of the board members agreed that "pornography" was a sexually explicit photography, painting, drawing, and design that would offend the sensitivities of a Mexican individual or family. Yet, no board member could define exactly what is pornographic.

We were about to be tested on the true meaning of pornography sooner than we had anticipated by someone that had the juice to bring the subject to a head. That someone was a person very close to me, and only by coincidence did I happen to be on the Board of the Chamber of the Publishing Industry.

The person invited me to lunch to explain that he was about to try the pornographic law on for size. Inasmuch as *Playboy* had been legally banned from distribution and sale in Mexico, my friend, a publisher himself, had purchased the photographic rights to all *Playboy* materials. That included editorial, photos, and cartoons. The idea was to change the magazine title name of *Playboy* to a Spanish language title, develop a "dummy" copy, and submit it to the publishing industry chamber board for approval for distribution and sale. He knew he would have a fight on his hands, so he took certain measures to help his approval case with the board.

First, he made sure that the certain parts of a woman that would be objectionable to some individuals or groups were not visible by carefully selecting the images. All that showed in the photograph was the nude body of a woman with carefully draped clothing over those areas that could offend the viewer. The photograph was now no different from a painting or photograph that you might see in a museum or art exhibition. The editorial content was focused on subjects appealing to men. He detailed some sports activities, men's fashions, healthcare, entertainment, dining and wining, and so on. The cartoons were non-sexual. The bottom line was that he had put together what would be a men's magazine with some lovely, young, semi-dressed images of models.

He wanted to know what I thought of the strategy. I told him what I always thought about pornography, that people identified it to suit their own morals, sometimes lax and other times rigid. What I didn't know was just where the rest of the board stood on their idea of pornography. Mexico had been on a so-called high road, as far as morals were concerned, that was laughable. With political corruption, industry robber barons, mistresses, black-market goods, and more, Mexico was not in a position to set the world's moral standard. Nevertheless, the administration went along with the pretense of superior morals for public, domestic, and international consumption. Unfortunately, print media was an item that was easily available to the masses across the board and easy for the government to attack in defense of a supposed high standard of morality. Frankly, I told my friend, I didn't know which way the ball was going to bounce. I did say I would defend his case based on my own moral code.

The board would send out an agenda two weeks before a meeting so there was time to prepare individual schedules. The next meeting included my friend's case up for discussion concerning approval for distribution and sale of his publication. Separately, each of the board members received information concerning the line items on the agenda. In the case of my friend, we were all supplied with a "dummy" copy of his magazine proposal in full color. The "dummy" copies included real editorial content so that no conjectures would be made. It also included a letter from my friend stating that no major deviation would be made in the photographic or editorial content in any and all future editions of the magazine.

Unlike the United States, where fifty dollars and a driver's license is enough for any individual to become a Notary Public, in Mexico notaries must be a graduate attorney-at-law or an actuary to qualify as a Notary Public. Whatever needs to be notarized is handwritten in a large official notary ledger and duly signed by all parties. This notarization then becomes a legal document and subject to fines and even imprisonment if not carried out to the letter. Putting everything together, it would appear that my friend had a solid case for of approval of his publication for distribution and sale.

THE TEST.

The meetings were always held in the boardroom of the offices of the National Chamber of the Publishing Industry. There were twelve members on the board, including myself. Three of the members were periodic magazine publishers. One was a women's publication along the lines of *Good Housekeeping*. Another was a combination sports magazine reminiscent of *Sports Illustrated*, and the third was

a soap opera update publication of the actors and actresses. Three
other members represented newspapers. One member represented
the paper industry, the printing industry, and finally the ever-present
government representative. Supposedly, he attended the meetings
only as an observer, but in reality he was there to intimidate that voting would favor the government.

Although it was always my policy not to make friends with
individuals I would someday have to strongly disagree with, three
of magazine board members seemed to be open-minded and would
deal fairly with the issue at hand. Still, I didn't know how these three,
or any of the other board members, would react to my friend's case,
which was first on the day's agenda.

The chairman of the board was the representative of one of the
newspapers and was a self-important type of individual and arrogant to the extreme. While everyone had been looking at his copy
of the proposed sample of the magazine, he was tapping the table
with his finger and giving the impression his mind was made up. The
other members were flipping the pages, reading some of the text, and
appearing to mull over their thoughts. The chairman looked hard at
each one of us and asked for comments. There were none.

The owner of the proposed magazine requesting approval was
a powerful influence in politics and business. I don't think anyone
of them would want to go up against this man. On the other hand,
some would seem to be anxious to welcome the opportunity for payback of some previous personal or business affront, and yet they held
back. Finally, the chairman took the bull by the horns. His comment
was that the images incited an individual to be sexually aroused. In
his opinion, the magazine should be classified pornographic.

What a stupid remark, I thought, but I noticed the chairman look
over at the government representative, both smiled and winked to
each other.

This seemed to be the discussion icebreaker. The second one
added that the models were obviously the typical American girl next
door, which made arousal worse, since women, albeit beautiful women
of the kind you find in the Crazy Horse Saloon in Paris, give impres-
sions of highly paid prostitutes and do not arouse a man in the same
way, while wholesome, cheerleader-type beauties were the kind you

brought home to mother and were certainly not for sale. Therefore, these childlike images would inflame the senses pornographically.

I couldn't believe my ears. What a ridiculous conjecture. I wondered what this authority on morality was doing in the "Crazy Horse Saloon" to begin with. It was not exactly a Cub Scout den. Another said that American women were "easy," and by their mere presence caused arousal and therefore gave an allusion of pornography. That line of thought was a slap in the face to me, and I would deal with it later. The rest of the board members began to chime in with justifications of various kinds to declare the magazine to be pornographic.

Every country had its own ideas about what constituted pornography, but no government had been able to describe it in detail. This included the United States. Moral, or morals, is simply based upon what somebody's conscience defines as right or wrong and really has nothing to do with pornography unless sex and morals are connected. So, is an individual sexually moral or not?

I now knew what strategy I would have to take if the magazine had any chance of qualifying for approval by the board. It was also going to give me the opportunity to attack verbally the board member who classified American women as "easy."

"*Que dices tu, Roberto?* what do you say, Roberto?" said the chairman, now leading the pack.

"Art," I said in a low voice, "very definitely art." None of my fellow board members made an effort to speak. I sneaked a look at the government representative, and he was beginning to perspire and was obviously not pleased with my response.

The chairman took the lead again. He smiled at me, but it was a meaningless smile.

"Do you mean the images are art or the magazine is art?"

"Both."

"Unbelievable," he said. "You must have a good reason you would call the photography and the magazine art, so why don't you explain yourself. I hope you're not going to take us down some artsy-fartsy road nobody but queers, hair stylists, and a gang of *haute monde* transvestites understands."

This guy wanted a war.

"Certainly, I'll lay it out so that even you will understand my explanation. First, I want all members of our board to know that I do not take lightly the statement made by the representative of the printing companies that American women are available for sexual favors simply by the asking. He is supposedly a well-educated and well-mannered member of this board. I do not know him socially, nor do I care to, but it is clear his ethical behavior is sorely limited. He is, according to his biographic profile, a wealthy and articulate individual that is here to assist us in leading our country in the righteous path of so-called sexual morality. Articulate not only means that he is supposed to be able to have a good command of the language, it also means he is supposed to know the subject well enough to have an intelligent discussion with another person. That is apparently not so.

"I have an American mother and a variety of American female relatives scattered around the United States and Europe. I'm not going to forget this man's egregious statement. I do not want an apology. It would mean nothing. Besides, an apology from him would only make the statement worse coming from a worthless piece of humanity. He is wealthy by virtue of inheritance; he never worked, he never had to meet a payroll, he reaches certain high levels of society by virtue of paying the entrance fee. He is a fraud that has to be protected by a half-dozen outlaw bodyguards."

The man's face was flushed. His jaw was set. He wanted to say something, but, like all cowards, he backed down facing retribution. The rest of the board members remained quiet at their seats, smoking or drinking coffee or both.

It was time to try out my strategy. I looked at each board member, hesitating two or three seconds before I went on to the next one. I skipped the board member I had humiliated, but he was avoiding me as well and was looking down at the papers on the table.

"Now to the issue at hand," I began. "What you consider art, I consider pornographic. What you consider pornographic, I consider art. Let me give you some examples. In front of a sushi restaurant here in the city there is a stylized statue of *Aphrodite of Milos*, better known as *Venus de Milo*. It is a bust. No head, no arms, no legs below the knees, but her breasts are clearly visible. An absolute horrible sculpture, and were it not for the plaque in front of the so-called statue, no one would be able to know it was supposed to be an interpretation of Venus de Milo. I consider that statue, located in a public place, as pornographic.

"Another exhibition of pornography is *La Diana Cazadora*—Diana the Huntress. Here we have a totally nude sculpture of a woman in the middle of *Paseo de la Reforma*, Reforma Boulevard, one of the most famous and beautiful avenues of our city for all to see regardless of their so-called sexual sensitivities. Even the League of Decency formed by Mexico City's leading women citizens opposed having the statue in plain sight and finally forced the sculptor to add a loincloth, which has since been removed. I find that statue sexually offensive and pornographic. Speaking about the hypocrisy in sexual morals, art, and decency, one of my friends is having an affair with a member of the women's League of Decency organization.

"My final example is *La Maja Desnuda*—The Naked Maja. I realize Francisco Goya y Lucientes, Spain's most celebrated artist, painted this masterpiece. It is said his imagery of women is unmatched by any artist of his time or any other time. Be all that as it may, *The Naked Maja* offended some religions sufficiently that Goya had to paint a *dressed* Maja. I'm not trying to establish anything about his approach to art and women; I'm only saying that *The Naked Maja* is pornographic to me."

The group just stared at me. Some with their mouths open, some shaking their heads, and the three magazine publishers I considered to more or less side with me just smiled quietly. When push came to shove, I didn't think they would really take my side, but at least I didn't feel they would strongly oppose my position. In any event, the die was cast. The rest of the meeting would be more than interesting.

Before anyone had a chance to speak up, I said, "These are only three examples of what I consider pornographic and probably all of you consider them to be art.

The chairman finally spoke up.

"You can't be serious that what the rest of the world considers as masterful art, you consider pornographic."

"I am taking this position to demonstrate how ridiculous it is to identify some nude women as pornographic and others as art based on the presentation and who painted or photographed the image. You insist the young women in the magazine are pornographic simply because they appear in a publication that you know nothing about. You consider my other examples as art because somebody said it is art when, in fact, nobody has really defined art.

"For example, does anyone sitting at this table know what the word 'Maja' means? From your silence I take it no one knows the meaning of the word 'Maja.' It was given to women of a lower class from Madrid who were characterized by a lack of social restraints and strong self-confidence in dealing with others, especially men. So you are totally unaware what the name of this painting really means and you want to be the all seeing, all-knowing experts that will define pornography so that our country's citizens will be safe from offensive and insulting pornography."

I stopped there but was ready to go on if needed. I got up and went to the coffee bar and poured myself another cup with cream and sugar and walked slowly back to my chair, waiting for someone to say or do something. Nothing happened. They made faces, scratched themselves, drank coffee, and took puffs on their cigarettes but did not speak.

The silence left the chairman no choice but to begin his final dialogue. His frustration and anger were obvious as he stumbled with his words. The government representative was fed up as well. He kept staring at me with murder in his eyes. I supposed he thought he could visually coerce me into backing off. Neither of them expected the meeting to take this direction.

"We have all had an opportunity to express our respective opinions relative to the publication in question. The owner is asking for official approval to distribute and sell his publication in the Republic of Mexico. We now must proceed to a vote. Our bylaws allow that the vote of this august group be confidential. In this case, we will use our blackball system."

Calling us an *august* group almost made me throw up. The blackball system consisted of giving each member a black and a white marble. The member would then insert his hand through a special opening in the box and drop his choice of marbles. The second marble would be handled in the same manner, deposited in the non-voting section of the box. The results of the voting of my friend's publication for sale and distribution were three against and eight for approval. Looking at the results, the chairman gritted his teeth and decided to drop the hot potato to buy time. He proposed a waiting period of two weeks to give us an opportunity to rethink our position on the voting. Everyone agreed, and we moved on to the second line item on the agenda.

The second subject on the agenda would cause as much of a disruptive scenario among the members as pornography. Requesting approval for distribution and sale was the magazine published as the official theoretical journal of the Maoist International Movement (MIM). The *Partido de la Revolución Democrática* (PRD) is Mexico's official communist party. Yet, the government does not favor communism but does pay lip service to the party for public consumption. Considering the subject and all its facets, our discussion pumped up our adrenaline but went nowhere. Again, the government representative did not look too happy, but I couldn't figure out if he was in favor of or against giving approval to the publication. Mexico's policy for communism was very complex and always tried to ride the fence on most points of discussion. His presence at our meeting was only as an observer, and he had no voice, so I really didn't care what he thought. On the other hand, some board members felt it was to their benefit to "stroke" the government representative to call in the chip at some future date.

By the time we were finished discussing the MIM theories magazine, we had come to the end of the workday. The MIM Journal was shelved until the next meeting. Our arrogant and self-important chairman stood up, posed, took a drag on his cigarette, and said, "The two items left on the agenda can also wait for our next monthly meeting. They are just small potatoes."

Of course, he was not the interested party of those "small potatoes" magazines, so it didn't matter to him. Why be concerned about the two publishers who had been sitting in the reception area for hours? Just let the assistant say they would be advised when to return and send them home.

A date and time was discussed for a special meeting two weeks later to finalize the request for approval of my friend's magazine.

Finally, after thirty minutes of batting it back and forth and studiously reviewing their respective business calendars, the board reached a consensus. I didn't open or look at my calendar. Whatever the time and date, I would be there, standing tall, giving them my explanation of pornography, whether they accepted it or not. In the end, if a publication was to be denied approval for distribution and sale, the denial had to be unanimous. Everyone knew that I would vote for approval. Under those circumstances, I believed the rest of the members would vote with me. They would then avoid having to face the owner of the magazine in question and the retaliation that would follow. By law the vote would have to be made public and would appear in the *Diario Oficial,* Official Government Diary, of that day's official governmental activities. The board members would now be in the clear with both the government and the owner of the magazine seeking approval. In two weeks the vote would be official, and my friend would have his magazine's approval for distribution and sale in the Mexican Republic.

Technical Oversight:
MEXICO CITY

SABOTAGE. As I walked in my office, my secretary came rushing over to me and said Roger had called four times in the last four hours. She said he had scolded her for not having a number where I could be reached in an emergency, and this was clearly an emergency. I had always told her never to respond to Roger when he was in a black mood because it would only make matters worse. Fortunately, and like a loyal soldier, she didn't say that I told her not to give anyone the number where I was when I didn't want to be disturbed for personal reasons.

Roger's senior management experience had risen to the top. He was in complete control when I finally reached him. From the sound of his voice, I didn't think it was only a money matter. Something else was really troubling him. After he finished recounting what had happened, I knew why he sounded so distressed. How could the corporate logos of two major corporations get mixed up one with the other? The photographic image of the product and the advertising tagline at the bottom of the page had the corporate name and logo of the competitor. The original advertiser's corporate name appeared only in the body copy of the message. Both had similar product lines easily mistaken by the layperson, so the error was not easily detected. The advertising space used was a four color, double-page spread that was scheduled to run twenty-four times per year. It was the reputation of the magazine with all the Madison Avenue advertising agencies that Roger most feared. His enemies would try to tear him to pieces, and Roger had enemies, but then so did I.

At this point, I had no answer for what would surely be a costly mistake and a tremendous blow to our reputation as an advertising vehicle. First things first. How and why did it happen?

"Roger," I said, "we have to work on this quickly before the ink dries. You start your investigation on your end, namely the production department, and I will do the same. If you trust Benny, our New York production manager, use him to check out anyone that in any way had access to the color films for this advertiser. The mistake, if it was a mistake, had to be made by altering the corporate name and logo on the black film. Also, have one of your attorneys be with Benny so that he won't be intimidated by anyone in Customs. The courier service that moves the press pouch from one terminal to another to make the flight connections also needs to be investigated. Finally, have the flight crew interviewed to see if anyone claiming to represent our magazine had reason to open the press pouch. I'll get to work here."

I hung up and began to go over the series of events from the beginning. Roger told me that a run-of-mill subscriber in Cochabamba, Bolivia, had stumbled across the ad and called the magazine's office in La Paz to point out the error. It turned out he was a graduate mechanical engineer and decided something had gone wrong in the printing of the ad with one company taking the credit for all advantages of the product and another company saying they were the best manufacturers of this type product all in the same advertisement. It was like seeing an ad with the headline that read "Drink Soft Drink X" at the top of the magazine page and then at the bottom of the page saying "You'll love Soft Drink Y."

So the gentleman didn't drop the matter but called our New York office, asked to speak with the president, namely Roger Fielden, and in perfect English described the problem to Roger. Without hanging up, Roger asked for a copy of the magazine and sure enough, there was the mixed-up ad. Roger thanked the man from Cochabamba, took his name and address, and began calling me.

The situation was simply confusing. The magazine's technical help that work on the film in New York just threw up their arms in frustration. I called the printers in Bogotá, Colombia, Santiago, Chile, and Buenos Aires, Argentina, and explained the problem, asking them to do a careful investigation of the their respective press pouches. By law they were not allowed to dispose of the pouches, so at least that one line item was on our side. The printers in each of the four printing plants simply check the initial signatures off the presses for color and register. They didn't catch the mistake either. Of course, no one did until the faithful subscriber in Cochabamba, Bolivia, brought it to our attention.

In Mexico I decided to have a meeting of those most closely involved in the production, distribution, and sale of the magazines. The executives I selected were key and senior enough to understand the seriousness of the matter. They were also in some way connected with the production of the magazines. Those who joined me included Hector, our CFO, who was well aware of how a blunder of this magnitude could affect advertising revenues in the future by scaring away advertisers. Second in line was Juan Rodriguez, our production manager and a logical member of this meeting. Third and fourth were David Flores and Jesse Brant, the two managers of our printing plant. Finally, Pepe Colmenares, who I would turn to if anything underhanded was taking place.

We began our investigation in the most logical place, and that was the offices of our Customs broker, where the press pouch containing the film arrives. The three principles and the five clerks answered our questions with a yes or a no. Other than that, they all just looked at us with a blank stare. Oddly, one of the brokers, who was generally a jovial person, always joking and laughing, was very quiet. In fact, more than quiet, he was nervous.

We went back to my office and kept dissecting the crime. As far as I was concerned, it was indeed a crime, and we would find the perpetrators. Everyone else agreed, and we began eliminating suspects. The advertising agencies? No. The corporations? No. Our people in New York? No. Our people in Mexico? No. The Customs brokers? Yes. Why? The Customs brokers had no axe to grind in hurting us this badly. They were forced to do it, but why? Everyone involved realized it would be discovered quickly but not before some long-term harm had been done to the magazine and to the advertising credibility of our publication. At least that's what the perpetrators thought, but with some damage control we could turn this around to our advantage.

DAMAGE CONTROL.

Right then we needed to know who did it and what their real motivation was. Instead of going through a long process of who and why, I asked Pepe Colmenares to recruit three or four of his hard case headbusters and pay the Customs brokers a visit. This was the best way to cut to the chase. The following day Pepe got a phone call, and we had our answer. It was, as some of us had suspected, the owner, president, and publisher of *El Futuro*. He had said it wasn't over when we beat him in the newsstand wars, and now it was payback time for him.

El Futuro's goons had visited the Customs broker's office and threatened serious bodily harm unless they had access to the press pouches for twenty-four hours. *El Futuro's* technicians altered the films, returned the pouches to the Customs broker's office, and that was that. The *El Futuro* president knew the altered films would be discovered in short order, but he also knew it would be too late and that the ad would run in all of our magazine's editions.

For damage control, the first thing to do was for us to admit to the incident. We sent out press releases to all the major newspapers and magazines in the U.S., Europe, and Asia under the headline "Leading Magazine Sabotaged." The tagline read "Enemies of Free Enterprise and Freedom of the Press do their best to squelch major Latin American publication." The accompanying story detailed what and how the intrusion had happened. We did not mention *El Futuro*, but I knew some of the ambitious and aggressive newspapers would snoop around until they uncovered the perpetrators. The story was picked up in Europe and the U.S., and in the end we were vindicated.

Roger asked me to fly to New York, and with Leo we visited with both advertisers and their respective agencies. In all honesty, we walked in each of their lavish offices with hat in hand. They knew they had all the power in the world to make or break a business or, in our case, a magazine. This was not the time to offer a rerun or anything as trite as that.

We were surprised that when we entered their offices they were all smiles. In the end, we were able to save the accounts after they took into consideration that their respective products were well publicized in most countries in the world. We thanked them and hurried out. In the cab, Roger and Leo thanked me for the fast action in solving the problem and getting the press coverage in all the right places.

When we got back to headquarters, Roger invited me to his office. He and Leo were all smiles. Roger handed me a large manila envelope and asked that I open it. Inside was a complete explanation of my new compensation plan, a stock participation agreement, and official notice of my election to the board of directors.

"We know you're in a hurry to get back to Mexico City," said Roger, "so get going. You can read it carefully on the plane. We think you will be pleased."

Rest & Recreation:

ACAPULCO

A CHANGE OF PACE. Flying home, I thought it might be a good time to take a few days off and try a different scenario and celebrate my good fortune. The compensation plan, stock agreement, and election to the board of directors were everything I wanted and more. Besides, I felt like I had been on the MLR too long and needed a bit of R&R. Several days earlier I had received an invitation to attend a birthday party for Mr. Acapulco, and what better time to enjoy life and my continued success?

Through the years, many people have given themselves the title of Mr. Acapulco, but if anyone had a right to claim this crown, it was the birthday boy. He was Teddy Stauffer, or Mr. Teddy, as he liked to be called. There is much to be said about Mr. Teddy, playboy, big band leader, husband to several Hollywood stars, and friend to many others, both male and female, and the man who put Acapulco on the map as a world-class resort.

To attend the birthday party and visit with old friends would certainly be a change of pace. Partying was a period of my life that I had more or less written off. I had not written it off because I was ashamed of any part of it, but rather because it was so non-productive, so lacking in initiative and any desire to do something worthwhile and contribute to some small part of civilization. All that interested me at the time was "wine, women, and song." Still, it had been a wild ongoing party for me and probably still was for some of those people from yesteryear.

Back in Mexico City everything was back to normal. I was in touch with all the major offices in Latin America and all was quiet as well. My only call of any importance was from Lorenzo Leone from Buenos Aires. I was hoping that he would not present me with some sort of crisis.

"I spoke with Bette," he said, "and she was overwhelmed how everything worked out for her father and the whole family."

"It was beyond my expectations as well," I said. "I had only meant to clear his name and get him off the 'persona non grata' list, but as it turned out, they will treat him like a visiting dignitary in the States, and he can call on the U.S. Embassy in Buenos Aires for anything of importance."

"They're looking forward to your next trip to B.A. They want to throw a party for you in appreciation of what you have done for them. I know the extended family is also anxious to meet you. Be prepared, you'll be in for a real treat.

"Bob, there is something else I need to speak with you about. However, I cannot discuss it over the telephone. All I want to know right now is if you're planning a trip to Argentina in the near future. Please don't answer now. I know you can get a message to me through several sources, so I'll wait to hear from you. This is not an emergency, so don't drop everything and come to Buenos Aires. Take some time off, you deserve it."

It was as if Lorenzo was reading my mind.

"That's exactly what I'm planning to do. I'm flying to Acapulco tomorrow morning and will be there for three, four, or five days living like I used to. I'll just lie around and allow myself to be pampered in the lap of luxury. I'll let you know what my travel schedule in a few days. Take care of yourself and stay out of the rain. Say hello to your brothers and Bette if you see her."

Roger and Leo were out, so I left a message with Leo's very trust-worthy secretary where I would be for the next few days and how I could be reached. In my message I said to leave me alone unless there was an emergency or a matter of life or death, since I didn't plan to leave Acapulco until I was good and ready.

Two of my friends who had also been invited flew with me to Acapulco. Miguel and Jorge were the two friends I had introduced to the obnoxious *gabacho,* disparaging word for American, CEO at the University Club meeting that ended up a disaster. What took place at the U-Club didn't matter to Miguel and Jorge and certainly didn't matter to me. That was gone and forgotten.

Together, we had been part of the "fast and furious" group of the past, which included the Birthday Boy and all his entourage of artists, singers, bullfighters, real and pretend film stars, bohemians, wannabes, millionaires, and those who didn't fit in any category. The three of us had somehow survived the previous life and become hard working, clean-cut, law abiding, taxpaying members of the human race. When we quit the fun and frolic, one of the young women in the bunch had labeled the three of us "lost members of a misunderstood generation." I never knew what she meant, and I didn't care either.

Walking into the birthday boy's hotel was like walking into something out of the Arabian Nights. It was a hotel in a manner of speaking. We actually registered at a reception desk and were assigned a room. Bellboys were available to carry anything as small as an overnight case or set of luggage. A few guests would arrive with nothing, having flown from Mexico City on a whim, and would buy appropriate clothes in the various shops. There was room service, laundry service, and even a message center. However, no telephones were available in the bars, restaurants, the pool, or any other public area. If you received a telephone call, you would be handed a message, and you would have to return the call from your room. More importantly, no children or anyone under the age of eighteen were allowed on the premises. The hotel was definitely not a place for business or minors.

My friends and I changed in our respective rooms and met at the pool bar. The bar was arranged in such a way that you could walk in and sit at one of the barstools or, if you preferred, a barstool inside the pool. The part that was in the pool was half shade and half sun so you could have it both ways. Mr. Acapulco had thought of everything to make life pleasurable during our stay in his hotel. Among the many characters that had walked in and out of my "previous" life was a gentleman who only served one kind of drink in his home. After years of serving the same drink at parties that he hosted practically every day in the week, the drink became famous. Bars, saloons, restaurants, and hotels served it and identified it by the gentleman's last name. Miguel, Jorge, and I decided that would be a good way to start the day, so we ordered the famous West and East Indies rum known as *Rhum Negrita* and Coke soft drink for each of us.

Drinks in hand and smiles on our faces, we began to scope out the scenery. With few exceptions, most all the guests were what are called "beautiful people." The women were outrageously beautiful with slim bodies and tans. A few of the men were past their prime but carried it well. The male guests included millionaires, movie producers, artists of all kinds, actors, and even a couple of bullfighters I recognized. In their swimming trunks you could tell which of the men cared enough about their physical appearance to work out and those who knew that with money, position, and power, looks didn't matter.

ENTER THE PARTY CRASHERS.

The next day, about eleven o'clock in the morning, we were sitting at the pool bar eating oysters on the half-shell when I noticed people at the bar began looking behind me with considerable interest. I turned to see what sort of attraction was getting most everyone's attention, although not much of anything would surprise me at Mr. Acapulco's home of fun and games. I looked to the cabana side of the pool and making a grand entrance was the owner, president, and publisher of *El Futuro.*

Good grief, I thought, *isn't there a place where I can get away from my ongoing pulp fiction, dime-novel thrillers with the likes of this piece of human debris?*

I knew very well he wasn't invited, but somehow he had heard about the party and bribed or coerced his way in. You needed a ticket personally signed by Mr. Acapulco to gain entrance, so something underhanded had taken place. The protocol in Mexico is that if you have a legitimate invitation and you bring along your own guests, they must also be accepted. That accounted for the two women that he had on each arm and his usual outlaw bodyguards, who were always a few feet away. He had left two of his bodyguards outside to look after his customized Cadillac, and probably because he doubted he would have need of any strong-arm action once inside.

The two women who were with him were what we called a *naca*. Loosely translated, that means trailer park, low-rent type creatures. The two *nacas* were bursting out of their bikini swimsuits. There was nothing attractive about the women. Simply put, they looked obscene. The ape bodyguards wore white cotton trousers, sandals, and white *guayaberas*, tropical sport shirts. Mr. Boor had on a trunk-type swimsuit with bathing suit legs that reached to his knees and a gold monogrammed *guayabera*. He had on several gold chains about his neck and at least two gold rings I could see. He looked like a fool as he made his way towards the indoor part of the bar. No one spoke to him on the way in. Either he didn't know anyone there at the hotel, or the guests who knew him were ashamed to be acknowledged by him.

I couldn't help grimacing and moaning at the sight that made my two friends take notice of the look on my face. There were six intruders, not counting Mr. Wonderful: two women, fours thugs. There we were, sitting in the pool by invitation at a no children allowed hotel having a cool one and watching all the pretty women, and then it starts raining on my parade. I had to tell my friends an abbreviated story of whom and what this man was and the newsstand wars, the poster we designed for him, and his final capitulation.

"What about those four *naco* apes that are following him?" asked Miguel.

"That's his Praetorian Guard," I said. "They look and act like hard cases, but the truth is, I have some headbuster friends who took care of them during the newsstand wars, but that isn't the point. The point is, this jerk comes out of my real life to ruin my fantasy life."

"So what do you want to do?" asked Jorge.

"I don't know. Let's let Caesar make his move. He knows me by name, but I'm not sure he knows what I look like. We'll just play it by ear."

The *El Futuro* boss and his entourage made it to the inside bar, taking a stool, coincidently, across and directly in front of me. There was no room for his women, so he let them stand behind him while his apes made the two persons sitting alongside the boss move. Then he ordered a bottle of champagne and had the bartender serve him and his two *naca* girlfriends. He ordered nothing for his apes. They just stood there taking in the landscape since their boss had his back to them and couldn't see their wandering eyes. The bartender put the champagne in an ice bucket and asked the boss if there was anything else he could do for him. He nodded and asked for two-dozen oysters on the half shell. That did it. If this buffoon was going to remain at the hotel, the rest of my trip would be ruined.

Maybe he was just there for the afternoon. I slipped away from the bar and walked through the waist-deep water to poolside, flagging down one of the bikini-clad waitresses. In a whisper I asked her to check with the hotel registration for the name of the intruder and how long he planned to stay, and then I made my way back to the bar.

"What's going on?" asked one of my friends.

"Before we do anything to upset this beautiful scenario, I want to find out quietly if this clown is going to spend the rest of the day here or if he plans to stay longer. I had one of the waitresses check with registration to find out. In the meantime, let's have another cool one."

We ordered three more of the same and waited to get a message back from the waitress. A few minutes later the bar phone rang and our bartender gave me the message. Mr. Jerk signed an open-ended stay. Although the desk clerk said that open-ended reservations were not allowed, the four apes convinced him that it would be okay for him and the two women. All four thugs would be camped in a room directly across from their boss's accommodations.

"That is going to be unacceptable," I said to my friends. "I have to think of a way to get rid of him without a fuss."

One of my friends agreed, "I know we owe Mr. Acapulco the respect of keeping order among ourselves, but we have to do something, or our few days are going up in smoke. An option is not for us to move to another hotel. The owner of this hotel has personally invited us, and that jerk has just bullied his way in."

"This guy is a coward," I said. "Most bullies are, and this guy is definitely a bully. He uses his money and power to crush anyone in his way. He met his match with my people, and I'm sure he has not forgotten the beating he took and the humiliation he suffered among his peers. I'm going to frighten him quietly in a way that should work, given he's afraid of his own shadow."

It occurred to me that the best way to get this clown's attention under the circumstances was to write him a threatening note much like he would write to an adversary. I asked the bartender for some hotel stationary and a pen and began writing what I hoped would be a reason for him to leave double time.

The note read,

Sitting in front of you is the man responsible for your crushing defeat in our recent newsstand wars. Just look up, and I'll wink at you. You are here as an uninvited guest, bullying your way in with your thugs. I want you to leave immediately. I'll pay for your bar bill. You have one hour to return to your rooms and gather your belongings and leave the hotel. You will not be charged for the time you spent here.

If you don't leave, this is what will happen. My headbuster friends from the newsstand wars are close by. Soon your customized Cadillac will be blown up with your two bodyguards inside the car unless they can run fast enough to get clear. Then, quietly, those four clowns behind you will be picked off one by one. That will leave only you and those two streetwalkers. You may also come to bodily harm. Sometimes it's hard to hold back some of our headbusters who are eager to do a good job for a bonus. The two gentlemen sitting at my side are jefes, bosses, of the headbusters and are ready to move if I give the word.

These threats are against the law, but I will not land in jail. The mayor, governor, and even the president of our country are close personal friends with Mr. Acapulco. They have often visited him here and have enjoyed many days of his hospitality. I am his good friend as well. You can take one last sip of the champagne and leave.

Both Miguel and Jorge read over the note and almost burst out laughing.

"A bit wordy," said Miguel, "but I think he'll get the message."

Jorge just nodded.

"You two guys just keep a straight face when I have the bartender hand it to him. I put both of you in the note because you're all muscled up from your power lifting and should impress the scumbag that he's dealing with strength."

"Bob, you're a power lifter too," said Jorge.

"Sure I am, but I'm shorter than you guys. Anyway, let's stop chitchatting around. I'll send over the note with the bartender, and we'll see the reaction, and don't you guys laugh or even smile. Give him your hard-nosed face."

I called the bartender over and asked him to give my note to the champagne-drinking man.

"If he gets up and leaves, don't try to call him back to pay for his bill. I'll take care of it. Just hand him the note and move out of the way so we can see what his reaction will be."

The bartender took the note and said, "Gracias, señor." He handed it to scumbag and moved out of the way so we could get a good look at the man's reaction. He took a sip of champagne as he causally opened the note that had been folded over. At first, he couldn't believe what he was reading. He furrowed his brow and swallowed hard. He must have read the note at least three times and then closed his eyes, probably thinking about what he would do next. Finally, after several minutes, he looked up at me, and I winked without smiling. Then he looked at Miguel and Jorge. The three of us were sitting straight, not drinking, not smiling, just staring straight at him.

EXIT THE PARTY CRASHERS.

He didn't hesitate for long, taking the note and tearing it in several pieces that he placed in an ashtray and burned with some hotel matches. We just sat there, waiting for his next move, and continuing to stare at him. It was as I expected. After seeing the note burn, he got up, and with his two women and his *naco* bodyguards, he began walking out of the bar. From a distance I could see him entering the hotel lobby.

"Let's just sit here and see if he's going to change his mind and come back," I said to my friends. Twenty minutes later the doorman came running up and handed me a note from the exiting group. *This isn't over*, it read. He had said that at our last encounter, and it went nowhere. I passed the note over to Jorge who burst out laughing. Miguel, the ever more serious one, read the note, shook his head, crushed it, and pitched it to the bartender, who was looking at us with awe and admiration. Miguel asked him to trash it.

Terrific, with that bump in the road out of the way, we were in for whatever each of us wanted or needed out of the next few days. Even though we were close personal friends, we were about as different in character and personalities as you could get. Miguel was a quiet and dark person and a lawyer. He was fiercely faithful and loyal, and when he offered his friendship unconditionally, that's what he meant but he could be very violent. He could be described as an extremely talented street fighter. Jorge, on the other hand, was more of a footloose and fancy-free sort, suave, debonair, and a very handsome womanizer. If needed by one of his friends, he was always available as the best help you could get in any kind of fight. Why these two wealthy and well-connected individuals needed to step forward to prove their physical strength and courage time after time was beyond me.

For the next five days we had a beautiful time, in a beautiful place, with beautiful people, and were charged up enough to return to our respective places of business and personal responsibilities with a spring in our step. The pool bartender went to his supervisor and explained what had taken place and how we had avoided a vicious scene with some intruders. The supervisor went to management, and it finally reached the boss. Before we left, Mr. Acapulco personally thanked us for avoiding what might have been a "blood and sand" type of scene.

"You are welcome here anytime," he said.

Delegation of Authority:
MEXICO CITY

THE NEED FOR NEWSSTAND CIRCULATION. We had local newsstand circulation managers based in each capitol city of each country. They were also responsible for newsstand circulation in other cities within their country. For any major problems or troubleshooting, I personally had to get involved in the situation. As time passed and our overall magazine circulation grew, the newsstand sales area had become more and more important and more and more problematic. While not our forte, newsstand circulation served a dual purpose. In the first instance, the circulation sales contributed to our overall circulation guarantee to advertisers. The second but equally important reason for newsstand circulation was promotional. It was vital that when VIP executives from the States, Europe, or Asia made their trips "around the horn," as they would call any trip south of the Rio Grande, that our magazines would be visible and available from any nook and cranny our advertisers could see.

The Bolivia uprising was different; a case in point, I had to personally be involved due to the personalities that were taking their differences to an international level. More often than not, the problem could be fixed by someone from the "home office" with a bit of schmoozing and kid gloves. Generally, that someone would be me. Over time, it became increasingly clear that we needed a newsstand circulation manager to cover the whole of Latin America. Pepe

Colmenares would be the ideal candidate, but after the incident with the credit card, I didn't trust him.

His next in line was a quiet, low-profile young man and a very efficient person by the name of Diego Alarcón. I knew him to be hard working, yet easy-going. Backroom talk pointed to an honest person, who drank little alcohol and was married with one child. He was a "nice" person but nobody's fool, and all indications were he would be able to stand up to the toughest of the newsstand distributors if needed. All of those attributes were necessary for the job.

THE PLAN.

Covering the whole of Central and South America is a considerable undertaking. However, our man would be more on a supervisory position than on a day-to-day personal role. First, he had to know the newsstand distributors on a first-name basis and well enough to buy them a drink, lunch, or any of a variety of social amenities. Whether I liked it or not, the introduction phase was my job, but we were going to have to do it a couple of countries at a time. It was going to take several months depending on my own business availability.

My office opened up to our conference room. For me, it was the ideal place to spread out my papers, materials, and reference books when I was developing a plan of action. As I was studying the latest newsstand sales reports country-by-country and city-by-city, another thought came to mind.

While I called Nico to bring me a cup of coffee, I thought how unemotional I was in planning a country-by-country business trip in Latin America. Stateside I would be developing the plan state-by-state, county-by-county, or city-by-city. In my business arena I would be looking at countries ruled by a military junta or dictator or facing a terrorist group and how it would affect me and my company and my magazine. Stateside I would be looking at the results of a situational analysis and such line items as competition, target market, and marketing objectives, goals, and strategy. I rarely thought about the almost unbelievable differences of how I conduct my business affairs in Latin America and how I would do it in Texas, Ohio, or New York. I found it amusing when asked to describe my business by friends or family; I would just get blank stares in return.

These are some of life's choices that are sometimes made without the benefit of intelligently studying and analyzing what kind of a career you are embarking on and what it will bring over the long term. In my case, the choice was perfect. I couldn't be happier, more satisfied, and fulfilled with my life. I had no regrets and wouldn't change a day, week, or anytime, including the downtimes.

Back to my drawing board, I began to explain to Diego the machinations of the newsstand distribution business in Latin America. It was almost as if the distributors had all met at the Punta del Este resort and, amid wine, women, and song, had agreed to run their respective operations in like manner. It reminded me of the huge meeting of the mob bosses who met in upstate New York and got caught by the local's *gendarmes*, the FBI, and whatever other law enforcement agency they could dream up. This seemed to be the "modus operandi" because incredibly, the newsstand distribution operations were similar in every country. Each is a monopoly, and if you don't play by their rules, you don't play at all. This is the mistake many of the foreign magazines make, thinking the prestige and title of their magazine is enough to receive special treatment on the newsstand. Prestige and title of a publication means nothing to a wealthy entrepreneur who came up the hard way by kicking, clubbing, and fighting his way to the top of his "profession." If you try to get a distributor to cooperate with you based on the magazine's country of origin, reputation, and popularity in the rest of the world, he will throw your publication in the trash bin and no one, including the law, can make him take it back. So the best and *only* way to do the best for your publication is to have a friendly relationship with your distributors.

I spent more time educating Diego on handling and working with newsstand distributors, but he already had three years of experience doing the job in Mexico. Even more, his work in the Mexico City newsstand wars was of great benefit for him. The Mexico newsstand distributor monopoly was the largest and strongest in Latin America. No other country comes close.

The Amateur, Quito, Ecuador, Lima, Peru

SUPREME COUNCIL OF GOVERNMENT (JUNTA), 1976-1979; JAIME ROLDÓS AGUILERA, 1979-1981.

Ecuador is a small nation bordered by Colombia on the north and Peru on the south. By good fortune for the Ecuadorians, it also borders with the Pacific Ocean.

Geographically, it is approximately the size of Nevada. The population was in the neighborhood of ten million inhabitants. Just to make a comparison, the population of Mexico City is approximately twenty million. Our newsstand distribution was only in the major cities such of Quito, Guayaquil, Pichincha, Guayas, and Manabi. We also distributed to a few smaller towns that requested the magazines for local readers. As in a couple of other cases, circulation in Ecuador is only important in the overall picture of our circulation guarantee. It is also there for promotion purposes of the traveling advertiser VIP from the States, Europe, and Asia. Ecuador, like many of the other Latin American nations, has always been in a perpetual political upheaval. Since 1960 to 1979, Ecuador had six presidents, two military juntas, and two military officers as interim heads of state under the sponsorship of a military tribunal.

The trip plan was to travel to Quito, Ecuador, first and then to Lima, Peru. From Lima I would fly alone to Buenos Aires, Argentina. In order to get word to Lorenzo Leone, I thought the best way to do it would be by a U.S. Embassy diplomatic pouch. In turn, I would ask that they call Lorenzo and simply give him my airline, flight number, and estimated time of arrival. I went to the U.S. Embassy and asked to speak to Morvin Leibowitz, who was now handling my debriefings.

I explained the relationship I had with Lorenzo Leone and his connection with a person that may be in line for the presidency of Argentina. I told him I had spoken with Lorenzo, who had called me from a friend's home in Punta del Este, Uruguay. Punta del Este was a favorite resort for many Argentines and was a few minutes flight across the River Plate. A long weekend for Lorenzo would go unnoticed by whoever was tapping his telephone and keeping track of his every move. Of course, being chased around went with the territory when you are a close personal friend of the person who may be the next president of the Argentine Republic.

"Morv, what I want to do is get a message to my friend, Lorenzo Leone, about my flight plans using your diplomatic pouch. I will give you Lorenzo's telephone number, and the message will be short and will only include the airline, flight number, and time of arrival, and is to be given to whomever answers the telephone. Morv, it is in the best interest of our country, and we are not breaking any protocols inasmuch as I am in the employ of the United States Information Agency, albeit I'm not paid," I said half jokingly.

Morv mulled over my proposal and decided to go for it. One thing about Morv, he was not afraid of his shadow. Unlike most bureaucrats, Morv did not fall back to consult with his superiors, who would only have a meeting and probably not come to an immediate conclusion and then they would run it by Washington. If Washington went for it, the originators of the proposal would have their hands clean. Sometimes I wondered how our country became the biggest, wealthiest, strongest leader of the Free World with the kind of middle management featherbrains and lethargic bureaucracy in charge of carrying out their superior's orders. Thank our Lord for people like Morv and Jim Warren in government that kept the wheels moving.

My message went out in the next diplomatic pouch headed to Buenos Aires, Argentina. By day after tomorrow, he would have my message, which included a request that he not mention my arrival to Bette.

ON OUR WAY.

Diego had never flown before, and he was about to board a big DC 8 with a seat in first class. I wasn't about to have Diego in coach class while I enjoyed the luxury of the first class cabin. In my book, it didn't work that way. That would have been blatant discrimination on my part.

Diego had a notebook with him, and from the moment we sat down, he began to keep a diary of the trip. He realized he was being offered an opportunity few of his counterparts have had or would have, and he was going to make very good use of it.

We flew Avianca Airlines to Quito, Ecuador, via Bogotá, Colombia. Changing planes in Bogotá, I realized it had been considerable time since I had been there on a business trip. In spite of all the turmoil produced by the FARC (Revolutionary Armed Forces of Colombia) the country continued to move ahead productively. I needed to plan a trip to Bogotá, Cali, and Medellin as soon as I could.

Making a landing in the Quito Mariscal Sucre International Airport is breathtaking. The plane comes in for the landing in what appears to be the middle of the city. In fact, it practically is. There is one runway that can only be seen by the pilots. As a passenger, you are looking out of the windows, and you are certain you will land on top of a residential or business area. A perfect landing helps slow down your heart, but it was Diego's first time, and I could see he was somewhat uncomfortable. The plane taxied back to the main terminal, and we deplaned via the stairway onto the runway. The view of the surrounding hills and the city was really spectacular. Diego was standing still, taking it all in, and using his notebook and camera to chronicle the beginning of his trip.

With our briefcases in hand, we walked in the Immigration area and went through the usual routine of answering a few questions about our reason for visiting Ecuador and then having our passports stamped. Picking up our luggage was next with a perfunctory check by Customs, and finally we stepped out into the city of Quito, Ecuador. Getting through was quick. We obviously didn't look like anyone trying to bring down the government. In Ecuador, those kinds of problems were mostly domestic and not international.

THE SHRUNKEN HEAD.

A few days earlier I had called our country manager to arrange a "surprise" for Diego. Juan Javier Crespo, our country manager, was a born prankster and was delighted to go along with my plan. What we had planned for Diego was going to be something of a shocker.

After greeting Juan Javier, we began walking towards the parking lot. One of the Indians that were gathered under a group of trees several feet away began making his way in our direction. It was obvious he had something in his hand that was hidden by a cloth. When he was about two feet away, his free hand took the cloth off to show us what he was selling. Juan Javier and I knew what kind of wares he was about to show, so it was no surprise to us. Besides, Juan Javier had arranged for the Indian to approach us by bribing him with a couple of American dollars and the possibility of a sale.

It was a shrunken head. As expected, Diego was stopped in his tracks. He was about to bolt, but Juan Javier and I held onto him. Diego had done his homework and knew that the sale of shrunken heads was against the law in Ecuador and other countries, but he also knew that this "souvenir" was sold illicitly. A shrunken head is a gruesome sight, and although I am not squeamish, I almost turned away from the sight of the shrunken head. It was a real one and that made the scene more revolting.

It looked like Diego was about to throw-up, so Juan Javier and I turned him around and began walking away. The Indian didn't follow us. If he called attention to us, he would soon be in the grasp of the local authorities. For public relations tourism and other human sensibilities, the selling of shrunken heads was strictly banned and punishable by life imprisonment.

I knew there was other headhunting cultures scattered about the world but only the Jivaro clan was known for shrinking human heads. The Jivaro tribes live deep in the Ecuadorian and Peruvian Amazon. They are warlike and very dangerous and have thwarted many attempts by the Spaniards to conquer them. They fought off the gold-seeking Incas and later the conquistadors, and to this day their reputation for fierceness discourage outsiders from entering their territories.

Diego was not impressed by the surprise we had planned for him. It was more than he was used to even living in Mexico where witchcraft is rampant. However, being presented a real shrunken head by a Jivaro Indian who probably did the shrinking himself is enough to shake anyone up. He was still white as we climbed in Juan Javier's car and drove off. He didn't talk. I didn't know Diego very well on a personal level, so I didn't think a *joke* of this kind would affect him to this degree. After fifteen minutes, I broke the silence by gently patting him on the back and apologizing for my lack of taste in allowing the Jivaro Indian to approach us. If we had pulled that stunt in any but a public place, the Jivaro Indian would have had my head as one of his trophies.

Ten minutes later we arrived at our hotel set in downtown Quito. In fact, most hotels were located in the downtown area of the city. Years before the only hotel in Quito was the Hotel Humboldt. That hotel was someone's home converted into a type of guesthouse that received special travelers only. We checked in and met back at the bar after dropping off our luggage. The hotel we were in chose to call it a boutique hotel. I guessed the use of the word "boutique" justified their claim to the title partly because it was small with only thirty-one guestrooms and partly because it was remodeled along colonial lines.

I thought a glass of wine would settle Diego's nerves. The waiter recommended a Marquéz Cáceres white wine, which he served along with *tapas* for the three of us. Tapas are a very tasty Spanish bar snack. In Spain all drinks in a bar are accompanied by tapas. After a couple of sips, Diego's color returned to his cheeks.

THE SKIMMERS.

"The problem we have here," I said to Juan Javier and Diego, "is that we are being robbed of circulation and money. I was looking over the latest circulation figures from the cities in the provinces, and they do not add up. For example, you send five hundred copies of a particular edition to the city of *Cuenca*, they return one hundred copies as unsold, they pay for fifty copies as sold, and that leaves three hundred fifty copies that have gone up in smoke, along with the money. It's the same with *Ibarra* and *Ambato*, *Machala*, and *Esmeraldas*. Those are the ones I have been able to track, but I'm sure you have your own list."

"I agree with you, Roberto, but you know how those *caciques*, bosses, in the provinces operate. With the turmoil in the country, intensification of the "tuna war," terrorists raiding the countryside, and rumors that some of the administration was communist, our distributors joined other strong businesses in their area and decided to be their own mini-government."

"How did they react when you invited them to meet us in Quito for a one-day conference?"

"All were delighted with coming to Quito. Since we are paying the bill, it makes it all the more enjoyable for them. Manolo Larrea, our Quito distributor, will meet us later for dinner, and our Guayaquil distributor will be here in time for our breakfast meeting tomorrow. Both are aware of what's going on with the distributors in the provinces and are, of course, on our side."

The next day, Juan Javier, Diego, and I and the distributors met for breakfast in a private dining room but did not discuss business. From there we moved into a conference room with seating for twelve. I planned to use the same tactics I had used in Chile and Mexico City if I had to, and, if needed, I would bring in the eight-hundred-pound gorilla to the party.

We were not pals coming together for a college reunion, so I immediately moved to the number one line item on the agenda and began by saying sales and remittances were not being reported correctly. Although the numbers were rounded off, I slowly described the city of Cuenca example before I said that practice was unacceptable. The word "unacceptable" made a few of the distributors frown, others inhaled deeply on their cigarettes, and one other moved away from the table and leaned back, as if waiting for the next salvo.

I could not afford to be timid or hesitant in our position and began laying down what our plan would be in a definite way.

"For business purposes, my company needs to account for all magazines that do not qualify for our returnable policy. Let's use the Cuenca city example as a base. The three hundred and fifty copies of the magazine that were out there in Neverland should be either paid for or returned for full credit. What my company will do is return fifty percent of the monies that legitimately belong to us. We will make these payments to you on a monthly basis. The payments to you will be identified as Newsstand Promotion Expenses. I know what you're thinking, if you accept this proposal, you have just lost approximately half of the money you were illegally keeping. Don't be offended by my strong language, we've both been in business in Latin America far too long without having seen and participated in a variety of shell games and scams.

"We can open up the subject of the meeting for discussion, but be advised, our proposal and our decision are final. There is no wiggle room for negotiation, and your decision must be made before the meeting is over at lunchtime. I have an option that you or your administration will not appreciate. I prefer not to use it, but I will, and I have discussed it with several members of the administration, and they want to avoid it as well.

It was probably the word "administration" that did most of the talking for me.

One by one, the distributors stood, nodded, and said, "I agree." They were going to get fifty percent of what they had been stealing, and it was legitimate. It was like found money. They continued in the good graces of the government for as long as it held office. I had warned Juan Javier and Diego not to smile, laugh, or in any way change the countenance of their faces, no matter the decision taken by the distributors. For me it was another small war won without the need to present my eight-hundred-pound gorilla pet. The look on their faces was what the Denver Bronco fans looked like in January 1978, when the Dallas Cowboys totally devastated their beloved team in Super Bowl XII.

Our work was over. I thanked the distributors and said, "We will have a mutually beneficial future."

No need to socialize, so we drove back to the office to set up the accounting system to be used for our new Newsstand Promotion Expenses. Speaking to Juan Javier, I said, "You and Manolo Larrea will handle the accounting of this project. Diego, I want you to take careful notes of all you see and hear here. We have the rest of the day and all tomorrow. The following day we fly to Lima for your continuing indoctrination in the mysteries of newsstand circulation work. I'm pulling your leg about the mysteries work, but I'm serious that newsstand circulation is more serious and important to us than it appears on the surface."

I didn't speak to the trio until the next day at lunch. The reports from Juan Javier and Manolo on Diego were good. I wasn't surprised. Diego is not only a hard worker, but he is a quick study. As usual, he was taking copious notes.

LIMA, PERU.

During the flight to Lima I had the opportunity to give Diego a short course in Peruvian history. It had to be a short course because I didn't know much about Peru, nor did I care for it. Somehow, I found Peru and Lima, in particular, boring. Of course, I was wrong about Peru. The country has a rich and interesting history. In spite of all my travels, it was impossible for me to be completely immersed in the history of all eighteen countries I covered. There was the "bloodless coup" incident that was of major proportion, but nevertheless it was an isolated event, and then there was the weekend honoring the U.S. Navy that I did not include in this journal and may not account for it at all.

No matter how I felt about Peru, there is an Inca landmark that must be seen and explored. This is the site known as Machu Picchu. Any person traveling to Peru who does not take the time to visit this place has to be a certified fool. I had been a certified fool for several years during my travels to Peru. Now, wishing to change my status and following orders from my mother, I would visit Machu Picchu. By good fortune, we would be in Lima over the weekend, so it gave me ample time to make the short trip. I was sure Diego had already studied Machu Picchu, so he would be my partner on this sightseeing tour.

Although Peru had two of Latin America's most violent, aggressive, and fiendish terrorist groups, our newsstand circulation problems had nothing to do with terrorism. Our problems were of shipping and distribution and logistics. Circulation of our magazines was mostly along the Peruvian coast. Lima and the port city of Callao accounted for sixty percent of the circulation. The balance of forty percent was divided by Arequipa, an industrial center; Trujillo, a commercial center; Chiclayo, in the sugar district, and Cuzco, famous for its Inca ruins, a much-traveled tourist attraction, and a few smaller cities in the provinces.

Alonso Chavez, our country manager, and Luis Miguel, our newsstand distributor, picked us up at the airport and drove us to the hotel. Diego and I checked in, and we all met in my suite for our meeting.

"You have several priorities while here and ongoing," I said, speaking to Diego. "You will find Alonso and Luis two very capable, experienced, and highly trained managers in their respective fields of business. Alonso has been with our company for twelve years, and Luis and his father have been distributing our magazines forever. I say that facetiously, but it is quite the opposite. The Luis Miguel & Asociados (Associates) Company is one of the oldest and most reputable companies in Peru not only in magazine distribution but also as book wholesalers. I say this to you, Diego, so that in my absence, carrying out your instructions, you call on these two gentlemen for their advice and counsel.

I had one day to work with Diego before the weekend began. He and I gave a brief look at each point I wanted him to analyze. First, I wanted a complete review of our distribution system that included shipping and magazine returns. I wanted to know what, if any, promotions were being done and whether they were being handled by Luis or if he was giving the local distributors an allowance for promotion purposes. Diego was going to be in Lima at least ten days, but I would check in on him periodically from Buenos Aires or wherever I found myself.

MACHU PICCHU.

It was time for a bit of sightseeing. From what I had been able to research, Machu Picchu is a mystery. It's a mystery that many "experts" have come forward to explain and claim as the reason for its existence, but none have been officially accepted. What was it purpose? When was it built? Why was it abandoned? Why did the

Spanish conquerors never know about Machu Picchu? All this mystery was straight up my alley.

The most convenient way for us to initiate our trek to Machu Picchu was to travel to the city Cuzco. From there we would take a train to the town of Aguas Calientes. The train is not exactly the Orient Express, so travelers are happy to cover the last leg of the trip by bus to one of the most important archaeological wonders of the world. Speculations abound as to its reason for existence and the geographical site including military, religious, the mythical cradle of the Inca elite, and even an only female cemetery. The female cemetery didn't sound plausible to me considering the "macho" image of the Inca males. Whatever the reason, it will remain an eternal mystery and, I believe, is one of the most awesome landmarks to be seen anywhere in the world.

It was difficult to leave one of the most beautiful and enigmatic ancient sites in the world as Machu Picchu, but sadly I had to return to the reality of my job. On our return I met with Diego, Alonso, and Luis and explained that I needed to fly to Buenos Aires right away.

"You already have your 'marching orders,'" I said to Diego, "so just be careful; stay out of the way of the terrorists, and don't fall in love."

The three walked out of my suite with a wave from Diego. I picked up my bag and walked out behind them. An hour later I was at Jorge Chavez International Airport in Lima on my way to Buenos Aires on Canadian Pacific Airlines. My choice of seat on any airplane is on the aisle. I sometimes make an exception when flying over the Andes for what has to be one of most spectacular and exhilarating sights of mile after mile of snow-covered mountains with jagged peaks. As I gazed at this wondrous sight, I thought of my last call to my mother. She was well, and she reported that my good friend Sammy was now executive vice president of a major food-manufacturing company. He continued to live in San Antonio and was considered one of principal movers and shakers in the city sponsoring blood drives, Community Chest donations, and president of his son's private school Booster Club. Sammy was a childhood friend who made well. While Sammy was being the toast of the town in San Antonio, I was troubleshooting in places like Cochabamba, Antofagasta, Vergara, Corrientes, and many more cities with strange sounding names.

Intrigue:
BUENOS AIRES, ARGENTINA

MILITARY JUNTA, 1976–1981; RETURN OF DEMOCRACY, 1983; PRESIDENT RAUL RICARDO ALFONSÍN, 1983–1989

Lorenzo Leone picked me up at the Ezeiza International Airport. We gave each other a firm handshake and quickly embraced. He had a driver, so we slid into the backseat of his car where he had a small bar with small bottles of our favorite adult beverage.

"So what's happening?" I asked, curious about the "cloak and dagger" need for the call from Punta del Este and my response through the U.S. diplomatic pouch.

"I need your help."

"You've got it."

PRESIDENTIAL STRATEGY.

"Roberto, politics in our country is no more and no less complex than in most countries of the world, including yours. Our people, that is, the ones I'm associated with, are trying to plan for political and economic stability in the future. Right now, our new democratic restoration will be short-lived because of political turmoil. Even the Peróns have taken over the presidency, albeit for short periods of time. First, it was Juan Domingo, the 'gran lider' himself, and when he was removed from office, along came his wife Isabel Maria Estela Martinez de Perón, who was also shown the door. Then one of their henchmen, Ítalo Argentino Lúder, took the office acting for Mrs. Perón. Finally, and for the last time, she took office later for six months when a *coup d'etat* deposed her. It is known as the Proceso de Reorganización Nacional (National Reorganization Process)."

In order to handle stress, Lorenzo was nearly a chain smoker. He was smoking now, and I guessed he had something to tell me of considerable importance. With the car windows up it was getting a bit smoky, and I began coughing. I cracked my window and so did Lorenzo. We were able to get a bit of fresh air in the car and continued with our conversation.

I said, "There has to be a better word than *complex* to describe the word pictures you just painted. I don't wish to offend you, but possibly Machiavellian explains the situation better."

"That's true," he said "but we know we're on the right track now to put the right person at the helm of our country's destiny. I'm sure you remember the night at the Mau-Mau and the champagne that flowed like water."

I nodded.

"How could I forget?"

"The gentleman who kept sending over the champagne is a close personal friend. Even more, he and I are on the same page with regards to patriotism, assisting our country in taking its rightful place among the rest of the civilized nations of the world and eliminating communism, Marxism, terrorism, and any other kind of extremism that may exist in our country."

"You said a mouthful, Lorenzo, and I applaud you and your colleagues for this undertaking that Argentina certainly deserves. Now, where do I come into this picture?"

"We need your help with the U.S. Government," he said emphatically. "What you did for Bette's family proves your influence with Washington, and I need for you to use your contacts to help us develop strategy for our country."

"Hold it! Lorenzo, I do not, I repeat, I do not, have influence or clout in Washington. I was able to help Bette and her father because I do have a friend in the seat of government with a middle-level post that, in turn, has friends above him who were able to help. In addition, the case of Bette's father, *don* Vicente, was a clear case of mistaken identity and the injustice that goes with it. My friend is a do-good kind of fellow. He is all for truth, justice, and the American way, and he was able to convince others that it was in the best public relations interest of our country that this problem be solved quickly and favorably."

"You made it happen, Bob, you made it happen. That's the important thing. You didn't do a one-man march on the Washington Mall with a sign that read 'I know of an injustice that must be corrected.' Instead you went to the only contact you knew and got the ball rolling. That person might have been in the post office department or in landscaping or as a kitchen aide, but it was someone willing to help who knew others that would help and so on. What I'm going to ask you for is very, very important but very, very easy to do."

"Before you go any further, Lorenzo, I believe you are overestimating what I can do in Washington."

"All I want you to do is listen to what we have to say. If you don't like what you hear, then we'll just drop it and forget we ever discussed it. Okay?"

"Okay. As you suggested, I'm staying at the new Buenos Aires Sheraton this time instead of the Claridge, so have your driver point the car in the right direction. I don't know what all this cloak and dagger stuff is all about, but I cannot imagine I am important enough to have to play 'hide an' go seek' or whatever game we seem to be playing."

"All we want to do is make certain you will remain in good health in spite of being associated with us."

"Good grief, Lorenzo, you sound like a scene out of a black and white 'B' spy movie."

He looked at me and frowned. "We'll pick you up about seven-thirty. We'll be having dinner with some friends, and I'm sure you will be interested in what they have to say."

A HELPING HAND.

Two of the doormen came running over to the car to collect my baggage. I shook hands with Lorenzo and got out of the car. As I began walking towards the front entrance of the hotel, I noticed an older lady standing and then walking back and forth, looking at different parts of the hotel entrance and building. I didn't blame her. The hotel was a monument of glass, chrome, and plastic, and there was nothing similar in Buenos Aires. This was garish American architectural overkill and a marked difference to the architectural wonders of Buenos Aires.

I walked over to her and asked, "Do you like this hotel?"

"Yes, very much," she replied in a small, low voice.

"Why don't you go inside? It's very impressive in the lobby as well."

"I would like to, but the doormen won't let me in."

"The doormen won't let you in?" I asked bewildered.

Two the doormen were standing a few feet away from us and knew I would approach them with questions. One of them appeared to be more than a doorman, so I directed my questions to him.

"Why won't you let this lady inside the hotel?"

"Those are our orders, sir."

"Your orders about this specific lady or to the public in general, and if you know why, pray, please tell me."

"When the hotel first opened, we had hordes of people walking into the hotel as if it was a train station. They damaged furniture, valuable ornaments, and artifacts, made a mess of the restrooms and, in some cases, stole the pieces. Later, as we began to receive bomb threats, we realized our open-door policy had to be changed."

It was easy to understand why the hotel was such an attraction to the Argentine people. Buenos Aires is often called the Paris of South America. It is a European city in Latin America. Argentina's culture was mainly adopted from Spain and Italy. Churches and public buildings reflect Spanish architectural styles. To them the architecture of this hotel was something out of the future. The Argentine's culture was always strongly influenced by the French, Spanish, and Italian artists, painters, and sculptors. Buildings like their Congress structure, the Metropolitan Cathedral, and even the Colon Theatre Opera House were a long way from American architectural influence. It wasn't until the sixties that American culture began to make incursions in Argentina.

"Would you like to see the inside of the hotel?" I asked the lady.

"Yes, of course, but I do not want to make a scene and cause trouble for you."

I smiled, took her by the arm, and spoke to the doorman.

"I am a registered guest of the hotel. Here is my pass," I said, showing him my entry card. "This lady will accompany me to the hotel lobby, the shops, and the mezzanine, where we will have coffee, hot chocolate, or some other refreshment and some pastry. Then I will usher her out of the hotel, call a taxi for her, and return to the hotel. Please move out of our way."

With some trepidation he moved away and had the other doormen do the same.

The lobby of the hotel was just as dazzling as the outside. The lady took a few steps inside the entrance and just stood there and marveled at the décor, furniture, and the people who were either minding their own business or going about their duties. We stood there for a short while and then began walking about the lobby, the registration desk, and the post for the concierge, the shops, and every nook and cranny that seemed to attract her. After about twenty minutes of sightseeing, I suggested we have some refreshments, and I took her up a few steps to the mezzanine coffee salon. We took a table for two, and she preferred hot chocolate with cream and Danish pastries. I had an American coffee. In Argentina if you don't specify your coffee order by saying "café Americano," you will be served the small demitasse that is strong enough to use as motor oil in your car. I joined her with toast.

We had a pleasant chat about the hotel and how elaborate it was inside and out. After finishing our refreshments, I signed the bill with my name and room number. As I took her by the arm and led her to the front entrance, she remarked that the hotel was not only a glamour palace, but guests don't have to pay for anything. I walked her out to the sidewalk and hailed a taxi. She gave me her address, and I gave the driver enough money to pay for the ride, but before she got into the car, she kissed me on the cheek and told me that the Lord would bless me for my kindness.

A few days later I would thank the doormen for screening the walk-in traffic after an incident that justified all the hotel caution.

BEHIND THE SCENES.

Lorenzo picked me up at the hotel at ten o'clock. I wasn't pleased that Lorenzo had put me in this uncomfortable situation by over-estimating my importance, but also because he was exposing me to be aligned with a particular party in a foreign country. Through the years I had made a very strong effort to stay away from the politics of whatever country I was visiting. It was not only for personal reasons, but as publisher of our magazine, I could inadvertently give the impression that we were supporting a particular movement, party, or individual. It was hardly the right thing for a publication that celebrated a non-partisan position in Latin America. I didn't blame Lorenzo; he was only asking a good friend for a favor and didn't realize what the consequences might be.

We drove to a home in the *Recoleta* residential area, the city's most expensive neighborhood. There was nothing cheap about our conspirators. The gated entrance allowed us to step inside the home without being seen from the street. The house did not belong to anyone in our group so that this reunion could only be seen as a social gathering, should anyone have observed the car entering the driveway.

Like most buildings of that time era, the home was European style with a large foyer facing a grand staircase and several doors leading to other rooms. We were received by a butler, who led us to one of the double doors that opened to a combination library and study. It had the look of a comfortable room with leather sofa chairs, sofas, and captain chairs. The room was smoky from cigars and cigarettes, and most everyone in the room seemed to have something to drink nearby. There was a pool table, and two of the seven gentlemen were playing a game of snooker as we walked in.

One by one they introduced themselves. If they gave their real names, I didn't recognize them. I felt they were the kind of behind-the-scenes individuals who made most of the decisions of how a country should be run and let figureheads take the credit. However, this was only possible where there were civil-elected authorities. On the other hand, a military junta only took advice from themselves.

"Please have a seat," said one of the gentlemen, who would be the foremost speaker for the meeting.

I dropped down in one of the empty captain chairs and was asked what I preferred to drink by Lorenzo.

"Nothing for the moment," I answered, wanting to keep a clear head.

"Lorenzo speaks very highly of you. He trusts you unequivocally, and we trust Lorenzo in like manner. He explained what you did for don Vicente and his family, and we are impressed with your noble move to correct an injustice. We have also had a report from one of our operatives at the hotel about your very kind and generous gesture with one of our older citizens. We thank you for your kind intervention.

"Certainly you are aware that the *Guerra de las Malvinas*, incorrectly known as the Falklands War by the British, was lost by Argentina in the most cowardly way by the current Military Junta. The positive side of the war, together with our current devastating economic crisis and large-scale civil unrest, has forced a transition from military to civil rule. We are calling it the 'Return to Democracy.'

"We have carefully reviewed, analyzed, and selected two individuals whom we feel can honestly fill the position of president of our country in succession of each other. We plan to support them honestly and forthrightly. We are hoping our strategy will assist in having first one and then the other become president. What we would like to know is the reaction of the U.S. Government to these two gentlemen as leaders of our country. Before you say anything, I know they are not going to endorse anyone. All we want to know is, will the U.S. look favorably on these individuals if they are properly and honestly elected to the presidency? Therefore, it would be very helpful if you could confidentially inquire how some of your senior political leaders feel about these two individuals."

"You flatter me, gentlemen," I said. "Lorenzo is a good and loyal friend, and I'm sure he thinks I have contacts in Washington that can move mountains. That isn't the case. The situation with don Vicente was a stroke of luck. I do have a close friend who, in turn, has a friend in a more senior position that was able to investigate the matter. It was a case of mistaken identity, and it was easy to resolve. In spite of the bureaucratic morass that exists in Washington, some situations can easily be unraveled. In this case, I was lucky, my friend was lucky, and ultimately don Vicente was lucky—"

Before I could go on, he interrupted me.

"What we're trying to achieve here is very much like intelligence work. You put together bits and pieces from different sources and, much like a puzzle, it finally develops into an understandable mosaic. You should know this. Isn't that what the CIA, MOSAD, KGB, MI-6, and even the USIA do as a matter of course?"

Whoops. He stopped me dead. Lorenzo was standing next to me. "I'll have that drink now, my friend," I said.

He looked at me with a slight smile on his face and then took a sip from the cognac snifter he was holding and a long pull on his cigar. Through the few seconds of silence the other gentlemen and Lorenzo just stared at me. Okay. This was not an interrogation. I was caught off guard, but my friend Lorenzo was in the room and certainly he was among friends. This was no more than a friendly get-together, and I decided to be as helpful as I could.

"I'll see what I can do," I said with a smile on my face as well. "You know more how governments operate than I do, and sometimes intelligence you are looking for can pop up when and where you least expect it. I can't promise you I will get information of any import, and I want all of you to bear in mind that I will not expose my magazine, my company, or myself to any situation that will reflect negatively on us."

"We would not expect anything less from you, Roberto. Now, would you join us for dinner?"

I decided to decline. Two hours of trying to make polite conversation without falling back to politics would be extremely difficult. I expressed my regrets and explained I had a heavy travel schedule the next day.

"On another occasion," said the spokesperson. "I would like very much to meet with you in a social environment and look forward to the opportunity. I'm sure my colleagues join me in thanking you for taking the time and, to a certain point, the risk in meeting with us. If we can help you in any way, please feel free to contact us through Lorenzo."

"You can thank Lorenzo for arranging this meeting. I hope all goes well with your plan, especially if it's in the best interest of Argentina. Your country and its people deserve a new and fresh democratic start. You have my best wishes for success."

Standing, I held my glass high and silently toasted the group, taking the final sip from my drink. As I crushed my cigarette out in an ashtray, I motioned to Lorenzo and began walking towards the double doors. The butler ushered us to the front door and to a waiting limo. We drove in silence for a few minutes, and finally Lorenzo spoke up.

"Thank you," he said in a low voice. He didn't need to say anything else.

"Lorenzo, I want to call Bette and let her know I'm in town. I'll call her in the morning, and we can plan something for tomorrow night. I'd like to see your brothers as well, so perhaps we can put together a party like before."

It was two in the morning, so I was pretty well wasted. As we drove to the hotel, he began telling me about the terrorist acts that had been taking place recently. It was no surprise. Sadly, Argentina was no different from the rest of Latin America. Violence and destructive forces took the place of calm discourse and reason. What was bothering me the most was how Lorenzo and the gentlemen I met with earlier insisted I had influence in Washington. My gosh, that was really a stretch. All I did was to report to the USIA what I had seen and heard while on a trip to Latin America and that was it. I don't think anyone took my information any more seriously than what it was: eavesdropping on people's social and business lives. I just couldn't convince them I was just a guy doing his job. I was no more and no less than just a guy.

THE PARTY.

I spoke with Bette in the late morning, and we agreed to have dinner and an evening out on the town with Lorenzo and his brothers. Lorenzo and his girl picked me up at seven o'clock. He told me his brothers would join us later and right then we were on the way to pick up Bette.

I just sat back thinking about last night's events and still couldn't believe what had transpired. When we arrived at Bette's, the house was dark. I got out of the car and walked to the door to knock. Just as I was about to knock, the door was thrown open and the lights came on. Inside the house I could see a gang of people all smiling and shouting "*Bienvenido,* welcome!"

Bette was at my side. Lorenzo and his girl were right behind me. I soon met her entire family starting with her father, mother, and siblings all embracing me, the women giving me kisses on the cheek. Franco and Dante were already there with their girls. Following the Italian and Spanish traditions, wine and *maté* tea were the beverages for the occasion. The party stopped long enough for the usual round of toasts, and although many of the toasts were for me, I was embarrassed. I kept thinking, *I'm just a guy. No more, no less, just a guy.*

Then came time for Argentine snack goodies of *empanadas,* pastries of meat and cheese and other varieties, and *sandwiches de miga,* sandwiches made with crustless, buttered white bread and thinly sliced cured meat and cheese. It was a party Argentinean-family style, and although I was self-conscious, I truly enjoyed meeting Bette's family and friends.

About ten o'clock the party began to thin out, and I quietly said my goodbyes to Bette's parents and family. They thanked me again and again, and we were gone with Bette on my arm. It appeared I had friends here for life. Interestingly, no one approached me for help with Uncle Sugar. In some countries where I've lived, the "hangers-on" would have been all over me for a handout. That's what is known as *concha,* meaning "I don't care what you may think of me, I'll ask for something and maybe I'll get it."

We headed for Mau-Mau for old time's sake. Lorenzo's brothers had made reservations and were already there when we arrived. Again, champagne flowed. We danced, talked, told some jokes, and enjoyed each other's company in general. My relationship with Bette, Lorenzo, Franco, and Dante was over a relatively short period of time, but I had become very close to the four of them, and I was sorry the distance between Buenos Aires and Mexico City would preclude seeing them more often. We left the Mau-Mau about two in the morning. I said goodbye to Franco and Dante and their ladies. I didn't think I would be seeing them for some time to come. Dante let me use his car the rest of the night so I had transportation to take Bette home and didn't have to bother with a taxi, which can be dangerous at that hour. I promised to leave the car keys with the hotel concierge.

THE BOMB.

It was about four-thirty in the morning as I approached the hotel, and from a distance I could see blinking lights and could hear the sound of sirens. I managed to find a parking place close to the hotel and began making my way through the multitude to the entrance. Fortunately, I had my hotel guest pass that allowed me to get through the various police checkpoints.

The night manager of the hotel was in a heated discussion with a uniformed individual who seemed to be in charge of the operation. I pulled on his arm several times to get his attention until he finally turned to face me.

"What happened here?" I asked, half-shouting to be heard over the commotion.

The manager shook his head and with a very worried look recognized me and blurted out, "A bomb was exploded in the hotel. What is your room number?" he asked nervously.

When I told him, he jerked his arm free from my hand and looked as if he had seen a ghost. Then he went back to waving his arms and speaking loudly with what was now a small gathering of senior looking and acting authority figures.

There were few civilians milling around, and I wondered if some guests had already made plans to move to another hotel or if they didn't think lightning would strike twice and went back to their rooms. Besides the hotel management people, the rest of those in the lobby were security forces, bomb squad experts, and firemen. I just stood there in the lobby, wondering if I should go up to my room. Security people, firemen, and hotel employees kept using the elevators, so they were in working order.

Just as I was about to head for the elevators, Lorenzo suddenly appeared.

"I heard about the bomb on the radio and hurried back here," he said with a worried look on his face. "The bomb went off on the floor above yours, directly above your suite."

"That explained why the night manager had such a worried look on his face when I told him my room number," I said sarcastically.

"We think the FAL, *Fuerzas Armadas de Liberación,* Armed Liberation Force, is behind this act of violence."

"Wait a minute, Lorenzo. What do you mean 'we think' the FAL is responsible for the bomb? When you say 'we think,' the 'we' means you know one or more of these law enforcement officers. So what's going on, Lorenzo? How did you get in here with security forces crawling all over the place and stopping all unauthorized people from even approaching the premises?"

"Bob, I have a senior-level security clearance card that was given to me by the connections you have already met. My job is to be friendly with as many of the movers and shakers I can ultimately use or influence. First things first, do you want to move out of the hotel? I can take you to the Claridge or the Alvear Palace or even my apartment. You know I'm not married, and as such I have to live at my parents' home, as tradition dictates, but I keep a small bachelor apartment near my office for whatever pretty circumstance may be available. On the other hand, I've been up to your suite, and it hasn't been damaged. Apparently, the bomb was not designed for collateral damage."

"No thank you, Lorenzo, I'm staying here. My flight for Mexico City is this afternoon, so I think I'll go up, take a shower, and try to sleep for a few hours."

"I'm sorry you have to leave Buenos Aires under these circumstances, but with your experience I'm sure you have traveled this road before. I'm also sorry I didn't tell you about my security clearance before now. That kind of indiscretion won't happen again, and my friendship with you is as it has always been—unconditional."

"Lorenzo, you are a good friend, and be not concerned. I am well aware the measures that have to be taken in these turbulent times, and they do not always reflect the true feelings of the people that are involved." With a tongue-in-cheek smile, I added, "I'm glad I have a true high level, card-carrying member of the elite security forces so I can use your name the next time I get pulled over for a traffic violation."

We laughed, embraced, and shook hands. I walked to the elevators, and Lorenzo headed for the front entrance.

"By the way, Lorenzo," I said over my shoulder, "let me know who the bomb was intended for."

Lorenzo looked back at me and nodded.

A Simple Distraction:

MEXICO CITY
CARACAS
VENEZUELA

With only one stopover for a couple of hours, I had plenty of time to get some much-needed sleep. Avianca always had good food and drink and a first-run movie, so I managed to use up more of the eight-hour trip. During my waking time, I was taking notes, preparing for the upcoming debriefing at the embassy. They were really going to get an earful from this trip.

A BUMP IN THE ROAD.

By good fortune I had Hector as my trusty backup. No matter how long I was gone, when I returned, the office was still in place but, like it or not, there was always a bump in the road, whether major or minor, when I got back. This time it was in Caracas, Venezuela, with a country manager who had been dipping into the cookie jar. Making off with some company funds upset me, but I was more concerned that he had kidnapped a young woman.

According to our people in the Caracas office, Carlos del Valle, the country manager, took the girl and fled into the mountains. As these affairs generally go, he had to buy the woman's favors with gifts and money. When his access to money ran out, she dumped him.

Same old story, but we never learn. She was in her early twenties, and he was sixty-three. He had gotten in over his head financially over a woman who cared nothing for him, and he had no way to return to his family and his previous life.

Nico poked her head in my office, and I asked her for a cup of coffee from her freshly brewed urn. While Nico poured the coffee, Hector and I stared at one another and shook our heads. Once again, I was proven right. Women are so much more clever than men, but sometimes they go too far and get burned themselves. This was a case where both the man and the woman got burned.

"So what does Carlitos want?" I asked, fearing the answer.

"He wants a first-class ticket to a destination in Brazil, twenty-five thousand dollars, and for us to forget his financial pilfering."

I sat for a few minutes wondering where in the heck this was leading.

"What gives him the right to ask for anything in the first place?"

"He says he has papers that involve the magazine and you with an American oil company in money laundering, bribery, and corruption when the oil industry was nationalized. He claims he even has pictures of money changing hands."

"Good grief, Hector," I said, sipping on my coffee, "what a stretch. I can't imagine how he would concoct such a story when all we did was a series of articles covering the nationalization process. We obviously had to deal with the transnational companies as well as the locally owned oil interests. That work was done with the authorization of the president of Venezuela, Carlos Andrés Pérez Rodriguez. I don't need to explain anything to this thief.

"Let's call Benito Suarez in Caracas. I remember him. Good man. He's the number two guy in the office, but I'm appointing him number one now."

A couple of cups of coffee, and thirty minutes later, my secretary had Benito on the line.

"You remember me, Benito?" I asked.

"Yes, sir."

"I just fired Carlos del Valle. You are now the Venezuela country manager. Don't say anything. You can celebrate later. I want to handle this mess quickly. I assume you have a way to reach Carlos?"

"Yes, I do, through his brother."

"That's even better. As soon as we hang up, I want you to get Carlos's brother in our office and then call me. I want you to do this right away."

"Yes, sir. His brother is waiting for a call from you."

"Okay. Do it now."

"What do you plan to do, Bob?" asked Hector and chuckled.

"I'm going to give Carlos a taste of my pet eight-hundred-pound gorilla long distance."

Hector and I continued on with our other company business, financial statements, quality control of the printing in each of the four plants, and other routine tasks. About an hour later the call from Caracas came through.

"I am Carlos's brother. His demands—"

"Shut up," I said, interrupting the brother in a very loud voice. "Pay attention, because I'm only going to say this once—"

"But my bro—"

"Shut up! I won't say it again. This is what you're going to tell Carlos. He is to come down to Caracas and let the girl go. He will then go home, get on his knees, and ask for forgiveness from his family. They will forgive him. Then he will call Mr. Benito Suarez, our new Venezuela country manager, and arrange to meet him the same day. Mr. Suarez will have with him a promissory note that will be duly recorded by a federal notary public for the amount of twenty-seven thousand dollars and thirty-five cents, representing the amount he stole from our company. The note is payable in monthly installments for a period of five years at the going interest rate. If he fails to make a payment, Mr. Suarez is instructed to have the appropriate police take him to jail. Your brother can then dispose of the papers he tried to blackmail me with in the following manner. One, he can send them to the oil minister with my best wishes. Two, he can have them framed and periodically look at them and dream of what might have been, and three, he can save some money for his monthly payments by taking the papers to the bathroom where they belong. In addition, he has committed a federal offense punishable by long-term prison sentences in attempting to blackmail me and kidnap a citizen. Mr. Suarez is on the other phone, as instructed, and he will report to me by tomorrow afternoon that your brother has followed all instructions."

I hung up. Nico, smiling, brought me another cup of coffee. My secretary, Hector, and a few others who had heard my loud voice and were standing just outside my office, began clapping.

"That's how I can use my pet eight-hundred-pound gorilla long distance," I said to Hector.

THE CON.

"You know Hector, I never have liked Caracas. I don't even like Venezuela. The only thing I really enjoyed and can't forget was the stunt we pulled on those two secretaries from New York while on their tour."

"Yep, being poolside with the gals sitting at the table next to us was the perfect setting." Hector laughed for a few seconds and then went on with the story we had repeated to one another several times.

"Bob, when you started looking up at the sky, then down at your drink, and shaking your head with a sorrowful looking face and took a swallow, I knew what the next step would be."

As Hector said, I kept looking up at the sky and then down to my drink several times and finally when the two gals began looking at me in a compassionate and concerned way, I knew we had them hooked. I guess they just couldn't stand not knowing what was wrong with me, so the two got up and came to our table to ask if there was anything they could do. Meanwhile, Hector had his arm around me and was patting me on the back, I almost laughed out loud at that moment. The women were both very attractive, but the best looking one seemed to be the most worried, and she laid her hand on my shoulder.

"The set-up couldn't have been better," said Hector, chuckling, "if we had it staged by a theatre professional. The *coup de théâtre* was when I said 'my brother has been defrocked by the church, and we are on our way back to Texas to tell the family. He is brokenhearted.'

I was not distracted by the food and drink noisily being served at other tables by the waiters. People were into their own conversations, talking loudly and laughing, but you could have heard a pin drop at our table. Miss Salvation Army reached down, took my hand, helped me up, and we walked off towards the hotel's main building. She was so sincere, I almost confessed to the scam, but wondering where we were going and what would happen next won over.

"What names did we use that time, Hector?"

"You were Tito Macgregor, and I was Mario, your brother. As I recall, Bob, you said she asked you for the names of your entire fictitious family. I don't know how you did it."

"I just pulled the names out of the blue. Aunt Rachel, aunt Annie, uncle Fred, uncle Harry, cousin Tommy, cousin Ralph, even grandma Fanny and grandpa Horatio, and so on. It worked. She bought it."

DAYDREAMING.

It was time to get back to the drawing board with my plans for my trip to Colombia. As a matter of curiosity, I thought about where I would be and what I would be doing had I opted for a career in the States. Certainly not the wild and wooly adventures I constantly survived in every country in Latin America I worked in. At this stage I would probably be a regional manager in the States. It seemed everybody was a regional manager. I might even be a vice president. Vice president of what? I don't know, just vice president. I'm sure I'd be a wheel in the local Chamber of Commerce and a Little League coach, and I would attend Boy Scout barbecues and golf tournaments. Wait a minute, I don't play golf. What the heck, I'm just daydreaming. It was too late to take that road.

The Smell of Danger:
BOGOTÁ AND CALI, COLOMBIA

THE ROAD TO COLOMBIA. My first stop in Colombia was Bogotá, the nation's capitol. Bogotá's altitude is nearly eight thousand feet. It is always somewhat chilly in the city, surely due to the high altitude, but the chill doesn't stop with the weather. People are chilly towards one another even after formal introductions. At that time, men wore dark suits, dark hats, and carried dark umbrellas. The elite of Bogotá say they speak the best Spanish, or *Cartellano*, as they call it, in the Americas. Their pomposity and snobbishness leads to the claim that they are the best educated, have the best culture, are better informed, and are equipped with superb organizational skills than any other major, or minor, city in Colombia. The only ones whom agreed with those claims were the elite of Bogotá themselves.

Gustavo Prado was the country manager for Colombia based in Bogotá. He was bilingual having spent several years in the States and understood the American approach to business. Gus, as I called Gustavo, was a hardworking young man with a wife and two children. Unusual for Latin America, he was not a drinker, smoker, or womanizer. I could count on Gus for any job that was within the law.

As was expected, the sky in Bogotá was overcast, and the climate was chilly. Gus picked me up at El Dorado International Airport, and we hurried out to his car. We kept looking over our shoulders and in every direction. Gus was just as jumpy about the kidnappings as I was. Through the years, kidnappers had become bold and would strike during daylight hours almost anywhere in the city. The kidnappers didn't know who I was, and they didn't care. I was a foreigner, most likely an American by my clothing, and arrival on an international flight, and might bring a sizeable ransom into their coffers. If no one would pay for my release, they would just get rid of me. It was wise to be alert for any strange moves on our way to the hotel.

La Violencia. The violence in Colombia began in the middle fifties and lasted for ten years as a power struggle between the Liberal and Conservative parties. In the sixties, this turmoil led to the birth of The Revolutionary Armed Forces of Colombia (FARC) controlled by the Communist Party, which leans towards the Marxist strain of Communism. The FARC was a serious problem for the legitimate government of Colombia, as they became the largest insurgent group in the country. The majority of their funding came from kidnapping, extortion, hijacking, and the cocaine trade. For the FARC, kidnapping had two objectives. One was funding, but the other was to keep people of importance in the public and private sectors in a continuous state of anxiety and stress. To a foreigner's benefit, kidnappers preferred local dignitaries of substance and prestige to a foreigner, especially Americans, for whom the U.S. government would not negotiate.

THE RECRUITER.

"So what is this 'recruiter' problem, Gus?" I asked, warily looking out of the window as we sped by the industrial and warehouse area of the city.

Gus stared straight ahead as he drove and began explaining.

"The FARC realizes that almost one hundred percent of their army are rural farmers and the like. They are uneducated, and that makes them easily led, but there are few at the top hierarchy that truly understand their mission that, on the one hand, is to keep FARC growing and on the other hand is in a position to negotiate with top government officials. So they launched a campaign to recruit young men who have at least a high school education, some college, or degrees as premium targets. They are recruited with promises of rank, better pay, and stature within the organization. Some of these recruits are sent back into the mainstream as recruiters of other of their peers and use the same party line."

"You're telling me we have one of these so-called recruiters in our sales department?"

"We do."

"So why don't you fire him?"

"First, he is not a commission salesman. He is good enough at what he does that he was made an employee of our Colombian company a year ago before he became a recruiter. I don't have to tell you the labor laws that protect employees from so-called 'abusive' employers and what you have to do to get someone fired unless you have definite proof of wrongdoing. Second, he is well liked by his peers, and to explain why we are firing him might prove to do us more harm then good. So that's the dilemma, Bob."

"Has he been successful recruiting?"

"Two of our best salesmen have already left. In fact, once they're gone, you never see them again unless they are sent back as recruiters. I think this is the classic case of being between a rock and a hard place."

"Do you have any ideas, Gus?"

"No. That's why I called you in on the problem, but I didn't want to explain it in detail in a telex or over the phone."

"We need to plan his 'retirement' very carefully. What we don't want is to play into their hands and have it backfire. I think I may have a solution, but I want to some time to think about it."

We went straight to the office in downtown Bogotá not far from the Tequendama Hotel, where I stayed when in the city. The Bogotá office was grandly decorated to suit the status of the president of our editorial board, who was also a former president of Colombia. He was not often in the office, but we needed to do some business housekeeping work and were hoping he wouldn't come in today. He wasn't there, so we dug into the current financial statement and other administrative matters. It didn't surprise me that everything was in order. Gus ran a tight operation. When we finished, I served Gus and myself a cup of a special brand of Colombian coffee he had squirreled away for special occasions. We sat in silence, drinking our coffee, and I wondered why trouble seemed to follow me around.

I was finishing my coffee when the sales people began returning to the office to report, and looking forward to meeting the "recruiter" to see if I could understand his psyche. Four new salesmen were added, so Gus took the opportunity to introduce them to me. I suggested we meet them one at a time so I could size up our problem person without a distraction. He was in his early thirties but looked even younger. He wore dark, quiet clothes, but that was classic Bogotá style. The suit looked like it cost more than he could afford, and I was sure FARC wanted him well dressed and looking successful and had paid for the packaging. Whatever his age, he looked like he was going to be a tough customer to handle. We had a brief chat, and it was easy to see he was well schooled. I doubted he would respond to intimidation, and that meant I had to be careful how I would use my eight-hundred-pound gorilla, if at all.

After they had all left, Gus and I went over our notes and agreed that the recruiter had to go. The question was how to have him exit the company quietly, cleanly, and with the least amount of fanfare and trouble.

"Gus, I'm going to fly to Cali in the morning. I won't be there more than a couple of days, and I may have to fly to Medellin as well. Since it has to do with an editorial job, you needn't come with me. Altogether I'll be gone about four days. During that time let's think about how we can unload the recruiter. For certain he cannot stay. Little by little he will chip away at the organization, and by the time he's through those he was not able to convince to join him in the FARC will not be worth keeping. You will have to start all over again. For the good of the sales department, the recruiter definitely has to leave."

CALI.

When I first set foot in Colombia, the country was in the middle of *La Violencia*. The absurdity of this ten-year struggle for power between the liberals and the conservatives was that it accustomed the Colombian population to bloody encounters akin to civil war. My initial home was in Cali, and I was told not to stray from the city in any direction, as it could lead to harm, kidnapping, and even death. Still, all was calm among the citizens with the usual round of parties in people's homes or at the Country Club. The climate in Cali is semi-tropical with an average temperature of seventy-four degrees Fahrenheit—a delightful place to live. When The Violence ended in the mid-sixties, it was replaced by the organized rebel group known as The Revolutionary Armed Forces of Colombia, People's Army, or FARC.

Equally as dangerous was the creation of the Cali and Medellin drug cartels that began as marijuana growers and exporters. In the late seventies and the early eighties the cartels were swimming in money, and that money bought out the law enforcement agencies and officials who were trying to stop the drug trade. The Cali Cartel, in particular, was so powerful and so disrespectful of all authority that one of their "hit men" walked into the DEA headquarters in Bogotá and gunned down the special agent in charge of the office. Even several U.S. administrations tried to help in the eradication of the cartels, but all efforts failed. It was a cancer that grew and festered until it included Bolivia, Peru, and Mexico.

A CALI CARTEL INVESTIGATIVE REPORT.

My New York office wanted to know if there was a credible writer who would tackle such a story that would be more dangerous than to face up to an iron-fisted dictator. The cartels had eyes and ears everywhere, and a careless word or comment would have the person who uttered it disappear. To do a story on the cartels and do it right would require a fearless type of person who would put his pride of authorship above personal danger. I called our editorial "stringer" in Cali and asked him to meet me at the Hotel Aristi in downtown Cali. Tulio Ospina had been our "stringer" for almost ten years. He was a journeyman writer of magazine and newspaper articles and investigative reports. He had a regular column in Cali's daily newspaper and was highly respected in all editorial and journalistic circles. I had no doubt he would do a masterful job in researching and writing the report, but the problem was, would he, in the face of threats and danger from the Cali and Medellin cartels? Other journalists had been kidnapped, tortured, and murdered for writing detrimental articles about the cartels. I wouldn't blame him if he turned me down.

Tulio was drinking a cup of *tinto* when I walked in the restaurant. *Tinto* is a demitasse-size cup filled with incredibly strong coffee and at least four to five spoons of sugar. Tulio spotted me and quickly jumped up to give me an *abrazo,* embrace, and a very warm hello.

We exchanged pleasantries for a few minutes while I ordered a *Café Americano,* American coffee. I looked at Tulio, and we both knew we were about to discuss something of importance.

"Tulio," I said getting right to the point, "we want you to do an investigative report on the two cartels. I told New York you're the man to do it, considering you are homegrown and have deep roots here, as well as very senior level-type contacts to get the job done."

Tulio didn't hesitate. "Oh yes, Roberto, I can get the job done," he said as he took a sip from the tinto and stared back at me. "I can do it, but it's going to cost you."

"How much?" I asked. This was a side of Tulio I didn't know.

"It's not a question of money, old friend. Don't take it the wrong way. I've waited a long time for this opportunity, and now I have to take advantage of it. You know that I'm also the stringer for another American publication."

"Sure. The rule is that we have the option for the choice of articles, stories, or investigative reports."

"Correct," he said, then with much care, even holding back a bit, he went on, "I want to move to the States and take my wife and son with me. Doing the story on the cartels will pin a bull's-eye on my back. I won't last a week after the magazine hits the newsstands, and they are capable of killing my family. My plan is to do a report exposing these murdering terrorists and drug dealers for what they really are. My price is enough money to leave the country and get settled in the States. Call it a kind of witness protection program. Also, I would like to be considered for a journalist's position with your magazine probably writing under a *nom de plume.* What do you think?"

"I think it's a great idea, Tulio, and, no, I didn't get the wrong idea about your motives. but I don't have the authority to say yes. However, what I *can* do is use my influence with our company president to make this happen as you want."

"I don't want to sound like one of the terrorists, Roberto, but I must tell you I have already been made an offer by your competition."

"Sure, Tulio, I understand, just don't do anything until I get back to you by early next week or sooner, possibly even tomorrow."

"I don't care for the other magazine's editorial policy, and frankly I do not like the people I would have to deal with. They are not at all like you and Leo, and they don't speak Spanish."

"Hey, old friend, thanks for your kind words. The feeling is mutual and, of course, you would be dealing with Leo much of the time."

"Another thing, Roberto. When the other magazine contacted me, they wanted to do everything over the phone. You have to be crazy to discuss this subject over the telephone, you don't know who's listening to your conversation, so I wouldn't talk about the cartels. Then they suggested I fly to Bogotá, and again, I refused. Bogotá is not for strangers, not even Colombian strangers. I made them come to Cali or no deal. That infuriated them, and they showed it when they arrived. Having said all that, they have made me an offer and it isn't bad. You don't have to match the offer, all you have to do is meet the terms I outlined for you, or I'll have to take the other guys up on it. This is an opportunity I cannot afford to pass up. Now let's finish talking in my car. I remember during the dictatorship of Rojas Pinilla that you could be sitting at a coffee shop and if you even mentioned his name or any other comment that could be construed as negative, thirty minutes later several Secret Service thugs would come to pick you up. The cartels, the FARC, or both could be playing the same game."

The logistics were that Tulio would be the writer of the investigative report. It would take about a month to investigate and write and would include the Cali and the Medellin cartels. He was to get as many pictures as he could and pick some out from his own newspaper files. He would then have three copies of the report made and taken to Bogotá by his cousin. In Bogotá, he would turn the envelopes over to Gustavo Prado and have then sent by press pouch to Mexico City, our New York office, and our Washington Bureau. The investigative report would not be published until Tulio and his family were safely in the States.

As we drove around the city, it brought back many fond and enjoyable memories. The city looked the same, although larger, but it was far from being the Cali I knew when I lived there. I couldn't believe I lived in Cali when the first traffic light was installed.

"Tulio, you will hear from me in a day or two. I'm very confident your proposal will be a go. Since I have nothing else to do in Cali, please drive me back to the airport, and I'll get my butt back to Bogotá. Shuttle flights go out about every ninety minutes."

Roger accepted Tulio's proposal, and the report was published after Tulio was in the New York area with a job as a senior editor under an assumed name. He lived in New Jersey and, as an extra precaution, mailed his work to the office.

Kidnapped:
BOGOTÁ, COLOMBIA

THE RECRUITER. On my return flight, I lay back slightly in my seat, studied the stewardesses going back and forth along the aisle, and tried to decide how I felt about doing away with the problem of the "recruiter" in Gus's sales department. I knew, hook or crook, we were going to have to get rid of this person. It was probably not going to be pleasant, but I consoled myself with the thought that while I would feel no remorse, neither would there be any pride or sense of accomplishment to unload a really small player in the overall scheme of things.

"Have you thought of anything, Gus?" I asked as we drove from the airport to his office.

"The only thing I can think of is to confront him with what he's been doing and that we have enough facts to get him fired."

"Yep, we can do that, but then we'll have to get a lawyer and prepare a case and then go before the labor tribunal and so-on and so-on. What would you think if we promoted him?"

"Promote him?" he turned to look at me with a serious frown.

"This is what I'm thinking, Gus. We promote the man, giving him a temporary title of sales-manager-at-large. Our rules are that he must work out of his home to give him the maximum freedom of movement. He will have a spectacular commission arrangement and a car allowance. His territory will be the entire city of Bogotá. We will help set him set up in business as an independent contractor, and he can hire as many salesmen as he likes, but he will be responsible for them financially. To do this he must officially resign his position with our company. Once he has his own organization up and running, he can call himself president of the company that we will help name, such as 'Subscription Sales Agency of Colombia.' Believe me, he'll drop the sales-manager-at-large quickly enough.

"If he goes for this offer, two things will happen. One, he will be successful, and that will only benefit the magazine with added circulation. With the additional monies he stands to make, he may forget all about FARC and become a true capitalist. The other possibility is that he fails. Since he has officially resigned from the company, he can't come back. Also, it will be easy to prove that he left of his own free will to pursue true entrepreneurship. It will cost us a bit of time, effort, and a bit of money in helping him get started, but either way, we're rid of him."

"Great," said Gus. "Let's do it."

Gus and I talked over our plan, how to approach the "recruiter," and how to set-up the trap. This guy didn't know me from Peter Pan, but he did know my name and that I was one of the magazine's senior executives. He also knew that I would occasionally swoop down on the Bogotá office for major "consultations" that would determine the fate of our business enterprise and those who were part of it. At least that's what he thought.

We took a couple of days to sell him on the idea. We talked about his position as president of the new sales organization and that he would select office space, outfit if with furniture, and hire the salesmen. The more we talked about it, the more he became enamored with the idea. By the morning of the third day he agreed to go through with the plan.

First things first. We had him sign a resignation from our Colombian company, including a clause that he would not ask any of the current salesmen to join him. With a city map we outlined the territory that would be his exclusively, including some of the suburbs. The territory was an area of the city that Gus's current sales team did not work. He went for it. As promised, Gus began working on a budget for the new operation that included monies that would come from the recruiter's own salary and substantial commissions he had earned and would earn. It was a win-win situation for us.

THE FATAL LUNCH.

With the recruiter problem almost solved, I decided to take some leisure time for myself. I called an old friend and asked him for lunch, but it had to be that same day, as I was flying back to Mexico City the following day. He was happy and surprised to hear from me. In spite of having traveled to Bogotá many times in the past couple of years, it seemed I was always too busy to get together. My friend enthusiastically agreed to lunch; giving me his office address, he told me not to be alarmed at the security precautions that had to be taken.

The building was tall and fairly new. When I arrived at the building and got out of the taxi, I was met by two stout looking, well-dressed men in suits and ties. They seemed to know me, perhaps by my clothes, or they had been given a physical description of what I looked like. The gentlemen ushered me through the front entrance doors and once inside, they patted me down. Satisfied I had no concealed weapons, we stepped into the elevator.

A dozen or so floors later we stepped out of the elevator and faced two more stout gentlemen. The first two retreated back into the elevator and, I suppose, went back to their posts on the ground floor. The two new security men frisked me again, and we stepped into a second bank of elevators. We went up another half dozen floors and stepped out into what appeared to be a reception area, only this time the receptionist was a male. He asked me for my passport, which I always carried with me for identification purposes. Actually, it was a copy with official stamps verifying its authenticity. He left me in the company of the second two gentlemen while he disappeared through a door behind his desk. I later learned that the two banks of elevators were for the exclusive use of my friend and certain members of his staff, including the security group. Anyone else visiting the building, including employees of his company who worked in another part of the building, used several other elevators that stopped one story at a time.

The receptionist returned and nodded to the two security men. They led me to the double doors that appeared to be the entrance

290 / ROBERT AMPUDIA WHITT III

to my friend's private office. I could hear the doors being opened from the inside. After a few seconds, half the door was opened, and I stepped inside. My friend jumped up from behind his desk and came over to shake my hand and embraced me. We were truly happy to see one another and said so.

"My gosh," I said. "This is like a fortress.

"You ought to see where I live."

"Tell me, old friend, why are you doing this?"

"Take a load off your feet and sit down, and I'll tell you why I'm living with the protection equal to that of the Pope."

Although I knew of cases around Latin America where senior American executives lived in medieval-type fortresses protected by a small army of hired mercenaries, I was curious to know what motivated my friend to choose this kind of life.

"I'm fifty plus years old," he said with a certain amount of self-satisfaction. "I have small children from my second marriage. In one year, more or less, I will retire anywhere I want in the United States. Not many people retire at that young age with a substantial income. I will have a chance to play a large part in raising my children. I will have a large home with a couple of acres, horses, dogs, and a fully stocked small fishing lake. If I prefer, I can settle on the beach somewhere with equal accommodations or in the mountains or wherever I choose. That's why, old friend."

With his choice of *modus operandi* out of the way, we chatted some more and began catching up when we remembered we were going to have lunch. My friend took me by the arm and we walked over to a private elevator that was located in his office and was sort of hidden by a bookcase. The two bodyguards that ushered me into the office also joined us on the elevator. This elevator went to the basement non-stop. Waiting for us as we stepped out of the elevator were three nondescript looking cars.

"These cars don't look like much," said my friend, "but they would do justice to the Indy Five Hundred"

One of our bodyguards sat in the front seat cradling a .45-caliber Thompson submachine gun. After we arrived at the restaurant, we sat in the car for a bit while our bodyguard's colleagues stationed themselves at several key positions. We were given the go-ahead to get out of the car and quickly walked to the door of the restaurant.

"That's a lot of trouble just to go have lunch at your favorite eatery," I said, shaking my head.

"You're right," replied my friend. "Most of the time I eat at my office, or at least once a week, sometimes twice, I go home for lunch, and I don't return to the office."

It was a small restaurant with the front door right at the sidewalk, which was only about ten or twelve feet wide. By parking at the curb that had been reserved for us, it took only seconds to cross the sidewalk and make it through the door and inside the restaurant. There were only well-dressed and proper-looking patrons at four tables. The maitre d' approached us, rattled off the specials, and we made our selection. He recommended a Spanish wine from the Rioja Valley that we accepted, and finally the preliminaries were over.

Then we got into some serious catching up. He told me he took the job for five years with the condition that he would be allowed to retire with all the goodies he had been describing. His home in Bogotá was in a compound surrounded by a high fence. Four other expats and their families lived there as well. The children were home schooled with series of tutors that had previously been screened not only for academic quality, but also to eliminate possible terrorists. They had movies brought over by the embassy and books, many, many books. Twice a year they were escorted by heavily armed Marines to the airport and allowed to fly home for a three-week vacation. They generally took the vacations at Christmas and during the summer months. Of course, they also had to put up with the nuisance of having Colombian paramilitary individuals as guards twenty-four hours a day.

He found my own business lifestyle of jumping around from country to country and putting out fires not at all attractive. I told him that it might be bizarre, but I found it exciting and interesting, and I liked it because I was good at it.

When we finished eating, we both had coffee, American style, but we turned down the Cuban cigars offered to us by the maitre d.' I didn't like cigars, but I said jokingly, "We can't smoke a Cuban cigar when they're banned in our own country. That would be unpatriotic."

My friend chuckled at my little joke. We were relaxed, leaning back in our chairs and continued to talk.

"What about your wife and family, how do they feel about living in a sort of jail while Daddy has his neck out doing the business of his company and continuing to add favorably to the bottom line?"

"The mistress of the house doesn't have a choice. Before we married, I explained that this and even worse could happen, and I suggested to her not to make the marriage commitment if she couldn't handle it. She agreed to take on whatever came her way. Not too many of those kinds of ladies these days. The children don't know the difference. According to them, they are having a glorious time. The compound has different kinds of games, there are other children to play with, and they're fascinated with the guards. Of course, they're four and six years old, so they don't require much to keep them happy.

About two-thirty we had our coffee, and our catching up was over. My friend insisted on paying for lunch. He paid in cash, saying he had no use for a credit card during his "tour" in Colombia. That was understandable. The windows in the restaurant were shuttered from the inside, but as we walked towards the front door I could see sunlight creeping in from the bottom of the door. A bright sun was uncommon for Bogotá, and when we opened the door, I was blinded by the brightness, but the first thing I noticed was that the two guards that were standing by each side of the door were gone.

There were shots being fired, people scrambling, and when I got my bearings and my eyes got used to the strong sunlight, I realized my friend and I were being kidnapped. Several men pushed us into the backseat of a big Mercedes 500. We had a kidnapper on each side of us holding an Uzi submachine gun. The kidnapper riding shotgun in the front passenger seat looking back at us was also armed with what might have been a Polish, Finnish, or even Russian machine gun, but what difference did it make? Our car sped away, escorted by two cars. One car took the lead and the other was our rearguard. The occupants of each car were all involved in the kidnapping.

As I began to collect my senses and concluded I was actually being kidnapped, I asked myself, *How could this be? I'm nobody. I have no friends in high enough places; my company, while successful in our own right, is far from wealthy. If* they want money for my release, they won't get any. If they want the U.S. Government to intervene, they are out of luck. Not only will my government not negotiate with terrorists, I am nobody to negotiate for. As always, I was just a guy.

On the other hand, it was clear who they really wanted was my friend. He was the CEO of a giant transnational corporation loaded with money who would certainly pay handsomely for his release. That is, if he lived through the ordeal or, for that matter, if we both lived through the ordeal that could possibly take months or even years.

We both turned to look at each other at the same time, but we didn't make a face or try to talk. I felt somewhat guilty that we had gone out for lunch and that we had taken so long in eating and catching up. That gave the terrorists time to plan the kidnapping. Surely one of their confederates had seen us leaving his office building and followed us to the restaurant. Within minutes, the kidnappers knew exactly where we were and made their plan, which wasn't much of a plan, but the execution of brute force. They had to have caught our bodyguards off balance, not thinking anyone would attempt a snatch in the middle of the day. By the same token, they might have had a couple of our guards on their side all along, waiting for the right time to strike. Turncoats were bountiful in Colombia and difficult to screen and identify. The terrorists, in this case FARC, paid their people well with ill-gotten monies from kidnappings, raids on small, unsuspecting villages, and robberies of all kinds. Still, my friend preferred to go out for lunch instead of having lunch in his office. So be it. I couldn't think about that anymore.

As I sat there, fear began to crawl quickly through my body and brain. I had been afraid many times before and it was probably why I was still alive. To have fear is healthy. To succumb to terror will get you killed. In order to survive, I knew I had to control the fear and not freeze so I could think clearly. I managed to calm down and to breathe evenly.

To begin with, I thought, *if all they wanted was to kill us, they would have done it on the sidewalk in front of the restaurant. That meant we would stay alive until the terrorists unfolded their ultimate plan. In spite of my fear, I had to continue to control it, hoping for some sort of break to escape.*

Remember, Bob, you've been in tight spots before. You've jumped out of military airplanes sixty-five times, you've faced hostile men with automatic weapons much like these terrorists, and there were more nip and tuck situations, but you survived. Maybe my friend and I will survive this hellish act as well.

My friend turned to me and began talking. He was perspiring but steady as a rock. He probably figured they wouldn't do anything to hurt either of us since the object of the snatch was money.

"Bob," he said somberly, "I think you might have a better chance of surviving this mess."

"*Callate!* Shut up!" said the man riding shotgun, who apparently was the leader.

My friend kept talking, "Tell my wife that I love her and the children very, very much."

"*Callate!*" *again from the front seat.*

"Tell her my company will pay the ransom and I'll be home in short order, and we'll be together again soon."

This time, the terrorist next to him hit him hard in the ribs with the butt of his machine gun. My friend doubled up in pain.

"You'll be telling her that yourself," I said and got the same treatment from the terrorist next to me, who hit me hard enough to break a couple of ribs.

I knew my friend's company would pay the ransom for him, but what about me? Who would pay for my ransom?

The one riding shotgun looked at me long and hard.

"*Y quien es ese buey?* and who is that fool?" he said, pointing his weapon at me.

"*Quien sabe,* who knows?" said the man sitting next to me, shrugging. "*Estaba con el otro,* he was with the other man."

"*Botenlo,* get rid of him," came the response from the leader.

Wow, I said to myself. I wanted action, I wanted excitement, and I wanted the international business arena with all the fabulous rewards. After everything I had been through, I was about to pay for them with my life.

"*Pero no lo maten,* but don't kill him," came the order from the front seat.

THE POWER OF LIFE AND DEATH.

Was he playing with me? I looked at him, and he just gave me a trace of a smile, which could also have been a sneer. I didn't have a chance to say anything to my friend, and the next thing I knew, the car door was opened as we turned a corner and I was pushed out onto the street. I don't know if my airborne training helped, but as I hit the street, I tried to do a PLF (parachute landing form), and maybe it worked because other than a ruined suit and a few bumps and bruises, I was okay. I sat there on the side of the curb and looked around. I couldn't believe I had been kidnapped by terrorists and was set free. I looked in every direction, but there were no people to be seen. It appeared to be a warehouse area, and I later learned the car holding my friend turned the corner and disappeared into a warehouse. When they emerged, it was a totally nondescript car headed for a safe house. The other two cars had gone in different directions to confuse anyone following the caravan. In all, it took less than ten minutes from the time we were snatched to the time I was pushed out of the car. No military or police cars followed in that period of time. It was an unexpected kidnapping by everyone on our side of the law.

I'm Alive:
BOGOTÁ, COLOMBIA

EMBASSY DEBRIEFING. With no idea where I was, I began to slowly walk back from what I thought was the right direction. A few minutes later a speeding car came to a screeching stop and picked me up. I guessed these were the good guys, but I wasn't sure. At least they were not pointing weapons at me, and they drove in the opposite direction from the warehouse area.

There were two other cars behind them who kept going. In the car were four Colombian Secret Service officers who didn't talk, other than to identify themselves. These four appeared to be hard-nosed individuals by their demeanor and physical presence. Colombia was known to have some of the fiercest law enforcement groups in the Americas. This was especially true of their SWAT teams. The SWAT teams were all about frightening tactics and brute force, and the Colombian government simply said it took fire to fight fire. As a terrorist group, FARC in particular, was a serious entity to reckon with and used their own form of brutality, including kidnappings. They were known to kill hostages just to show they could do it and nothing could stop them. Hence, the Colombian SWAT teams meted out justice to FARC members in the same manner. The Colombian law enforcement agencies had an informant network all over the country that were well paid for their information, so in order to avoid falling into a trap, the FARC carried out their operations at unlikely times and places.

The Secret Service officers took me straight to the U.S. Embassy, and after some talk between one of the guards and some embassy officials, I was ushered into the offices. The guards drove off without a word, and I turned my attention to my new hosts. It was debriefing time, and the questions went on all afternoon and into the night with only bathroom breaks, sandwiches, and soft drinks to give me a rest. I must have told the story a half dozen times or more. How did I know my friend? Why did we go out for lunch? Who picked out the restaurant? What was I doing in Colombia, specifically in Bogotá? The questions went from the personal to professional and back.

That did it. I was very tired but mostly angry over how the interrogation was being conducted.

"Wait a minute," I said, taking a swallow from my soft drink and pushing my chair away from the conference table just to give them pause and me a chance to let off steam. "The kidnapping is a tragedy, but you're acting as if I'm the bad guy. I have a question for you. Do any of you, in your infinite wisdom, know why they let me go?"

"I do," said a tall, well-dressed man sitting away from the interrogators. He had not taken part in the questioning but had sat calmly observing and taking a few notes. "That is the way the FARC lets us know they have the power over life and death, no matter who the hostage or hostages are. They have been known to allow dozens of hostages to go free, and at the same time they have slaughtered hundreds. You are free because they have sent us a message: 'Yankee Go Home.'"

I knew there was more than one group of terrorists operating in Colombia but this group wanted us to know who they were. I was told it was the FARC who carried out the snatch. The kidnappers purposely left a small FARC battle flag on the street. The design was a map of Colombia superimposed over the Colombian colors, two crossed rifles, and an open book located between the barrels of the rifles with the initials FARC located in the center. Bullets and education were their mission.

Finally, I was told I would be taken back to the Hotel Tequendama where I was staying but I was not to leave and was to be available for more debriefing the next day. Swell. There went my flight scheduled for the next day.

My ride was a late model station wagon that held six people, seven counting me, all armed to the teeth. I was escorted across the lobby to the elevators and right up to my room, which they opened and gave a once over. Finally, they were gone. I sat at the edge of the bed for a while thinking about my friend and his wife and children. I knew I had to go and see her and give her my friend's message. I undressed and got into the shower for about half an hour. In bed I was so keyed up I couldn't sleep for thinking about my friend and what his fate might be. I didn't leave a wake-up call, but the phone rang at eight-thirty. It was the embassy. Could I be available at ten? There were a few questions they wanted to go over. I agreed but told them I needed to visit with my friend's wife and children in the afternoon and would leave Bogotá for Mexico City the next morning no matter what.

The only person meeting me at the embassy was the gentleman who answered my question about why I was allowed to live. He walked over and closed the door to his office.

"I have tragic news for you," he said in a very solemn voice, "your friend is dead."

I was speechless, feeling I had been hit a powerful blow to my stomach. I just stared at him and slowly sat down in the chair behind me.

"Why? How?" I said, regaining my voice and composure.

"The terrorists did not leave the city, probably fearing they would be identified and caught on a highway making their way back to their country fortresses. Since this kidnapping was obviously not planned, our guess is they decided they would hide out in a Bogotá safe house for a few days and then slip out. The Colombian SWAT team had several FARC safe houses locations and had informants stationed around the houses to report any unusual movement. It didn't take long for the SWAT team to be made aware which of the houses was holding the hostage.

"Unfortunately, the Colombian authorities didn't consult with us or tell us they were going to attack the safe house. They made their move about two in the morning. Had we known in advance about the attack on the safe house, we might have asked for time to include our professional input and some of our men, but they went ahead guns blazing. The team went from room-to-room shooting anything that moved until they made it to the last room. As they burst in the room, a terrorist was standing next to the hostage, whom they had sitting in an armchair, his wrists tied to the chair's arms. He was blindfolded with tape across his month. The terrorist was holding a .45 up to the hostage's temple and shot him as the SWAT team came into the room, cutting the terrorist in half with an AK-47.

"We arrived on the scene shortly thereafter, too late to do anything except pick up the pieces. His body is here at the embassy pending arrangements to send him home. That will probably be tomorrow, so if you want to visit with his wife and children, you better do it today."

SAD CONDOLENCES.

The same station wagon and the same guards drove me to my friend's home in the compound. I could only imagine what was going on in her mind, so I decided to give her my friend's message, my condolences, and leave. Other women were consoling her and preparing food. The children were not totally aware of where their daddy was and were outside playing with other children. Children are so resilient, I was sure once they knew what had happened to their dad, they'd bounce back quickly.

Dreading to go into the house, I walked in slowly and sat down next to her on a couch, not knowing what to say other than the usual platitudes that mean nothing.

"First," I began, "I am at a loss for words to tell you how badly I feel that this outrage took place, especially since I survived. He figured I had a better chance to make it through the ordeal, so just before the terrorists threw me out of the car, he told me to tell you he loved you and the children very much, and that, God willing, he would see you again once this mess was resolved." I held her hand and squeezed it. "He was a very good friend, and although we had not seen each other in a couple of years, I will miss him. I will especially miss him when I think that I was with him almost at the last and survived. I was told the way these animals show the control they have over life and death is by letting one go when they have the power to snuff out his life."

She thanked me with tears in her eyes but didn't respond. I sat there drinking a cup of coffee and nibbling on a cookie. The children ran in, but they didn't recognize me, so they went to their mother asking if they could have dinner at one of their friend's home. She nodded her head, and they ran off.

"I don't know what I can do," I said, reaching over to hug her, "but if there is anything you need or want me to do, anything at all, please let me know. I'll leave my card on the coffee table with my address and phone number. Please let me know where I can reach you in the States. Again, I'm sorry. Have a good trip home."

She was crying now and didn't answer. I turned and walked out of the house where two of the embassy guards were waiting for me. They drove me back to the hotel but left me at the door this time. I went up to my room and thought about what had taken place in the past twenty-four hours. It seemed like a bad dream, but it was real and very frightening. Only a couple of times before had I faced a nip and tuck situation like this one, but as the old saying goes, "Close but no cigar." I wondered when it would catch up with me.

I called the airline and confirmed my flight for the next morning. Then I called Gus and asked him to come to the hotel and to bring any unfinished business, including an update on the new sales office and the recruiter. I pulled out my journal and took notes for the debriefing in Mexico City. Boy, did I have a laundry list of everything that had taken place during my trip to Colombia. Problem was, I had to leave out the kidnapping. I had to be careful not to slip up about the terrible incident that had taken my friend's life, even though it was the U.S. Embassy in Mexico City that would debrief me. We were all on the same team and yet sometimes we were playing a different game in a different stadium. The tall Colombian Embassy officer had told me that I was not ever to speak about the terrorists, the kidnapping, or who was kidnapped. It was a matter of National Security, and if I made the details public, I was subject to a fine and imprisonment. Was that to be forever?

Gus had the recruiter matter well in hand, and I was sure he would stay with it and work it out favorably.

"Gus," I said, "we might make a capitalistic dog out of the recruiter."

"Yeah, he's really into it. I've been with him looking at possible office sites, and all he can talk about is how he plans to run his operation. He's got ideas for the staff, the sales policies, commissions, everything."

"You're doing great, Gus. Let me know if there is anything you need, and keep me posted on our recruiter friend."

We said our goodbyes, and Gus left. I began packing the small bag I had brought with me and decided to get something to eat from room service. I didn't feel up to going to any of the hotel's restaurants and having to speak with the maitre d' and the waiters.

On to the Future:
AROUND THE HORN

HOMEWARD BOUND. The next day I was at the airport promptly at seven o'clock for a flight at eight. No problem going through Immigration and Customs, although I felt like a sleepwalker showing my passport and then having a perfunctory check of my baggage since I was on the way out. I sat in the waiting room, just staring ahead until the first-class passengers were called for boarding. The attractive stewardess offered me coffee that I gladly took with two lumps of sugar and some cream. Thirty minutes later the rest of the passengers finally boarded, and we were on our way. I was looking forward to the flight home, but since I didn't sleep well the previous two nights, I decided to have a glass of champagne, hoping it would help me sleep.

About an hour later as I was dozing away, we landed in Panama so that the passengers could deplane and do their duty-free shopping. The flight from Bogotá to Mexico City could easily be made without refueling. Classic in the Latin American way of doing things, I was sure Avianca had a special arrangement with the Panama Port Authority, the retailers, or the government to make this stop for duty-free buying purposes. Panama was known as having the best selection of duty-free merchandise in the world and, certainly, someone was making a good amount of money each time the flight landed there. Under ordinary circumstances, it gave me a chance to deplane and buy my own duty-free goodies. However, this time I was in no mood to deplane, shop, and talk to strangers, so I remained onboard.

My arrival in Mexico City was normal. I chatted with several of the senior Immigration and Customs officers and gave them packs of cigarettes from a carton I had in my briefcase, then I went straight home from the airport, grabbed a sandwich, and drove back to my office. I didn't want to sit at home and think about my friend, his family, and how I had survived on the whim of the terrorist leader.

As usual, I waved and said hello to the office staff with a forced smile on my face; although I had only been gone less than a week, it was the usual homecoming. Hector was standing nearby, and I asked him to make up an agenda of work with problems, if any, at the head of the list. In the interim, I went through my mail and phone calls. The only calls of any importance were one from Roger to call him as soon as possible on my arrival and one from my contact at the embassy.

There wasn't much exuberance and energy in my report, that included the recruiter and other bits and pieces, leaving out the kidnapping and the fate of my friend. Roger noticed I was a bit on the down side and said so. I passed it off as being close to exhaustion and not feeling well in general. Taking advantage of the call, I asked if it was okay to take some six or ten days off in my hometown of San Antonio. Roger was quick to give me his blessing.

Leo was next on my call list. I gave him the same report as I had to Roger.

"By the time you get back, we'll be putting the finishing touches on our European version of the magazine," he said excitedly, "and it will be published in four languages; English, Italian, French, and German, simultaneously. We will have our offices in London, we will do editorial in Paris with our French partners, and we will produce the magazine in Milan or Verona, Italy. How does that sound?"

"Terrific," I said with as much enthusiasm as I could muster.

"You'll play an important role in this venture, Bob, so hurry back."

Before I could make my call to the embassy, Morv Leibowitz, the head of USIA Latin America, called. He asked that we meet the next morning, but instead of going to the small conference room, I should come directly to his office. He would leave word at the front entrance so I would be ushered to his office on another more senior floor. I assumed he'd been advised about the kidnapping and the outcome. As it turned out, that is exactly what we discussed.

In advance of my week's stay in San Antonio I met with all department heads of the magazine: editorial, production, advertising, subscription sales, newsstand circulation, and accounting. There were no problems to deal with, and I felt at ease about leaving on vacation with Hector in control.

SAN ANTONIO, TEXAS, A NOSTALGIC TRIP.

It was only a two-hour Mexico City to San Antonio flight. Nevertheless, I was in first class to get away from children and crowded seating arrangements in coach and to have the space and quiet time to think. I declined the offer for lunch, knowing my mother would have something special for me.

As I thought about my friend and his family and the events of the past few days, I had no desire to have an alcoholic beverage before landing in San Antonio. I was determined to walk in my hometown, where I was born and raised, with a clear head, ready to carry out my plan.

Before I left Mexico City I called my mother and gave her the airline, flight number, and time of arrival in San Antonio. I was my dear mother's only son and her pride and joy, but I was not always a considerate son. When I enlisted in the paratroopers in San Antonio, I was allowed to go home to return the next day. At the kitchen table I asked my mother if she had plans for the next afternoon because my train was leaving for California, to take basic training, and I wanted to say goodbye to her there. She was speechless and just stared at me. She was well aware of the Korean War, but I was the only son of a widowed mother. I was about to enter college, and I certainly didn't have to go if I was drafted. She just started crying.

Again, I did the same thing when I left for Latin America and when I went to live in Colombia and Chile and through many, many trips in Latin America and Europe. I always told her my plans at the last minute. I truly regret being so inconsiderate with my mother.

She was at the airport and took me straight home, where she had cooked some of my favorite dishes for lunch. We spent the rest of the day talking about my exotic trips, accomplishments, promotions, and more. Nothing about the tight spots I had been in and certainly not about the kidnapping. Later in the evening I called some of my friends to tell them I was in town and arrange to meet somewhere for a drink the next early evening, "Happy Hour," as they call cocktail time.

Of the four I called, one said he just couldn't make it during the week and preferred to meet over the weekend. However, he spent half an hour telling me about his two children and their academic and athletic accomplishments. He invited me to a neighborhood barbecue the following Saturday.

"Sorry, Bob, no beer, wine, or liquor due to the children."

I declined saying I had a previous engagement.

Two of the other three agreed to meet me at one of our old watering holes. We met at five-thirty in the afternoon, and by seven they were on their way home.

"It's a weeknight, Bob," they both said almost at the same time. "You understand, we knock off early." It was just as well; they were close to boring me. One of the two friends did most of the talking and pointed out what a dirty campaign was run against him for the position of the President of the Chamber of Commerce. However, he showed them by winning anyway. The other friend was very involved in a Little Theatre Group and offered to give me two free tickets for any performance I chose. I accepted to give them to my mother and one of her friends.

The fourth one was more or less as I remembered him. He picked a place with a generous "Happy Hour" that included snacks, salsa and chips, and other "finger" food, as they call it in the states. He was a beer drinker and nothing more, so I joined him with the one of the new light beer.

We had been talking for about an hour and a half. I described some of my misadventures and activities in the world I lived in, to which he would take an occasional sip from his beer and a deep drag on his cigarette and would occasionally roll his eyes.

"It's been over twenty years since I began living and working in Latin America. I've been thinking of coming back to cook-outs, the Easter Bunny, and Thanksgiving with turkey and all the fixings. What do you think, Paulie?"

"We've been friends all the way back to elementary, junior, and high school when you were a troublemaker and were always looking for excitement. From what little you've told me about your current life, I'd say you wouldn't make it up here. You are not programmed for fundraisers, garden parties, and the breathtaking excitement of dollar-limit poker games."

"You're probably right, but I feel I should give it a try. I have some thinking to do in the next few days before I'm really definite on the idea."

"Just like that, Bob, you're going to give your life a one hundred and eighty degree turn just so you can give it a try?"

Paulie looked at me, shook his head and said, "Good luck, Little Beaver."

"You betchum,' Red Ryder," I said laughing.

We finished our beer and walked out of the beer joint.

The next few days I spent driving around San Antonio in my mother's car. It was a nostalgic trip driving past Woodlawn Elementary School, Horace Mann Junior School, and Jefferson High School. I went into the Texas Ice House and had a cold beer. I drove out to the "Outskirts," a beer-joint hangout where you took your date when you were playing the role of a BTO, Big Time Operator, and had five dollars in the back pocket of your Levis. I drove by Alamo Stadium where we played our high school football games. I checked out the Pig Stand Drive In, our unofficial headquarters, and found it replaced by an office building. For closure I went to look for Top Town where we parked and tried to make out but found our lovers lane overrun by row houses built after the Korean War.

That was enough cruising and driving along memory lane. I was convinced, or at least I thought I was convinced, I should try to spend the rest of my life in the States. I loved New York City, but living there was not an option. It was too busy, too hectic, and too out of control, or so it seemed to me at the time. The next day I visited with my banker and asked him for the name of a person or company in the business of identifying companies for sale. I was moving fast now. The die had been cast. My meeting with the broker was short. I wanted to buy all or part of small or medium-sized publishing company based in San Antonio. After he did his research and sent me a prospectus, I would let him know if I was interested, and we would go forward from there.

This was the beginning of the biggest mistake I ever made in my life and what would prove to be a personal disaster for me that came close to destroying my career as a creative, passionate, and productive individual.

Next I called Roger and Leo and asked to see them as soon as convenient. I booked an early flight to New York with departure the next morning. I could then stay with my mother the rest of the day and evening. This time I told her my plans, and she was overjoyed. I warned her that it may not work out, but at least those were my plans.

THE BEGINNING OF THE END.

Roger, Leo, and I spent several hours together the day of my arrival discussing the bombshell news of my departure from the company. The three of us had dinner and drinks that evening and spent the better part of the next day, including lunch, on the same subject. They did most of the talking. How could I give up a growing and successful career? Where would I replace the adventure and excitement of Latin America? How can you do this after all we've done for you? Obviously, they knew nothing of the kidnapping that was foremost in my mind and enough adventure and excitement to last for the rest of my life, or so I thought.

Roger offered me more money and stock. Leo offered to introduce me to world leaders in Europe, including the Pope. Big time offers, but my mind was made up. When they finally realized I was not going to change my mind, the matter of how the Latin American operations would be managed was next for discussion. I had to agree to stay with the company from ninety to one hundred and twenty days while we figured out new strategy. They thought I might change my mind during that time. After all, although they didn't know it, I didn't even have a publishing company to go to. I also had to agree I would help Leo kick off our European magazine venture. That part

I liked. It meant travel to England, France, Italy, and Germany, with side trips to other countries of my fancy.

Back in Mexico City I had a long meeting with Hector. Actually, it was not the usual formal business meeting, but a conversation of why I planned to leave the company. I wanted his help in restructuring the Latin America management plan of action, but I asked him to keep it confidential. I needed time to think what direction to take and who should play what role in the overall scheme of the operation. I thought about having one of the regional managers take over my responsibilities, but none had broad managing experience and none had sufficient command of the English language to deal with the New York office. There was also the matter of the trouble spots that popped up in any one or more of the eighteen Latin American countries at any given time. Our regional managers were all very regional, very into their own countries. Finally, they would never fit in with Roger and Leo.

The thought about bringing in an outsider was a consideration, but to identify an individual with the proper publishing experience in Latin America and fluent in both languages would be near to an impossible task in two or three months. Even more, an outsider would have to know how to handle the idiosyncrasies of each country personally. Would an outsider know how, where, and when to use my eight hundred-pound pet gorilla? Would he take an old lady by the arm into the lobby of a hotel so she could see firsthand the invasion of American art and culture, or could he handle interviewing a head of state or be witness to a bloodless coup? The dilemma I was in was my fault. First, I had never considered a successor to my position, and second, I thought only of myself when I made the decision to leave the company.

The other option I had was more practical and doable. I would name regional managers, who would be responsible for his country and surrounding countries of lesser importance. For example, the Mexico manager would be responsible for Mexico, Central America, and the Caribbean. Our Colombia manager would handle Colombia, Venezuela, and Ecuador. From Santiago, Chile, the manager would be in charge of Chile, Peru, and Bolivia. Lastly, Argentina management would look after Argentina, Uruguay, and Paraguay. The delicate situation in Brazil would be left up to Leo in New York. Hector would be the go-to guy by the three regional managers for trouble in Latin America, and he would consult with Leo on what action to take. The regional managers had seen me in action on problem situations in their respective countries, so they would be able to follow my lead.

Two weeks later I got a call from Leo. He wanted me to fly to Milan, Italy, to see about setting up production for the magazine. From there I was flying to London, where we had our new offices, and then Paris to meet with our French partners to discuss coordination of editorial with production. It was a fun trip, and although I had been there before, this time was special. It was the birth of a new venture being handled by professionals. Launching the new magazine was a glorious period of time. To see it come to fruition almost made me change my mind about resigning from the company, but it was too late. By now I had received a prospectus of a small publishing company with two magazines that attracted me. The company was based in Austin, Texas, and that was near enough to San Antonio. I flew to Austin to meet my two new partners, and although they were perfectly decent and honest people, we had absolutely nothing in common but the magazines. That should have been the tip-off.

FAREWELL.

The European magazine was launched and was an instant success. Advertising from Europe, Asia, and the United States in four languages poured into the magazine. We celebrated in Maxim's Paris restaurant with our French partners. Some of the beauties from The Crazy Horse Saloon and Follies Bergere joined us. It was the stuff of dreams and a night to remember. It was an event that I never was able to duplicate, and for years later I wondered why that didn't stop me from leaving the company and my beloved magazine. Of course, I knew the answer, and the answer was what had happened to my friend and me back in Bogotá.

It was necessary to fly to each of the regional offices to promote the managers to their new positions. I also prepared a *modus operandi* manual to be used in carrying out their new responsibilities. Making my rounds of each of the regional offices, the newly appointed manager threw a party in my honor. I began to feel nostalgic as I was saying goodbye for the last time to the regional managers and other employees I dealt with from time to time. I didn't think I would ever see them again. The regional management structure I put in place for Latin America was accepted with enthusiasm and appreciation. The plan was functioning well in the few weeks before I left Mexico on my way north.

Until now, saying goodbye to our newly established regional managers was not especially difficult since our relationships had been mostly business oriented. Saying goodbye in Buenos Aires to Lorenzo, his brothers, and Bette was another matter. In spite of the relatively short time we had known each other, we had become more than just friends. There was a bond that brought us together, and it was the thought I may never see them again that made my departure so very sad. Little did I know that in about three years we would be renewing our strong friendship.

For now, my excuse was that I was burned out and needed to try something different. They couldn't believe it. Why, at the peak of my success and that of my magazine, did I just pick up and leave? I wished I could tell them about Bogotá, but I didn't.

I also met with Bette and her family. Her dad was beside himself, thanking me again and again. Bette's tears flowed, and I was hard put not to join her. Beautiful young woman that she was, she would soon have gentlemen callers, and I would become only a memory. I vowed to stay in touch with all of them, knowing it would be hard. Again, I felt I shouldn't be leaving. I shouldn't be making this decision under the dark cloud of the kidnapping. Still, the wheels of the future kept moving, and the next thing I knew I was on an airplane going to my destiny.

IF IT'S BROKEN, FIX IT.

As planned, I was in Austin, Texas, at the appointed day and time, not knowing I was soon to begin the downward slide of my personal and professional career. My first wrong step was to arrive twenty minutes late for a party given in my honor by one of my partners. Somebody made the snide remark that by being late, I thought my time was more valuable then theirs. From there on it was down one step at a time. I didn't fit in. Austin didn't like me, and I didn't like Austin. I made no friends. I did everything I thought I was supposed to do. I bought a nice boat, joined the yacht club, had a home built on a Country Club and thought I was living the American dream. I realized how wrong I was in less than one year. It took me another two years to negotiate my way back to the international world.

In Latin America, there are still many more events, actions, and outrages where I played a large or small part. There was the military junta of General Pinochet in Chile, the Peruvian Tupac Amaru Revolutionary Movement and the Shining Path, both terrorist groups, and their atrocities. We were witness to the battle of corruption in Ecuador and the nightmare in El Salvador of the disappearance of dissenters, and I was there when a rebel group overthrew Anastasio Somoza, Jr., Dictator of Nicaragua, and when President of Venezuela Carlos Andrés Pérez was forced to resign for corruption. Lorenzo's friend became a candidate for the presidency of Argentina and ultimately became president.

Of course, those stories and more belong to the next twenty years.

1. Author's note: Idlewild International Airport became John F. Kennedy International Airport in the early sixties. Many travelers who visited New York City frequently continued to call the international airport "Idlewild" because they didn't like Kennedy, or they wanted to boast about being experienced and frequent fliers, or they simply didn't go along with the change.